# Praise for **Leveraging Your Links**

"Leveraging Your Links *is as eclectic and purposefully unruly as the subject of social media itself. It's chock full of concepts and practical examples that show how relevant content has an impact in the real world. Allan's brilliant book is a must-read for all businesspeople who want to connect with online consumers and networks.*"

- Barbara Corcoran, Real Estate Industry Leader,
TV Commentator and Celebrity, and Best-selling Author

"*Allan delivers yet another prolific and intelligent interpretation of the relevance of social media today and continues to be a pioneer in our industry. His insightful perspectives and in-depth knowledge never cease to amaze. This book is a must-read for everyone who wishes to maintain or gain success as a real estate professional in today's multi-media rich, consumer- and information-driven environment.*"

- Rei L. Mesa, President & CEO, Prudential Florida Realty,
Florida Real Estate Services

"*I commend Allan in taking the initiative to write a book that will undoubtedly serve as a guide for every real estate agent and broker who wants to thrive in this next generation of business. Whether you love or fear social media, this book is a must-read for your continued success in the real estate industry. This is not a fad; it is the new foundation of both marketing and communication.*"

- Sherry Chris, President & CEO,
Better Homes and Gardens Real Estate LLC

"*Once again Dalton addresses the current and future needs of real estate practitioners. His remarkable and unique insights will help agents and brokers learn how to effectively integrate this transformational new medium. Once they embrace and use social media in the manner outlined in this easy-to-read and highly informative book, they will be on their way to even greater success.*"

- Dick Schlott, President & CEO,
Gloria Nilson, REALTORS®, Real Living®

"*Allan Dalton has been a soldier for the betterment of the real estate industry for over 30 years. His commitment to real estate brokerage, REALTOR.com and to Top 5 are examples of someone who deeply cares about this industry and the agents who serve it. His ability to communicate and his willingness to support agents with tools that are relevant has always been a hallmark of his trade and his love of the industry. Congratulations, Allan, on this missive. I am certain that those who read it will gain real value and understanding of the conversion of their job from owners of proprietary information to those who seek a true and deep consultative relationship to the external public.*"

- Ed Krafchow, President & CEO,
Prudential California/Nevada Realty

"*In this book, Allan Dalton has successfully demystified social media for the real estate industry and in a way that only Allan can—he's articulated the differences between social networking, social media and real estate social marketing. Allan's focus on content marketing, purposed for the consumer that goes beyond presenting the listing itself, and his belief that this new media offers a transformational opportunity for those in our industry who engage, is right on the money.*"

- Scott Dixon, President, *The Real Estate Book*,
Network Communications, Inc.

"*Social media in real estate is an evolving and unsettled medium that requires a seasoned, forward-thinking real estate professional. I have known Allan for 20 years and he has always created the tomorrow of real estate.* Leveraging Your Links *is just another example of Allan serving as a real estate pioneer.*"

- Gino Blefari, Founder, President & CEO,
Intero Real Estate Services

"*When you combine Dalton's mastery of marketing and media with Hundley's technology and systems wizardry, you get a combination that works as well as peanut butter and jelly.*"

- Mark Stark, CEO, Prudential Americana

"Real estate success will more than ever require that agent and company business plans devote adequate attention toward effectively harnessing the potential of social media. To that end, this book and RISMedia's content leadership is indispensable."

- Bob Lefever, Industry Leader, Speaker, Consultant

Dalton (and Hundley) embrace the online world with fervent passion and, more importantly, with purpose. Leveraging Your Links *is an indispensable guide for moving beyond the simple act of just amassing followers and friends. It is a compelling read with actionable, clear-cut strategies for creating a relevant and meaningful online presence that meets the needs of existing clients and attracts new ones. Goal-focused real estate pros will value this go-to source for defining activities that lead to results.*

- Deborah Madey, Broker, Peninsula Realty Group

"Allan Dalton's and Steve Hundley's research, findings and overall mastery of the subject make this a book that will be a must-read for every one of our agents!"

- Steve Rodgers, President/Owner,
Windermere Exclusive Properties

"Allan Dalton has uniquely distinguished himself for his marketing contributions to the real estate industry and he now turns his critical eye to a subject matter greatly in need of his, and RISMedia's, insights and recommendations: connecting to and with consumers via compelling content."

- Richard (Rick) Higgins, Chairman & Founder,
The Higgins Group

"Most books on this subject are either too philosophical, way too technical or unoriginal. Allan's interviews with megastars like Gregg Neuman, Valerie Fitzgerald, Krisstina Wise and the rest of his 'Real Estate Dream Team' keep this masterpiece practical and, most of all, real. It is without question the best book I have ever seen come out of our industry."

- Gee Dunsten, CRS Instructor, Real Estate Educator

# Dedication

To Carol, for being a saintly and brilliant wife and best friend for 38 years, our beloved daughters, Ginnie, Becky, and Laura, and our precious grandchildren, Reagan, Max, Aiden, Noel, Harrison, Grace and Shane.

To John Featherston, for his immense contribution to the media needs of the real estate industry for over 30 years, for making this book possible and for being an exemplary husband, father and friend.

To the innumerable, high-quality real estate professionals throughout North America for the profoundly positive impact they have on the lives of millions of consumers.

# Introduction

Social media and its interrelated and complementary concept, social networking, have transformed millions of people from being merely consumers of information to *producers* of information. Social media, empowered by technology, has forever changed the way in which people connect, communicate, organize, and interact. Yet, as is the case with all change, the manner in which individuals respond to this online transformational opportunity varies, and real estate agents are no exception.

Predictably, when it comes to effectively incorporating social media into real estate business practices, there are those in real estate who will resist, or even refrain from, its use; others who will embrace the opportunity; and then there are those who will be the most adaptive. These are the individuals who will excel in harnessing, managing, and maximizing social media's vast potential through the creation of their own social media strategy.

Judging by the results of the *2010 Dalton/Hundley Real Estate Social Media Census*, featured in this book, it appears that the majority of real estate agents have not yet developed their real estate-oriented social media plan. It is my fervent desire that the contents and concepts of this book materially contribute to the social media-related pursuits and practices of the forward-thinking, open-minded real estate professionals who read it. I am referring to professionals who are committed to providing greater value to consumers, which will consequently enable them to reap the greater professional rewards they deserve. In order to best appreciate the order of magnitude surrounding the inherent changes caused by how modern-day individuals connect and communicate, it might be helpful to first examine the perspective on change expressed by the German philosopher, Georg Wilhelm Friedrich Hegel, in the early 19th century.

Hegel postulated that all monumental change, when examined retrospectively, reveals three distinct points or phases:

*"In preparing for battle, I have always found that plans are useless, but planning is indispensable."*

– Gen. Dwight D. Eisenhower

# Introduction

1. That the particular change was necessary;
2. That the change was beneficial, and;
3. That the change required a correction, or period of adjustment.

Indeed, it is precisely in regard to this third aspect of the change cycle—the period of correction that Hegel suggests, or his "synthesizing step"—that compels me to comprehensively examine, and then address, the relationship between social media, social networking, and real estate-career application, as it will clearly prompt some obvious areas for necessary adjustments and corrections. In this book, I address my concern that many real estate agents are displaying a predilection toward the *networking* aspect of social networking, presumably where they feel more in their element, more than they are gravitating toward the content-dependent *media* opportunities that are connected to social media. Moreover, I also carefully examine why much of our industry appears to be significantly overlooking the relationship between social networking, social media, and classic marketing business principles.

The lack of marketing integration in regard to social networking and social media can be explained by virtue of the fact that many real estate professionals are being more technologically tantalized or seduced by online networking rather than by the value of actionable consumer-centric real estate content or the opportunity to respond to the real estate needs of the overall marketplace that social media presents. *It is becoming apparent that there are too many real estate professionals who are more inclined to employ social networking/social media to chat rather than to convey; to socialize rather than to educate; and to participate rather than to lead.* Of course, activities pertaining to conveying information, educating consumers, and leading online communities will require a concept and commitment to content that goes far beyond the traditional role the real estate industry has been limited to—one of providing only the most basic information on available properties and ancillary services tied to the transaction.

Clearly, as an industry that has always put more emphasis on its networking activities than on providing robust, timely, and expansive information, it most likely comes as no surprise that for many real estate agents, their first social networking/social media forays have been directed toward the goal of connecting versus producing consumer-actionable content. Regrettably, social media's technologically empowered applications and platforms will require real estate–related refinement and distinct strategies in order to meet the needs of consumers and clients, as well as generate acceptable ROI levels. Central to such strategic development is ensuring that real estate content is congruent with the unmet real estate informational and decision-making needs of the various online communities.

In fact, when it comes to leveraging your links, I would like to contribute a new word to the English-speaking world: contentsequences. "Contentsequences" is a hybrid that represents a significant merger between the words "content" and "consequences." I am hoping this new word might serve as a memory device to remind us that when content is not used as the vital link to connect social networking and social media, there are indeed "contentsequences"—specifically, missed opportunities for those professionals who seek to increase not just their reach, but more importantly, their influence online.

While I'm sure he didn't have real estate agents in mind, legendary UCLA basketball coach, John Wooden, once stated, "Never mistake activity for achievement." This quote succinctly summarizes a real estate social media conundrum: when social media is misused, it could result in some real estate agents doing *less* business than they did when their activities were strictly performed offline. Social media/social networking success will not be assured due to expertise in blogging, tweeting, or amassing friends, followers, and online users alone. Nor will it be guaranteed by the number of networks, communities, and tribes in which you are a dedicated participant. I make this assertion because, in my view, *connectivity without content* will not create clients.

Future client creation will be dependent upon how effectively content and contacts are skillfully connected and integrated. Regarding the role of how content will influence the way in which consumers select a real estate agent, I respectfully offer this cautionary note: ***Any real estate professional who believes that real estate content is not critical to how consumers will go about seeking real estate advice and representation will be passed over by increasingly enlightened consumers.*** If you believe that consumers will continue to exhibit selection behavior based upon social reasons—i.e., a friend in the business—online as they have for decades offline, then you might be inappropriately dissuaded from elevating your relevance online. The Internet, social media, and social networking, in particular, are now enabling consumers to look through a monumentally larger window into the various levels of professional real estate comportment and content sophistication. Unquestionably, the way in which consumers go about forming their perceptions of real estate excellence will forever be altered due to social media.

Leading real estate agents and their companies have a historic opportunity to change the way consumers perceive them. Accordingly, we must now transition from a predominantly transaction-based model by evolving in a way that causes our clients to more substantially rely upon us for our thought leadership, skills, and services. These professional attributes need to be inserted before, during, and after transactions. While this observation may appear to some as being unnecessarily obvious, assuming these expanded responsibilities will not be quite that simple to all and especially to those real estate professionals who are bereft in terms of providing consumer-centric content.

I suggest that there will be those who will be challenged by this shift of emphasis, because, historically, our industry, when defining its consumer relationship responsibilities, has only sought to claim the *center* of the transaction and not the *entire* real estate experience. This mindset is one that consumers are reminded of on almost a daily basis. One example is when we announce to consumers, both offline and online, "When you are ready to buy or sell a home, give us a call." What consumers infer from our message is, "Mr. and Mrs. Consumer, what we really mean is that until you're ready to buy or sell, don't bother us. However, *we* will continue to bother *you* with our promotional pumpkins, refrigerator magnets, calendars, and announcements of our statistical achievements"—ritualistic real estate practices that relentlessly manifest that our industry is comfortable remaining in a perpetual state of being *interviewed* versus elevating our value by becoming more *informational*.

This circle-the-wagons-around-the-transaction mentality has also ironically served as a call to arms by many industry leaders who unstrategically cry out, "We must keep real estate agents at the *center* of the transaction." This misplaced strategy only emboldens industry competitors to engage with real estate consumers earlier in the real estate continuum...i.e., online. This abdicated opportunity by our industry enables these middlemen to charge what they would call a referral fee, but which is, in actuality, and as I have been saying for years, a tariff.

There's also a meaningful nexus, one that should garner industry attention, between social media and issues tied to referrals, fees, and overall value proposition. Social media will now enable us to not only better facilitate real estate transactions, but to also become more instrumental in educating consumers on the unique benefits that consumers can derive from real estate.

The power of social media can become particularly important when real estate markets are experiencing a so-called downturn. During this period, the question becomes: Who has the responsibility to inspire unilluminated consumers regarding where their present real estate opportunities can best be found? Historically, this role was one—due to the excessive cost of offline print and, specifically, newspapers—that the industry abdicated to traditional media. At the same time, the real estate industry instead elected to adopt a keep-in-touch strategy with its promotional materials, as opposed to taking on the responsibility of proactively influencing public opinion regarding real estate. The recovery of real estate markets has never been influenced by our industry's most prominent content, that being either classified advertising or personal promotion. But now it can be, through the strategic deployment of social media-driven real estate content.

So too, social media will enable our industry to convey to consumers that the industry's greatest leaders and coaches are not the ones who are producing seminars and speaking at conventions about how real estate professionals can ascend to higher productivity plateaus, but rather those best and brightest who are coaching, educating, and leading consumers on how *consumers* can prosper. For this level of consumer-centric coaching to become a reality, it will require research, resources, and relevant content. To that end, RISMedia is not only publishing this book but playing a unique role as an industry content provider.

RISMedia's B-to-C (Business-to-Consumer) content, along with what I am now labeling B-to-C-to-C (Business-to-Consumer-to-Consumer) content, along with technologies such as 1parkplace content management, provide the real estate industry with an enviable asset—robust and actionable real estate content. Such resources, when strategically integrated into one's social media strategy—and thus, one's real estate career—will lead a transformation to where content share determines both personal and company market share.

'LLAN DALTON, recipient of the first annual Harwich Award
Merit for high school journalism and Miss Helen Murphy.
member of the English Department at Hyde Park High School
(Sally Baier photo)

*My first foray into media, long before it became "social media," when I wrote about my local community, led to a high school journalism award.*

To best ensure that the content in *Leveraging Your Links* is helpful regarding the aforementioned objectives, while writing this book, I have endeavored to draw upon the practical experiences of many successful real estate-related social media mentors. I have also included RISMedia's *2010 Dalton/Hundley Real Estate Social Media Census*—along with its results and our analysis of the data—so that readers will not only be exposed to a theoretical, abstract, and cerebral approach to the subject of social media, but also benefit from the concrete examples of successful applications regarding these important concepts. My spirit of intent is to provide you with both an important *message*, along with an invaluable *method(s)*. One without the other misses the mark and is less than either you or consumers deserve.

## For Want of a Nail

*For want of a nail the shoe was lost.*
*For want of a shoe the horse was lost.*
*For want of a horse the rider was lost.*
*For want of a rider the battle was lost.*
*For want of a battle the kingdom was lost.*
*And all for the want of a horseshoe nail.*

—Centuries-old, unattributed Proverb

## For Want of Relevant Content

*For want of relevant content*
*The respect was lost.*
*For want of respect*
*The consumer relationships were lost.*
*For want of consumer relationships*
*The real estate transactions were lost.*
*For want of real estate transactions*
*The fees were lost.*
*For want of fees*
*The career was lost.*
*For want of the career*
*The financial security was lost.*
*And all for the want of relevant content.*

—Allan Dalton, 2010

# Author Bios

**Allan Dalton** is Chief Marketing Officer of RISMedia and Co-founder and President of RISMedia's Top 5 in Real Estate Network®.

Dalton is the former president of Move's Real Estate Division, and served as CEO of REALTOR.com. Dalton has 30 years of leadership experience, including being the former president and co-owner for more than 20 years of a 32-office real estate brokerage firm.

Ranked by NAR's *REALTOR Magazine* in 2006 as one of the industry's 25 Most Influential Thought Leaders, Dalton has been a keynote speaker at numerous industry events throughout North America and Europe.

Recognized as a pioneer in creating innovative and effective marketing systems for real estate professionals and companies, Dalton co-created Century 21's Customized Marketing System as well as ERA's Value Added Marketing System and Value Added Career Development Book. He also developed the NRT Full Service Marketing System and created three major marketing systems for Better Homes and Gardens. Dalton also created the Real Estate Move-Up System and the Real Estate Financial Planning System and is the creator of the Real Estate Social Networking System℠ and Co-creator of the Real Estate Social Marketing System℠. A former Boston Celtics draft choice, he is also featured in *Atlantic Monthly Magazine* as "America's number one pick-up basketball player" (http://www.theatlantic.com/past/docs/issues/2000/04/harper.htm (Part 1) http://www.theatlantic.com/past/docs/issues/2000/04/harper2.htm (Part 2)

Dalton also authored *The Truth About Real Estate*, *Real Estate Team Coaching* and *Value Added Career Development*. Dalton and his family reside in California and Connecticut.

**Facebook:** http://www.facebook.com/people/Allan-Dalton/100000541151160?ref=search
**Twitter:** http://www.twitter.com/allandalton
**LinkedIn:** http://www.linkedin.com/in/allandalton

As CEO of 1parkplace, Inc. **Steve Hundley's** passion is to develop cutting-edge real estate marketing systems and technology solutions for America's top REALTORS and brokerage firms. He founded 1parkplace in 1995 after a successful 10-year real estate career listing and selling homes in the Silicon Valley of California.

1parkplace is an industry-leading, real estate marketing and technology solutions provider that develops custom lead generation solutions, contact management systems, website technologies, hyper-local BLOGGING systems, strategic SEO services and real estate social marketing systems for maximum sales results.

Hundley is also recognized as an industry educator and recently formed the 1parkplace University where he has hosted exclusive training events. He is also a former faculty member of the University of California, Los Angeles (UCLA).

**Facebook:** http://www.facebook.com/1parkplace
**Twitter:** http://twitter.com/1parkplace

# Acknowledgments

This book not only focuses on the virtues of contribution, community, connectivity, and collaboration, but it owes its very existence to such laudable principles. Therefore, I wish to extend my gratitude to all of those who were meaningful contributors to *Leveraging Your Links*.

My deep appreciation to John Featherston and Darryl MacPherson, partners at RISMedia, for approving, being patrons of, and publishing this book. To Steve Hundley, CEO of 1parkplace, for his immense contributions, his vision, and the significant time and effort he expended to ensure the book's success. To Maria Patterson, executive editor at RISMedia, for her wondrous and impeccable editorial vigilance. To Patricia Bahner Porco, for her momentous effort in structuring, organizing, and copy editing this book from the beginning to its completion. To Cathleen Stack, for her invaluable thoughts and insights, and her leadership in selecting and organizing our Social Media Mentors. To Kelli Cahill, for her indispensable and magnificent execution of the book's design, graphics, and physical layout needs. To Christy LaSalle and Susanne Dwyer, for the physical production of the book. To 1parkplace's Steve Fox, for his statistical compilation and analysis of the *2010 Dalton/Hundley Real Estate Social Media Census*. To Dr. Virginia Taylor and her associate, Nicole Ferrari, for their illuminating work on the possible correlation between social networking and social anxiety. To our cartoonist, Adam Fontenault. To Carol Dalton, for her remarkable intellectual and practical consultative acumen and the consultation she provided to me on every chapter I wrote. And, of course, my greatest appreciation is for each Social Media Mentor, be they practitioner or analyst, who willingly shared their systems, ideas, and overall best practices for the betterment of the reader.

Given the considerable time and effort I expended in the writing of this book, I also want to make note that there is not one word that portends to be from me that isn't. I feel the need to acknowledge this point as we are in an age of ghost writers and an age where individuals feel no guilt whatsoever in lifting the thoughts and words of others in their writing. Moreover, the major premise behind social media is that now all of us as "citizen journalists" possess a greater opportunity to express ourselves than ever before. I have taken this opportunity to write and I resoundingly encourage you to do likewise, both off- and online.

*A lack of nuanced thinking is often at the root of not fully capitalizing on an important movement. Just as many interchange the terms Internet and Web when they actually refer to two completely different things—the Internet represents the hardware and the Web refers to the software and the wealth of information it provides—they also make no distinction between social networking and social media. The difference between these two terms, however, is quite substantial. Prepare to become enlightened.*

—Allan Dalton

# Leveraging Your Links
## How to do more business off- and online

## The Social Media Mentors:
*Insights, Inspiration and the Individual Social Media Strategies*
*of Real Estate Leaders Across the Country*

# Contents

# Leveraging
## Your Links

### How to do more business off- and online

▷ Convert Friends, Fans & Followers
Into Customers & Clients

▷ Create Your Personally Branded
Business Social Network

▷ Convey Your Real Estate Social
Marketing Value

# Foreword

*By John Featherston*

As founder and chairman of a media company, I, along with my partner, Darryl MacPherson, our Executive Editor, Maria Patterson, and our entire RISMedia family of real estate journalists, must acknowledge we are thrilled that the overall concept of media is taking on unprecedented importance within the real estate industry—in the form of social media.

It is important to note, however, that not everyone, as is the case with all transformational change, will significantly or similarly benefit. Those who *will* thrive in our new social media environment will be the real estate companies and real estate professionals whose strategies satisfy what I view as three preconditions for social media success:

1. They must possess a clear and deeply embedded understanding of both the difference between social networking and social media and how to integrate the two.
2. They must be committed to first accumulating and then providing relevant real estate-related content to distribute online to specific consumer communities and markets.
3. They must develop and then implement a strategic social media plan.

In *Leveraging Your Links*, Allan Dalton comprehensively addresses each of these preconditions. He does so by approaching the subject in both a compelling philosophical manner, as well as in a highly practical and readily transferable fashion. Allan, as the book's author, although possessing a remarkably extensive and diverse background in real estate brokerage, marketing, technology, and media-related endeavors—as exemplified by his role as former CEO of REALTOR.com, his many years as an owner and leader of his own major real estate brokerage, and his recognition by the National Association of Realtors as one of the industry's "25 Most Influential Thought Leaders"—goes well beyond his many personal examples and experiences by also generously including the best practices of some of our industry's most exemplary social media practitioners. Allan's approach to writing his book on social media fittingly symbolizes what social media is truly all about: networking, listening, learning from others, connecting, interacting, educating, participating, and providing thought leadership.

Accordingly, the reader benefits from his highly collaborative treatment of a highly collaborative and participatory phenomenon—social media.

As Publisher and CEO of RISMedia, I am happy to say that this approach pleases me immensely. The cooperative and networking approach to business development has been a practice I have fostered through RISMedia's events, conventions, research, and our esteemed industry best-practices panels for more than 30 years. RISMedia remains committed to providing the industry with such participatory platforms so that real estate's leading practitioners can continue to share their priceless experiential knowledge with valued colleagues in a trusted environment.

RISMedia has been and will continue to be steadfast in its commitment to being a valuable media partner to the real estate industry. This dedication is reflected both in our creation of important B2B (Business-to-Business), as well as highly relevant B2C (Business-to-Consumer), content. I trust that you will find Allan's unique and groundbreaking work, on how the relationship between the real estate industry and consumers can become a richer one through the effective use of social media, consistent with RISMedia's role as a leader in providing real estate-related information.

I'd like to also take this opportunity to thank you, the reader, for your commitment to ongoing social media development. I know you will both enjoy and greatly benefit from this book.

John Featherston
CEO & Publisher
RISMedia

# Chapter 1

# Something's Happening Here

*"There's something happening here.*
*What it is ain't exactly clear."*

—Lyrics from "For What It's Worth" by Buffalo Springfield

With apologies to Buffalo Springfield and all Generation Xers and Yers who may not be aware of this Baby Boomer-revered song, "For What It's Worth," perhaps these iconic lyrics best express the current state of understanding—or lack of same—surrounding how to best utilize social media for greater real estate brokerage success. I selected this musical metaphor as it is consistent with the thoughts expressed by many real estate professionals who participated in the RISMedia and 1parkplace social media research project, which was conducted by Steve Hundley and me. As a component of our project, I personally conducted countless seminars and focus groups. Additionally, Steve and I created, interpreted, and summarized the *2010 Dalton/Hundley Real Estate Social Media Census*, which appears later in this book. During our exhaustive research, we were struck by the realization—in fact, I see it as somewhat of a conundrum—that while most real estate professionals embrace the notion of social networking and social media, and many are engaged in their own versions of these activities, few can point to their social networking and social media activities as being responsible for any windfall of real estate transactions. Moreover, our research, involving thousands of Realtors, revealed that while they are devoting countless hours to Twitter, Facebook, LinkedIn, blogging and a host of other social networking-related activities, they disappointingly cannot tweet or even chirp that they are experiencing any significant increase in their incomes from these time-consuming pursuits. This feedback reinforces what I wrote in my introduction, in reference to the illustrious UCLA basketball coach, John Wooden, who once said, "Never mistake activity for achievement."

My research has also caused me to conjecture that the reason for such a lack of reported results (for many, but not for all) might be because the majority of real estate agents approach this social networking and social media movement in order to principally advance their own agenda, as opposed to devoting the proper attention to employing social media and social networking platforms to advance the interests and needs of their consumers and clients. Moreover, I have not observed any real estate professional who has devised a strategy for converting friends, fans, followers, network and community participants, or visitors to their websites/blogs into their own personally led and branded real estate social network where consumers become deputized as members. The significance of this void is that the real estate industry has quixotically aspired to create "customers for life" without success for decades. After years of witnessing massive consumer mutiny against this ill-fated attempt, perhaps we would have been better off emulating how those more successful than we create lifetime loyalty. That would be the myriad of companies, churches, political parties, civic and social leaders that establish more estimable records for consumer retention due to their willingness to offer "membership" opportunities to their consumer following.

Consequently, many real estate agents are not experiencing the results they desire—despite the enormous amount of time some report devoting to social networking and social media. One plausible explanation for this expectation shortfall might be that they either on their own embraced, or were taught to embrace, this movement from the wrong perspective—with the wrong spirit of intent. I say this because in my view, tens, if not hundreds, of thousands of real estate professionals were principally motivated to participate in social networking because they inferred that social media's greatest utility was in providing a way for them to connect and communicate with individuals and communities in a social, or promotional, fashion. They neglected to realize that if they were to use emerging technology to produce and/or provide informative real estate content to as many targeted consumers as possible, they would become greater beneficiaries of social media.

Is it fair, therefore, to ask if the real estate industry's rush to social networking and social media judgment has been less about embracing the media possibilities within social media—which clearly benefits consumers—and more about gravitating or even succumbing to the *networking* elements of social networking in order to satisfy its own needs to prospect, become more visible, and aggregate online contacts? How do consumers benefit from all of this? Clearly, consumers, from all accounts, have never experienced a real estate agent "famine," and they don't need to be apprised, via our social networking, of the large number of real estate agents who are available to list their homes. However, while there is no shortage of agents, there does exist a monumental void regarding how our industry responds to the informational needs of technologically savvy real estate consumers. A survey by Actionable Research reveals that consumers are disappointed by how we engage them. The study concludes that consumers, therefore, often go to friends, instead of agents, for real estate information. Ironically, due to social media, consumers will now be able to satisfy these real estate informational needs online with or *without* us.

Another question that might require reflection is, "Why has our industry initially resisted most major real estate-related changes that consumers advocate, yet not in the case of social networking?" The more I searched for an explanation, the more I realized that the reason might be because we perceived that the other changes, which were clearly in the interest of consumers, were not similarly in *our* best interest. Conversely, we interpret social networking as being in our interest—which is why we may be selectively adopting only those aspects of social networking and social media that benefit us more than those that are clearly in the best interest of consumers.

Who can argue that there wasn't an almost pathological opposition to making home property data available to consumers via the Internet when the opportunity first became available? It didn't take a major research and development effort to recognize that while much of our industry resisted this change, consumers embraced it. You may remember that even recently, many industry decision-making leaders were also passionately against IDX. Was such disapproval due to consumer interest or industry interest? I am happy to say that, now, both of these major movements—Internet marketing and then IDX as an iteration of the same—are supported by earlier real estate industry recalcitrants. This phenomenon, regarding how change is typically resisted in all personal and professional sectors, also gives credence to what the German philosopher, Hegel, said, as I explained in my introduction: all great change has three phases: the thesis (that the change is necessary), the anti-thesis (that the change is beneficial), and finally, the synthesis (that the change requires a correction or a period of adjustment).

In the case of the relationship that many real estate professionals have with what they either call social networking or social media, the *thesis* might be: Social networking is a great way for me to stay connected with my friends, family, and personal referral base; to insert myself socially among the friends of my friends and their friends; and, if this is also a way for me to attract buyers and sellers to either my listings or me, all the better. The *anti-thesis* would then be: I've gone to numerous courses or conventions over the past several years on social media training; I am networking with an "industry subculture" comprised of those who are the most active and successful at social networking; I have dramatically increased my number of friends, followers, and fans, and I also have a blog; however, I seem to be spending so much time managing my social networking responsibilities, that it's actually taking away from my ability to make more money in real estate. And the *synthesis*, or as Hegel would posit, the correction period, becomes: One needs a social media strategy whereby the process of social networking and social media is sufficiently strategic and systematized enough that the proper professional prioritization of time and results is achieved.

This is the reason why a significant part of this book will focus on the need for real estate professionals to integrate social networking and social media in order to create a necessary convergence—that being *real estate social marketing*.

Given the importance of creating this convergence, Steve Hundley and I will provide you with an example of a real estate social marketing system and show you how you can customize your own. John Featherston, founder and chairman of RISMedia, and chairman and co-founder of RISMedia's Top 5 in Real Estate Network®, when discussing social media, is always quick to point out that social media, like any invaluable resource, can be both beneficial and harmful. His examples are: We need water to live, but it can also *drown* us. Fire can heat our homes or *burn* them.

This book, *Leveraging Your Links*, is entirely geared toward enabling forward-thinking and consumer-centric real estate professionals and companies to progress from their perfunctory practice of utilizing social networking to become vastly more connected, to learning how to dramatically increase not just their range and reach, but the influence they can have with increasingly sophisticated consumers. This is a critical step as today's consumers have, figuratively speaking, developed antibodies to the self-promotional efforts of real estate agents and are desperately seeking substance and informational value from them instead.

Noted journalist Eric Sevareid said that in this age of information, we need to change the traditional order of placing data first, information second, knowledge third, and wisdom fourth, to an order where wisdom comes first, then knowledge, then information, and lastly, data. Social media is making available, for perhaps the first time in history, integrated communication platforms that can deliver the wisdom and knowledge of trusted advisors, like you, in a way that consumers will find irresistible when it's done effectively. This is where you will leverage your social media links.

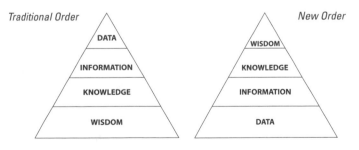

*Which pyramid reflects your Social Media Strategy?*

Achieving this lofty goal will require that you first have a very deep understanding of the differences between social networking, social media, and real estate social marketing; and second, that you construct your *own* customized and specific real estate social marketing strategy.

# Chapter 2

# Social Media to the Real Estate Rescue

D r. Timothy Leary, most noted for his exploratory "work"—both professionally and personally—regarding psychedelic drug use, and for being the founder of the League for Spiritual Discovery, a religion dedicated to the worship of the drug LSD, is also credited with a quote that I believe has a significant nexus to the relationship between social media and how the real estate industry needs to change the way in which it relates to consumers. Dr. Leary, who received a Ph.D. in psychology from the University of California, Berkeley, was a former West Point cadet (for a limited time), an assistant professor at Berkeley, the director of psychiatric research at the Kaiser Family Foundation, a lecturer in psychology at Harvard University, as well as a writer, futurist, and published author. In his 1982 book, *Changing My Mind, Among Others*, he wrote (in what I am sure was, for him, a transcendental moment), "If you want to change the way people respond to you, change the way you respond to people."

## Social Media to the Real Estate Rescue

Perhaps Dr. Leary's words regarding how we respond to people do not create a natural high for you, but they do for me. These are words that should be seriously considered as we attempt to repair, redefine, and even rescue our industry's relationship with consumers. In fact, I am devoting this entire chapter to my own exploration of how our industry can utilize social media-enabled technology to communicate more effectively and create professional social bonds with today's more sophisticated and technologically enabled consumers.

I must begin by asserting that our industry's potential to employ social media for the purpose of *rescuing* our image with consumers, *rescuing* our relevance, and *rescuing* our results, begins unsurprisingly with our first identifying what, if anything, needs to change within our industry and how this change intersects with social media opportunities.

I have always valued the saying, "When we are through changing, we are through." Thankfully, we as an industry will never be through, because we always have made and always will make the necessary changes directly connected to our survival and relative success. Undoubtedly, however, unless we are flexible and open to making the changes that consumers value the most, our professional rewards will be significantly limited, if not in outright jeopardy.

Real estate professionals, like virtually all people, when first encountering any significant change, typically assess the change's direct impact on them. That is, how the change or innovation can specifically either enhance or threaten their success or careers.

Unfortunately, unlike the hundreds of millions of people who are already engaged in social networking and gathering friends, fans, and followers, and involved in online community organizing and interactive connectivity for purely social reasons—and not principally to sell or market goods and services other than perhaps themselves—real estate agents have to wrestle with how to promulgate both their services and their clients' interests. The challenge then becomes: *"How can I ensure that I don't violate the friendship boundaries of those online, who only want to connect with me socially, by inserting my business interests, while at the same time, avoid being perceived as superficially social to those within my networks who are seeking my business expertise?"*

Consequently, it is to be expected that this conundrum—when coupled with the new business need to devote considerable additional time to real estate-related social networking and social media activities—is causing many in real estate to experience acute frustration and even anxiety (which I discuss in another chapter).

My research also reveals that many in the industry are beginning to question the return-on-investment (ROI) relevance of social networking. Real estate has always been, and remains, an incredibly time-consuming career. Now, with the advent of social networking and social media, there are even more demands on a Realtor's time. This new development has also led some agents to consider using their online social networking activities as an alternative for, instead of a complement to, other modes of prospecting, networking, etc.

In order to change the way in which we use social media to better respond to the needs of consumers, one first needs to respond to this seminal social media-related question: "Why do I want to be engaged in social networking and social media, and what do I hope to accomplish?"

>> Is it to amass a larger social network online?

>> Is it to aggregate a larger online social network and then attempt to convert your friends, fans, followers, etc., into buyers, sellers, and/or clients?

>> Is it to convert social networking contacts into your own personally branded real estate social network—one, as I recommend, that creates a consumer membership enrollment opportunity as a feature of your website/blog?

>> Is it to build your brand online?

>> Is it to save money from reduced classified and/or display advertising and personal promotion spending offline?

>> Is it to organize or lead online communities?

>> Is it merely to participate in online communities?

>> Is it to establish yourself as a trusted real estate advisor to more folks?

>> Is it to generate more traffic to your website and/or blog?

>> Is it because you enjoy feeling more connected to more people?

>> Is it to better educate consumers?

>> Is it to more effectively stay in touch with clients and past customers?

>> Is it to appear "with it" or be perceived as a highly evolved and techno-savvy real estate professional?

>> Is it to avoid other less comfortable means of prospecting?

>> Is it because social networking provides you with a sense of greater professional accomplishment?

>> Is it to cultivate greater professional relationships within the industry and attend networking conferences formed on the basis of a shared interest in social networking among your peers?

>> Is it so that someday you might be better able to sell your "Real Estate Book of Business" or database of online contacts and networks?

>> Is it a means to keep in touch with friends and family that you miss and don't get to see face-to-face often enough?

>> Is it to enhance the lives of consumers?

>> Is it to be viewed as a real estate thought leader?

>> Is it to better serve your clients?

>> Is it to improve your SEO?

Do many or all of the above possibilities apply to you? If so, you will discover that the purpose of this book is to help you create an integrated approach and system related to social media based upon your objectives. Otherwise, you might become unduly frustrated and begin to lament, "SO MUCH INFORMATION, YET SO LITTLE TIME!"

Ultimately though, as a real estate professional, your professional use of— or your motivation for excelling at—social networking and social media must result in a benefit to the overall marketplace and to various niche marketplaces in order to realize personal gain.

Accordingly, *in order to provide value in the marketplace, it is imperative in my view, that you "own" the distinctions that separate communities, networks, and markets.* Herewith, I have provided generally accepted definitions of the three categories:

> **Community:** a group of people who live near each other and who are currently interacting with each other. Since the advent of the Internet, the concept of community no longer has geographical limitations, as people can now virtually gather in online communities and share common interests, regardless of their physical locations.
>
> **Network:** a system connecting people or things. A **Social Network** is a group of individuals who connect and congregate in groups, based upon common interests or needs.
>
> **Market:** a market is any place where the sellers of goods and services can meet and interact with the potential buyers of those goods and services.

My reason for including these three distinct definitions tied to communities, networks, and markets is because if real estate companies or professionals do not subordinate their specific online strategies based upon these clearly delineated needs, all that will follow will be confusing activity without results. This will contribute to many in the industry aggressively chasing real estate consumer problems that truly don't exist. The bottom line, from the consumer's perspective, is that there's never been a shortage of real estate agents attempting to connect with them. Only personally relevant material and communication will be of significance and value to most consumers.

In order for me to make it as clear as possible regarding whether you, as a real estate professional, are making the proper distinctions between online communities, online networks, and the needs of various online and offline real estate markets, it might be helpful for you to contemplate these questions:

> ▸ What is the name of the online community that "Expired Listing Homeowners" currently belong to?
> ▸ What community do prospective "Short Sale Homeowners" belong to?
> ▸ What is the community or network that "First-Time Buyers" or "Move-Up Sellers/ Buyers" call home?

Let's be clear; there are no such communities. And regrettably, this all-important distinction is not being adequately conveyed within conventional real estate-based social media tutelage. These aforementioned consumer groups, due to their unmet marketplace needs, represent *markets* more than they do networks or communities. To paraphrase the good doctor, Timothy Leary: *in order to have consumers properly respond to us, we must first properly respond to them.* Remaining true to this premise, I respectfully suggest that we must first subordinate our efforts to effectively respond to the needs of consumers to what many refer to as the "Law of Compensation." The definition I like best pertaining to the Law of Compensation is: Compensation is always in direct proportion to the quantity and quality of goods and services rendered.

This law suggests that we must respond to social communities and networks in a fashion that differs significantly from how we respond to distinct marketplace needs, which, in turn, form real estate markets. For example, the First-Time Buyers market represents needs that are directly connected to the Law of Compensation. This is why we tell clients, "I will be marketing your home online," as opposed to saying "I will be 'communitizing' your property online."

As you construct your social media plan or system, I recommend that you ask yourself, "Is my social media plan in alignment with marketplace needs? Or instead, is it merely limited to the shared interests of friends, fans, followers, networks, and online communities where marketplace needs may not naturally surface?"

Many years ago, there was a popular police drama on television called *Naked City*. At the end of each episode, the narrator would state in a serious demeanor, "There are eight million stories in the Naked City. This has been one of them." There are over one million real estate agents and each will have his or her own social media story. And there are also millions of online networks. But there are truly only several riveting real estate stories that need to be told online at any one time. You need to master these highly relevant stories and then match them to the right markets through the right communities and online networks. You must also provide the most enticing and relevant links to cause those with marketplace needs to connect to your website and/or blog.

There are essentially only three major markets, in my opinion, that most real estate agents should constantly reach and influence online:

1. Buyers/Investors
2. Sellers
3. Those who someday will be Sellers and/or Buyers.

For example, if you have concluded that you want to spend more of your time with home sellers, you first want to break this market down into several subcategories: those interested in resale, builders, niche markets of investors, waterfront properties, luxury markets, etc. Then you need to determine how to best reach and influence them online.

If you examine your markets at any given time, you will discern specific needs—but typically, only several. For example, what percentage of the home sellers in your market right now would be comprised of:

- ▸▸ Expired Listing Homeowners
- ▸▸ Short Sale Prospects
- ▸▸ Move-Up Sellers/Buyers
- ▸▸ Traditional Home Sellers who intend to put their property on the market in the next year or so

These relevant and distinct submarkets might very well cover a major part of the overall seller-side market, but they only comprise a very small percentage of the overall online communities and online networks at any point in time. This should vividly indicate to any strategically sophisticated real estate agent, who is attempting to be all things to all people online, that this is no more than a fool's errand and will spell digital disaster.

Accordingly, what is your social media plan to reach and influence these distinct markets online? How can you aggregate these folks into a distinct subset separate from the various non-specific online real estate communities and networks in which you participate? This requires social media seductiveness, which, in turn, requires customized-to-the-niche-market content. Later on, I will provide examples of what this online content should cover, and Steve Hundley and I will demonstrate how to connect social media content—through the use of real estate social marketing principles—in order to monetize your online commitment.

But first, let's revisit our industry's overall need to strategically employ social media *and real estate social marketing* for the purpose of rescuing our industry's image and relevance in the marketplace.

Regrettably, many consumers view the real estate industry in monolithic terms. They do, indeed, lump everyone in our industry together as one. This is not unusual, however, as people routinely treat most groups in a similar fashion. We all tend to stereotype people in specific professions—lawyers, engineers, pilots, etc. Another example regarding collective group characterization can be found in how most businesses aggregate all individuals—even when these individuals represent a myriad of different demographic subsets or distinct populations—together by using one word: consumers. One of the most important understandings that evolve out of what social networking and social media represent, and especially real estate social marketing, is that all individuals, groups, and markets must be nuanced in order to serve them and their distinctiveness.

The deeply entrenched practice of stereotyping professional groups is particularly problematic for the real estate industry. This is because when groups or professions are ranked, we don't seem to fare as well as most other professions, as illustrated in this Harris Poll study:

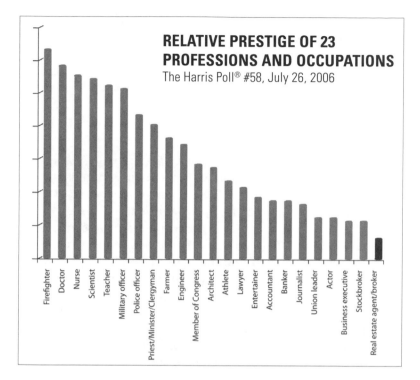

**RELATIVE PRESTIGE OF 23 PROFESSIONS AND OCCUPATIONS**
The Harris Poll® #58, July 26, 2006

Firefighter · Doctor · Nurse · Scientist · Teacher · Military officer · Police officer · Priest/Minister/Clergyman · Farmer · Engineer · Member of Congress · Architect · Athlete · Lawyer · Entertainer · Accountant · Banker · Journalist · Union leader · Actor · Business executive · Stockbroker · Real estate agent/broker

This denigrating categorization of all real estate professionals is essentially one that carries with it negative image consequences—consequences that social media can change, and perhaps rescue, but only if we properly utilize this transformational tool. Let's look at the consequences of the stereotypical treatment consumers afford to all real estate people offline—*which will also continue to take place online* unless we change consumer perceptions of our industry through the effective and strategic use of social media. As it is, the consequences of the lack of consumers' overall respect for our industry are:

1. When consumers erroneously conclude that all real estate agents are essentially the same, they expect less.
2. When consumers expect less, they generally receive less.
3. When consumers expect less, it stultifies industry-wide development because "less" becomes acceptable to the consumer and, therefore, to our industry as well.
4. When consumers expect less, they respect us less, and, therefore, tend to go elsewhere for real estate guidance (see survey), or resent us for the fees we charge because they see such fees as essentially only being tied to *transactional* assistance and not *content* assistance as well.
5. When consumers are more comfortable going elsewhere for real estate information, they often receive inferior and damaging information.

6. When consumers go elsewhere for real estate information, they become influenced by those who oftentimes discourage them from buying, moving up, etc., and who express negativity toward real estate professionals.

7. In real estate markets that require greater industry influence to stimulate the markets, when we are not turned to by consumers for such stimulation, markets tend to suffer more, which stalls economic recovery.

8. When consumers don't turn to real estate professionals for real estate information, both consumers and real estate professionals suffer.

All of these aforementioned consequences can be totally reversed if our industry employs information and content, and the appropriate social networking and social media platforms, to better respond to the needs of consumers.

At the root of some of these existing problems is the fact that, presently, we are not sufficiently educating consumers beyond their transactional needs. To illustrate my point, I venture to say that if you visited the real estate section of most bookstores, you would find that less than two percent of the books about real estate were written with the consumer in mind and are, instead, "industry"-generated.

Moreover, have you ever wondered why it is that our industry was not significantly blamed by Congress, consumers, or the media for the recent real estate-related meltdown? This was a real estate downturn that led to not only Fortune 10 companies, but *countries*, going bankrupt. Why weren't we harshly reprobated? After all, criticism should have been directed at anyone who was involved in encouraging people to buy properties and, in turn, secure mortgages based on utterly inappropriate advice and decision-making.

Could it be that the rest of the world is dubious regarding the real estate industry's power to influence consumers and instead views us as being materially insignificant regarding the decisions consumers make—even when those decisions are about real estate? Social media, however, if properly used, can now change consumers' perceptions in a positive way.

I must ask: at the present time, is any newspaper displaying this type of headline: "Real Estate Agents to Lead Real Estate Recovery"? The answer is no. However, I must say that the recent National Association of Realtors (NAR) ad campaign, thanks to Dale Stinton, Frank Sibley, and John Most, was spectacular in its relevance and in its positive message regarding reviving the real estate market.

But NAR and its marketing and media muscle cannot perform this strategic task unilaterally. It requires every Realtor's more effective deployment of his or her social media opportunities, and that, again, requires relevant content. By content, I mean relevant information that is disseminated to respectful consumers who are more trusting regarding real estate relevance in their lives.

This shift will entail individual real estate professionals employing social networking and social media as more of a real estate catalyst that impels people to buy and sell, as opposed to our merely posting, "Homes for Sale" content. Even worse is when the primary influence related to real estate decisions is being generated from those outside of the real estate industry.

Presently, the real estate industry is nowhere near as proactive as it should be regarding how real estate consumers can and should be influenced. For example, what do you think causes consumers to decide to purchase larger homes? Is it due to a change in their careers or financial status? Because they now have more children? Or would it be because real estate professionals contacted them when they were not even remotely interested in buying larger houses and the agents' content and consultative skills became the catalyst for stimulating their interest?

This is just one example of how we, as an industry, need to begin to view social media as an avenue for using *actionable* real estate content to expand consumers' interest in real estate. We need to bring them into the market, as opposed to only responding to consumers' needs when they decide to enter the market, and even then, by responding minimally—essentially only providing them with content tied to transactional assistance, i.e., pictures of homes with links to real estate agent contact information. From all appearances, the real estate industry's long-assumed offline role was more geared toward

*One example of how the world is dubious regarding the real estate industry's willingness to provide consumers with relevant editorial content is the best-selling book* Freakonomics, *which blasts the real estate industry.*

*facilitating* versus *causing* real estate transactions. Now, due to the unprecedented range, reach, influence, efficiencies, and economics made possible through the proper use of social media, our industry can become the appropriate catalyst for appropriate real estate decisions.

Since social media can uniquely respond to our industry's need to more effectively direct consumers, we must both re-examine and revise our old methods of consumer engagement so as to fully utilize the capabilities of this relatively new tool. We must, therefore, seize this social media opportunity as an industry—that is, unless we believe that consumers are making the connection on their own, offline, between our calendars and their downsizing; our refrigerator magnets and their moving up; our pumpkins and how they can appeal their property taxes; our park bench signs and why their homes didn't sell; or our supermarket cart advertisements and why they should buy an investment

## Social Media to the Real Estate Rescue

home near the university their child attends.

Speaking of supermarkets, I remember a Realtor in Chicago coming up to me after a seminar and saying, "Mr. Dalton, I am no longer advertising on supermarket shopping carts. Now, I only promote myself online through my social networks." I asked him what led to the change and he said, "I went home for dinner and my 6-year-old daughter was crying. I asked her what was wrong and she said, 'Dad, all of my friends at school think you are missing!'"

So, how can social media rescue perhaps your own, but at the very least, our industry's image, relevance, and results?

In my view, the way we can reboot our response and relationship to consumers is by becoming more strategic and skillful in how we disseminate the right content to the right consumer, within the right community or market, and in the way in which we communicate with them.

For that, it will require our industry to become more dedicated to conducting consumer-based research. Other than the great researching job done routinely by NAR, how many companies can point to their own research and development department? Moreover, how many Realtors are conducting significant research and development themselves, and specifically doing surveys within their local markets to determine the unmet needs of consumers? How many are then following up with the right strategies that allow them to respond to these consumer-validated needs online?

Furthermore, I encourage you, the reader of this book, to create a real estate survey for your particular marketplace and provide a link to it on your website or blog so that consumers in your marketplace can participate. This consumer-centric and sensitive effort on your part will signal that you care about, and are committed to, their/your community and marketplace needs. It will also convey that you, specifically, want to know how they'd like to be responded to online regarding your social media content.

More than 20 years ago, I created an offline survey that was distributed to approximately 50,000 homeowners. This major, consumer-focused effort on my part led to my company and myself being featured in major media outlets. This strategy then led to my creating the Better Homes & Gardens Home Information System℠ and selling my rights to this information system to the Meredith Corporation...a major, and highly regarded, media conglomerate.

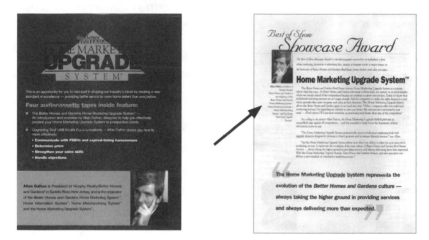

Presently, Steve Hundley and I, along with RISMedia and 1parkplace, developed the *2010 Dalton/Hundley Real Estate Social Media Census* so that we could learn more about our industry's use of social networking and social media. We also created the census to demonstrate to the industry that we are truly committed to *discovering*, through our research, the social media needs and practices of thousands of real estate professionals, and *sharing* the results in both this physical book and online, as well as at educational events that we facilitate.

Since I make numerous distinctions throughout this book, please indulge me for this particular one. What separates real estate professionals from others is that essentially every other person, when using the Internet or social media/social networking for business purposes, is only trying to attract consumers, buyers, and possible clients. THEY ARE NOT TRYING TO SERVE THE NEEDS OF THEIR EXISTING CLIENTS, AS ARE REALTORS. If we demonstrate to our clients—and specifically to home sellers (where seller agency applies)—that we manage our social networking and social media in a way that expressly benefits *them*, this will lead to consumers' overall better appreciation of our online value.

I witnessed firsthand how this responsibility was either neglected or misunderstood while I headed up REALTOR.com. It became abundantly clear to me that many of the Realtors were more interested in how they could generate leads from REALTOR.com for overall purposes, than they were in using REALTOR.com to better market the properties and serve the fiduciary needs of their home-seller clients. This is why, when I arrived, I changed a major program that existed at REALTOR.com from "I-Lead" to "The REALTOR.com Home Marketing System," which then led to the creation of the Company Showcase Program.

Interestingly, those Realtors and companies who more readily accepted and understood that REALTOR.com was of greater value to them when they used it as a vehicle for serving the needs of home-seller clients—rather than principally as a means to obtain new leads—experienced a far greater benefit because they were tapping into the needs of clients and not just consumers.

Regarding the use of social networking and social media vehicles to enhance our image and relevance, we will see results in this area only when consumers begin to discover that we are not only able to use social networking and social media tools for our personal prospecting, networking, and overall thought leadership purposes, but also to strategically advance the interests of our clients.

As an example, if you wanted me to be your home-seller client and you identified my home as one that would be ideal for "downsizers," I would immediately ask how you plan to use your real estate social networking and social media contacts to reach and influence this targeted market in order to serve my specific needs. This would be of greater interest to me than merely hearing about your massive collection of friends, fans, and followers. I would also be interested in seeing you tweet about the benefits of downsizing and accompanying your tweet with a link to a related article on your blog. This would impress me more than seeing you tweet that you are going to a convention—which essentially is announcing, "Come burglarize my home because I won't be there this weekend." How relevant is that?

It is for this reason that Steve Hundley and I will highlight, in another chapter, examples of how to best use social media in order to display your professional relevance through the use of a *real estate social marketing system* that we have developed.

But for now, let me pick up where I left off regarding the significance of delineating network communities and markets. The content I will share with you in the next chapter reflects the need to *customize* solutions for specific real estate markets online versus the misguided social media efforts of many in our industry, i.e., their inability to respond to the social needs of scores of disparate networks and communities through social media and social networking.

I'd like to rephrase, for our purposes, Dr. Leary's quote about changing the way people respond to you: *To change the way we are responded to, we need to change the way we respond to the market's needs.* If we respond predominately on a social basis, we should expect to be responded back to in the same manner, reinforcing the view that we are an industry that epitomizes the notion that success in real estate is based more upon *who* you know and not on *what* you know. If, instead, we communicate a willingness to respond to distinct unmet real estate needs that exist within the marketplace through our nimble use of social networking and social media platforms, we will find that the manner in which we're responded to creates an additional transformation—one that works in tandem with the monumental transformation spawned by social media-based technology. Again, this transformation is all tied to our content, and our content is tied to our social media spirit of intent; for that, I will provide, in this book, examples of how some of my social media writings address distinct marketplace needs in order to best convey the importance of matching the right content with the right consumers online.

**Whom would you more likely trust regarding advice on whether or not you should invest in real estate?**

**37.6%** Financial Planner
**17.2%** Family, Friends or Neighbors
**14.3%** Real Estate Agent
**7.0%** Attorney
**3.0%** Other
**20.9%** None of these

Source: Actionable Research May 2007

*Consumers respond based upon how they are responded to.*

Dr. Leary's most famous quote might be an appropriate way to conclude this chapter: "Turn on, tune in, drop out." Regarding social media, real estate professionals need to first turn on and definitely tune in, but please don't drop out as your efforts will enable you to reach greater real estate heights...if not "highs".

# Chapter 3

# Linking Marketing
# with Social Media

Of all the chapters within *Leveraging Your Links*, this particular one will be, for me, the most personal. My observations will reflect my deepest thoughts regarding the vast and infinitely complex field of social media and how it relates to real estate brokerage. I will also draw upon my own specific career experiences as they pertain, both directly and indirectly, to social media.

The degree to which I personalize the subject matter of social media is done with the implicit permission extended to all of us from the underlying premise of social media. Social media is defined by many as either citizen journalism or the democratization of information. We are now encouraged to make a conversion from where we traditionally were only consumers of information to where we now are empowered to be the producers or publishers of information. The consequences of social media perhaps even *mandate* our individual musings.

Concerning how citizen journalism relates to real estate professionals and their opportunity to convey professional content online, it also means that we can insert ourselves as thought leaders in a way that was, heretofore, unimaginable. This unprecedented online literary opportunity, however, must not be abused. Our approach to social media must be balanced, so that we not only express our personal thoughts and views, but are also willing to listen to, learn from, participate in, and interact with the thoughts and teachings of others. Citizen journalism, when undertaken properly, is a critical concept to absorb in order for the real estate community to effectively move forward. Since social media represents a shift from media conglomerates dominating most of the journalistic content surrounding real estate to where now the average citizen can also make individual content contributions on the subject of real estate, it would be tragic if average citizens alone—instead of real estate experts like you—assume the real estate informational role or fill the void that has been created by social media.

Regarding the necessary balance that this literary opportunity presents, and as it relates to this book, my personal postulations are far outweighed, in fact transcended, by the contributions within *Leveraging Your Links* that have been derived from RISMedia and 1parkplace research; our far-reaching *2010 Dalton/ Hundley Real Estate Social Media Census*; the expert and practical social media applications that the mentors featured in this book reveal; as well as from the information collected from countless hours of research and focus groups, conducted by Steve Hundley and me.

When interviewing scores of social media practitioners throughout North America, I always acknowledge, as I wish to do here, that one of the major reasons for my seeking and understanding their thoughts and practices on the subject of social media is that I am, admittedly, not a consummate social networking practitioner, but instead, one who is committed to being a dedicated social media analyst.

Although I am, or have become, a "self-proclaimed" social media analyst—which suggests objectivity and a degree of analytical distance—like any of us who approach any subject, my "take" on social networking, social media, and now on real estate social marketing, can be traced to the antecedent experiences that influence my writing.

Regarding my principal professional experience, I must acknowledge that when considering the three following words and concepts—Networking, Media, and Marketing—that my greatest emphasis and interest remained on the field or discipline of Marketing. Thus, I would be remiss not to disclose that I cannot help but forensically assess and evaluate the role that marketing can, or should, assume in any online relationship that is created between real estate professionals and online consumers—especially regarding how real estate professionals should seek to not only market themselves and properties, but also respond to the needs of the marketplace...not just one monolithic marketplace, but the needs of myriad niche markets that can now be better reached and influenced through effective social media strategies.

I believe that the effective utilization of marketing, as part of an effective social media strategy, begins with one's thoughts about marketing. The one definition of "marketing" that I have found to be both the most inspiring and the most instructional is one that I read many decades ago: *"Marketing means first determining the unmet needs in the market and then creating goods and services to satisfy such unmet needs."* If this particular longstanding definition is one that doesn't work for you, then I suggest that you Google, as I did, the definition of "marketing" yourself. You will find that there are scores of other definitions, although all of them seem to be essentially similar. For example, here's one from businessdictionary.com:

*"Marketing: management process through which goods and services move from concept to the customer. As a philosophy, it is based on thinking about the business in terms of customer needs and their satisfaction. As a practice, it consists in coordination of four elements called the 4 Ps."*

To satisfy your intellectual curiosity, the 4 Ps of marketing are price, product, promotion, and placement.

I have no doubt that a high percentage of the readers of this book have, at the very least, a vague recollection of these 4 Ps, while some, I am sure, are especially conversant regarding their significance. The appropriate question then becomes: To what degree does our industry derive its marketing direction, either offline or online, from these 4 Ps, since they are considered to be the building blocks, or arguably the DNA, of all marketing? More specifically, what might their significance or relationship be to the effective utilization of social media by real estate professionals?

This relationship between marketing and social media may not be, at present, one with which real estate professionals are consumed. My sense is that some readers—those who are approaching this topic with a narrow focus, or those seeking gift-wrapped or linear explanations of this complex social media subject matter—might even wonder how marketing, or the 4 Ps of marketing, could possibly be connected to social media or, more specifically, why this perspective requires illumination within *Leveraging Your Links.* Those readers will be especially puzzled if they purchased this book with the sole intent of learning how Facebook, LinkedIn, Google Buzz, and SEO work, along with how to effectively create or aggregate friends, fans, followers, communities, and tribes. Although many of these components of social media have been covered extensively within this book, I nevertheless remain unswervingly committed to ensuring that *Leveraging Your Links* goes well beyond the typical and perfunctory tutelage to which much of our industry has been already exposed.

One reason why my goal for this book is to exceed the mechanistic, and, instead, delve into what's missing in most instruction on the subject of social media, has to do with the disturbing findings that emerged from our Social Media Census, as well as from all our other comprehensive research. To be clear, if our approach and industry-centric teachings were not inextricably interwoven with unmistakably poor and unprofessional results, then I would not have become motivated to suggest a different perspective on social media usage for real estate professionals. All evidence points to the fact that the overwhelming percentage of real estate professionals who describe themselves as being engaged in social media are not able to claim any material ROI benefit from their online activities. Therefore, it is my considered opinion that the lack of ROI-related results is due to the fact that many in our industry are approaching social media as it relates to serving communities and individuals, instead of recognizing that social media/social networking must, first and foremost, in order for one's efforts to be monetized, coalesce into a personal online *real estate social marketing system*.

In order for social networking and social media to be integrated for purposes of real estate social *marketing*, a strategic synthesis or convergence is required. For this, one must first examine one's thoughts regarding his or her spirit of intent in using social networking and social media, and determine whether he or she considers social networking and social media to be one and the same. *For example, if one is to conclude that social networking and social media are interchangeable and essentially the same thing, it would, therefore, become virtually impossible to integrate them and achieve convergence. This is because, by definition, if entities are the same or indistinguishable, they cannot complement one another and, thus, be integrated. For example, you don't integrate the color red with the color red.* Yet, if you integrate the color red with blue, you create a convergence where you arrive at purple. It is stunning to me, in my research, to literally hear thousands of individuals asserting that social networking and social media are one and the same, and then go on to say that social networking and social media have to "work together." Out of respect for my focus group participants, I don't challenge them on their confusion or logical inconsistency. For the purposes of this book, however, I have elected to forcefully rebut this widespread, illogical conclusion to a complicated and nuanced subject matter that is crying out desperately for digital distinctiveness. To not have, as a starting point as one attempts to optimize social media, a definition of what it *is* and *is not* is an impediment...because thoughts matter.

Accordingly, I'd like to invoke the iconic words on a plaque that resides on my wall: "Watch your thoughts as your thoughts lead to your words; your words lead to your actions; your actions lead to your behavior; your behavior leads to your character; and your character leads to your destiny." If you accept this anonymously written, poetic-like postulation regarding the consequences of our thoughts, then your thoughts regarding social networking, social media, and real estate social marketing will lead to your words, actions, behavior, character, destiny, and thus, your results.

Perhaps the definition of marketing, as meaning first determining the unmet needs of the marketplace, might also significantly influence your strategic utilization of the available social networking and social media platforms. Now, if your thoughts regarding social networking and social media are not deeply rooted in a marketing definition—based on spirit of intent, where you are determined to employ social networking and social media first and foremost as a way to meet the unmet needs of consumers rather than your own needs—you might be experiencing social media burnout or futility. This could be because you are approaching this transformational opportunity from what might be considered a predominantly self-serving point of view or self-motivated manifestation. For real estate professionals hoping to assimilate the many wonders of Web 2.0 and beyond—which now enables connectivity, interactivity, sharing, listening, participating in communities, as well as building and fortifying your friends, fans, and followers—their greater utilization of social networking and social media, *if it does not emerge out of a consumer-centric prism*, might result in their experiencing a very unrewarding and even debilitating and distracting involvement with the concepts. Clearly, if you are not effectively harnessing the inherent and leverageable power of social networking and social media as conduits to creating consumer solutions, and thus bringing value to the "marketplace," you might find yourself seduced or even intoxicated by a never-ending personal quest to attain an Ashton Kutcher-like Twitter following, without having an accompanying strategic plan to convert your burgeoning list of followers into buyers, sellers, and real estate clients.

I'd like to go a little deeper into how thoughts lead to words, and ultimately, online real estate results. Regarding marketing, and, specifically, how our industry responded to the wisdom surrounding the 4 Ps, regrettably, while the rest of the marketing world found inspiration, clarity, comfort, and, ultimately, professional marketing instructions from the 4 Ps, the real estate industry was one of the only industries that opted out. This is because, in my considered opinion, much of our industry confused or failed to effectively delineate, for decades, the difference between *selling* a home and *marketing* a home. It wasn't until about 25 years ago that, as an industry, we began to own the distinction. For decades, real estate companies would never broadcast that they were the "number one top marketer of homes," but instead would claim that they were the "number one seller of homes." Clearly, every real estate company and agent now know and profess the difference. In real estate terms, when one represents the *home seller* (unless your practice of agency precludes this distinction), one is providing a *marketing* role that emanates out of a *marketing* plan; when an agent is representing a *buyer*, the agent is looking to *sell* the buyer any one of a number of homes as opposed to marketing a particular home. Yet, as simple and straightforward as that distinction is, the lack of such clarity has created massive confusion for consumers, undermined our value as an industry, and generated many additional, negative, and unintended consequences. Therefore, it might be helpful to know that since many in our industry—for decades and until recent years—confused the concepts of selling a home with marketing a home and considered the two as being one and the same, we as an industry, might be particularly vulnerable based upon this history of confusion over such a simple distinction.

Likewise, it stands to reason, therefore, that our industry also might not appreciate the difference between *social networking* and *social media.* Our real estate ancestors confused selling and marketing, thereby treating them as one and the same, and one has to wonder, whether their present-day offspring will now be confusing social media and social marketing?

As it is, most in our industry capriciously or whimsically select either social media or social networking to describe their beloved new activity in a fashion that recalls the old "You say, 'tomato' and I say, 'to-mah-to'" expression.

## Linking Marketing with Social Media

To be deliberately redundant, if you believe that social media and social networking mean the same thing and you use the two terms interchangeably— without the proper dedication to nuance and distinctiveness that is required for greater understanding and, thus, utility—then how can you possibly optimize each of their potentials separately? What's more troubling is: how can you scientifically and strategically integrate sameness? In order to understand and then effectively employ the *real estate social marketing system*—which Steve Hundley and I, along with our respective companies, 1parkplace and RISMedia, have developed—it is imperative that you grasp the significance of social networking and social media as parenthetical entities before you can accept their convergence leading to real estate social marketing, and specifically a *system* for real estate social marketing.

Distinctions, while very important if one is interested in clarity and potential convergence, unfortunately, are often overlooked or not made. Even those who profess to be social media gurus, actually consider the Internet and the World Wide Web as being indistinguishable. To the contrary, both the Internet and the Web are clearly different enterprises although, admittedly, symbiotic. If this distinction comes as a revelation to you, it might be helpful to understand that the Internet is more defined by its hardware and the Web by the software that enables links to content.

We all appreciate the consequences of what transpired due to our industry's not achieving delineated clarity regarding the concepts of selling real estate and marketing real estate. For starters, it empowered a consumer cottage industry called FSBOs. How could "For Sale by Owners" *not* conclude that if all we did was *sell* their homes, that they could do it, too? Perhaps if, 80 years ago, we realized that we were really *marketing* homes when representing the home seller, then consumers might not have become as emboldened in their own ability to become—not FSBOs, but "FMBOs," or "For Marketing by Owners." Being a FMBO and marketing a home requires a totally different skill set and value proposition than selling a home does. Regrettably, we unmistakably gravitated to the word "sell" because, as real estate salespeople, we defaulted to the notion that most people who sell anything are not considered marketing people. Although we did *both*—sell and market—rather than celebrate and properly educate the consumer as to how each required a different discipline, we, by default and until recently, celebrated the word "sell."

Our industry's overall lack of marketing dedication, also explains why, in my view, we latched onto price and essentially, for all intents and purposes, discarded 75 percent of the other Ps of Marketing (product, promotion, and placement). A classic example of this self-induced marginalization of our value can best be discovered in our marketing approach regarding why some homes don't sell and others do. Specifically, when we over-focus on price as the major or only reason why a home *does not* sell, we reveal that we have also symmetrically concluded that the only reason a home *does* sell is because of price. This unwittingly conveys to the consumer that our skills cannot be much greater than those of an appraiser. This simplistic, longstanding, and resoundingly communicated belief and acceptance within our industry that homes don't sell because of price has denied our industry the opportunity to achieve a higher purpose and one with greater clarity—that being that the only reason a home doesn't sell is because of *marketing*, because price is just a *part* of marketing, as are staging, negotiating, networking, and a host of other often overlooked, yet nevertheless valuable, real estate-related skills. The result of our industry over-focusing on price, and concentrating more on the word "selling," or using it as an acceptable and interchangeable word for "marketing," was that it deprived us of a full appreciation of marketing. This forced us to ensure that our minimalistic thinking would be validated by the following mindset, which I've heard expressed on hundreds of occasions from within the industry: "Allan, you could have five dead bodies in the basement of a home, but if you lower the price enough, somebody will buy it."

What this non-marketing thought process conveys to both our industry as well as to home sellers is: Even if the greater reason your home didn't sell was due to ineffective consultation and negotiation, inept staging, inadequate networking, or non-targeted marketing, if we just keep lowering the price enough, somebody will buy your home. Therefore, those other marketing activities are not germane because...don't you see?...the only reason a home either sells or doesn't sell is because of *price*. This attitude enables real estate professionals to get by with thinking and conveying that if they keep lowering the price enough, independent of anything else, somebody will buy the home, since it's all about price. Thus, we introduce a self-fulfilling prophecy. Considering that thoughts lead to words, words lead to actions, and so forth, ask yourself this question: If all you ever heard within the industry was the assertion that the only reason a home does not sell is due to ineffective *negotiating*, do you think there would be greater emphasis placed on negotiating skills? What if the real estate industry agreed that the only reason a home doesn't sell is because of inept staging? Would there be a greater emphasis placed on the development of staging skills? Clearly, there are a host of reasons why a home doesn't sell, and there is one word that includes all of them—*marketing*. Price is a part of marketing, but marketing is not a part of price. This lack of a marketing thought process emerges out of a lack of full comprehension of what marketing means to an industry that for years celebrated the word "selling." Now I am equally fearful that our lack of distinctive clarity—regarding the trilogy of *social networking, social media, and social marketing*—will carry with it significant negative consequences as well, when it comes to our value to consumers.

Perhaps the following example will bring greater clarity to my premise:

### What's Your Mindset?

| | | |
|---|---|---|
| Listing Presentations | or | Marketing Proposals |
| Listing Agent | or | Marketing Agent |
| Pre-Listing Packet | or | Pre-Marketing Packet |
| If You Don't List, You Don't Last | or | If You Don't Market, You Don't Last |
| Listings Are the Name of the Game | or | Marketing is the Name of the Game |
| Homes Don't Sell Because of Price | or | Homes Don't Sell Because of Inadequate Marketing (Because Price is a part of Marketing, i.e., Wrong Price = Poor Marketing) |
| I Strive to Sell More Homes | or | I Strive to Sell Homes for More |
| Personal Promotion | or | Property Plus Content Promotion, which Better Promotes the Person |

These distinctions will carry with them profound social media consequences as you strive to insert yourself as a real estate thought leader. I must confess that I am conflicted about our industry's lack of marketing focus. While I can empathize with those consumers who may not have had the opportunity to realize the greater value of our industry's most professional marketers, I must confess that I owe much of my career success—which enabled me to pay our three daughters' tuitions at Princeton, The University of Pennsylvania, and Boston University—to our industry's greater celebration of the words "listings" and "sales" versus "marketing." This void, or the insufficient emphasis placed on marketing in general, enabled me to co-create, for the following international real estate brands, this list of marketing systems:

SYSTEMS

**Better Homes and Gardens and Allan Dalton unveil Home Merchandising System at Convention**

*Allan Dalton presented the Home Merchandising System at Convention*

Reprint from Meredith Corporate publication.

➤ The former Better Homes and Gardens Real Estate Company
➤ The former Better Homes and Gardens Home Marketing System<sup>SM</sup>
➤ The former Better Homes and Gardens Home Merchandising System<sup>SM</sup>
➤ The former Better Homes and Gardens Home Information System<sup>SM</sup>
➤ The former Better Homes and Gardens Home Marketing Upgrade System<sup>SM</sup>
➤ The Century 21 Customized Home Marketing System<sup>SM</sup>
➤ The ERA Value-Added Marketing System<sup>SM</sup>
➤ The NRT Coldwell Banker Full-Service Marketing System<sup>SM</sup>

The German writer and philosopher, Johann Wolfgang von Goethe, said, "Before you can *do* something you must first *be* something." Therefore, allow me to respectfully ask you: Are you more of a social networker, a social media-ite, or a real estate social marketer? How about all three?

If you answered that you are more of a social networker than a social media-ite, or if you're not quite sure yet what it means to be a real estate social marketer—because that concept is not receiving the same attention as social networking and social media—and, consequently, your motive for using Facebook, Google Buzz, LinkedIn, Twitter, etc. is primarily, if not predominantly, social, then that reality might explain the following findings. As noted earlier, based on our extensive and exhaustive research, the overwhelming majority— well over 95 percent—of our focus group participants have revealed either a mounting frustration regarding how little money they can directly attribute to social networking activities, or a complete absence of real estate-related results altogether. We also learned that many real estate professionals are experiencing difficulty in resolving to what degree they should engage in social networking on a personal basis as opposed to inserting themselves in a visible way for business purposes. In other words, they're thinking, "I need to be careful not to be considered as one who is prospecting social networking communities for real estate business opportunities. While everyone else is tweeting about the Super Bowl, should I be chirping about my Super Listing?" Other agents are beginning to express concern that their clients could infer that the reason their real estate agent hasn't properly marketed or sold their home is because the agent has become diverted and is now an incorrigible online chatterer, as opposed to a world-class, strategic online marketer of real estate.

Now, of course, social networking *is* making a small percentage of Realtors much more successful, as is demonstrated by those real estate, social-media expert practitioners embraced by this book. They represent stellar examples of how successful real estate agents need to be not only social networkers but also, as *they* are, providers of media content, in order to differentiate themselves throughout their online social networking.

## Linking Marketing with Social Media

As I indicated earlier, I need to be as transparent as possible in disclosing what has influenced my view of social networking, social media, and real estate social marketing. It indirectly relates to Mark Zuckerberg, the founder of Facebook. I first became familiar with Mr. Zuckerberg and Facebook several years ago while I served as president of Move.com's real estate division. This position not only included my being CEO of REALTOR.com, but also entailed my being responsible for the performance of Top Producer, our Enterprise website division, Home Builder.com, and Rent.net. Admittedly, the vast majority of my time, knowledge, and impact was directed toward the flagship of our company, REALTOR.com.

As an officer of Move.com, I had the responsibility of presenting detailed reports regarding the real estate division to our board of directors. Our board was composed of a veritable Who's Who, or unofficial Hall of Fame of Internet, social networking, and social media visionaries. Mike Long, CEO of Move, Inc., and a gentleman whom I greatly admire and consider a great mentor and friend, was instrumental in the founding of WebMD and served as its Chairman & CEO before taking on the major challenges of righting Homestore/Move.com, which only he could. Another member of the board was John Doerr, a partner at Kleiner Perkins Caufield & Byers, and who, in John Battelle's book, *The Search: How Google and Its Rivals Rewrote the Rules of Business and Transformed Our Culture*, is credited with being instrumental in the funding of Google, as well as Amazon and Friendster. I remember Mr. Doerr saying that Amazon's original spirit of intent was to eliminate illiteracy in the world. I must say, I was deeply moved when I heard that.

*Two gentlemen, Mike Long and Bono, who have utilized social media for transcendental purposes. Mike to bring health information to the world as former Chairman & CEO of WebMD, and U2's Bono to bring humanitarian aid to the world. Is it just me, or do I seem more ebullient to be standing with Bono and Mike than they do to be standing with me...sorry, guys, but you're now a part of my "network."*

Another board member was Roger McNamee, the founder and chairman of Elevation Partners, who is internationally renowned as a technology visionary, and considered by Mr. Zuckerberg to be a close technological comrade. Also on the board were other individuals whom I also greatly respected: Geraldine Laybourne, who began as program manager at Nickelodeon and ended her time there as president; and Brad Williamson, dean of the UCLA Business School, to name just a few.

All of the exceptional people on the board, just as John Featherston has, have deeply influenced my thinking regarding social networking and social media. The reason why I am becoming an egregious name-dropper right before your very eyes is that I'd like you to know that my having had the privilege of being exposed to and associated with these much wiser, and far greater social media visionaries than I could ever hope to be, and my observing how every single concept or conversation they were engaged in always emanated out of the question, "What would be best for the consumer?" have truly influenced how I view and assess whether or not our industry, and all associated with it, are approaching social networking and social media from a similar vantage point—one where consumer and client satisfaction remain paramount—or instead are utilizing social networking in a more self-centered and, therefore, less-valuable manner.

Specifically, I believe that Mr. Zuckerberg created Facebook so that Harvard students could connect and form an online community—not so that they could sell their goods and wares to each other. This leaves me to wonder, based upon our research, if the reason why so many real estate agents are experiencing a lack of financial reward from their social networking exploits is that some form of social networking deity is punishing them for their digital misuse. I also wonder if another reason is that since our industry cannot resist personal promotion opportunities, it is overlooking the opportunity to publish and promote valuable real estate-relevant content and is demonstrating behavior similar to that which I observed while at REALTOR.com.

My experience as CEO of REALTOR.com, for the several years that I had the honor of being associated with the National Association of Realtors® website, represents the single-highest privilege of my professional life. This experience not only provided me with a uniquely widespread look at our industry-related online behavior, but it also prepared me for what was to come next: social networking and social media.

Regarding REALTOR.com, I must say that since I left the company, the improvements to its website—due to the collaboration of Errol Samuelson and Dale Stinton and their respective organizations—regarding how it serves consumers and Realtors and their clients is stunning; it is truly beyond anything I could have imagined. Moreover, in Max Pigman, a legendary REALTOR.com executive, the industry has an individual who possesses as much knowledge regarding the integration of real estate brokerage and technology as I believe exists. That said, even with the great resource that REALTOR.com is, it is interesting that so many Realtors did not originally gravitate to it on the basis of how it could best serve their clients and consumers and, instead, were determining how it could benefit them, with the result being that they were slow to monetize the site's greater value.

I don't make this observation with any malice, cynicism, or to malign any individual or company, as it is human nature to first wonder, "What's in it for me?." I am as much of an example of this as anybody else, as I will now reveal.

The reason why I can relate to the real estate industry's recalcitrance regarding the Internet in general is reflected by how in the mid-1990s, when I was president and co-owner of my previously mentioned brokerage, and at a time when the Internet made its first appearance in our company's consciousness, both Joe Murphy and I, like many brokers and/or owners, resisted what it represented. In fact, as a way to diminish the Internet's significance back then, I quickly created the *Real Estate Outernet*. The *Outernet*, while it did have the Internet at its center, was my way of reminding both my associates and consumers that while the Internet was a part of what we do, it was only a part; our greater value in serving their needs was over and above the Internet. This was necessary as many of the home sellers and builders I met with during marketing proposals and presentations wanted to see how the Internet was going to impact our marketing.

Please remember that this was in an age when many in real estate were beginning to talk about the threat of disintermediation—defined by Merriam-Webster's Online Dictionary as "the elimination of an intermediary in a transaction between two parties"—and how they feared the Internet would either displace their usefulness, like it did for travel agents, or at the very least, marginalize their value. During that period, as an owner owing all of my income to real estate brokerage, I was concerned that our perceived value would suffer, so, in response, I created the *Outernet*.

It is obvious to me now, as I look back, that my initial resistance to the Internet, regarding its relationship to our value, is an example of how I focused more on what we might lose versus what the consumer might gain. Those more prescient than I in-

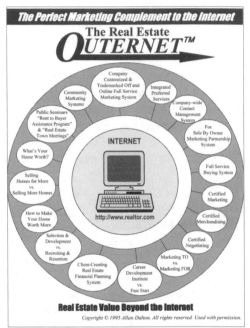

*The off- and online world will always have to be integrated. Just as my Outernet illustration showed in 1995.*

tuitively understood that the Internet needed to first be viewed for how it would benefit consumers and our clients. In the same way, we must all ask ourselves how social networking and social media usage can best serve consumers and our clients. But for that to happen, it will require a different thought process for many in our industry when it comes to how we view change.

Since you do not need this author to be the zillionth person to offer up examples of how people resist change, I'd like to instead address how I believe our industry has *responded* to change, and how we also have *resisted* the changes that the outer world (not the *Outernet*) has embraced. In fact, I'd like to ask you why our industry has resisted virtually all of the major changes that consumers have embraced, except for social networking. Could it be that many within our ranks not only did *not* resist social networking but, instead, were actually *giddy* about it, because they overwhelmingly viewed it as potentially benefiting them versus how they could use it to benefit consumers? The name itself, social networking, when relating to real estate agents, reinforces many consumers' opinions of agents; those consumers do not properly appreciate all that Realtors do and have come to believe that your success in real estate has more to do with your being social and a networker as opposed to your being a great salesperson, marketer, highly skilled negotiator, merchandiser, or thought leader.

This industry-enabling thought process has also led many consumers to unjustifiably perceive a real estate transaction as a fee-inflated event that they must subsidize in order to promulgate an inefficiently run industry. In plain language, they believe they're being overcharged because they think they can do what we do: "They can sell, I can sell. They're social, I'm social. They can network, I can network." And now, "They're on Facebook, I'm on Facebook. They tweet, I tweet. In fact, so does my 10-year-old." This is why real estate professionals will have to become more adroit at explaining how they have harnessed the combination of social networking and social media for real estate-specific purposes, and as a way to represent clients' needs, and, thus, have a real estate social *marketing* system.

I may not be right, but I am convinced that many in our industry will be slow to ascend to this convergence because I witnessed a slow period of adoption regarding REALTOR.com—most agents did not immediately recognize its full potential and only understood it years later. The evolution of the use of REALTOR.com by many is reflected by how most Realtors first viewed the site as a way to promote themselves: first in the directory, then via a personal website. They were not as quick to utilize the site's other features—i.e., enhanced listings, virtual tours, featured homes, and other contextual information that benefited consumers—which are now used by most Realtors. Eventually, many arrived at the conclusion that if you served the needs of the consumers online, before your own, you would realize a greater payoff.

Reflecting back on my own experience, in terms of how our industry responds to most major changes, I wonder if you agree with this illustration of how the industry is typically not in sync with the changes that consumers favor.

## Linking Marketing with Social Media

**Responses to Change:**

| Change | Industry's "Initial" (many, but not all) Response | Consumers' Response |
|---|---|---|
| Internet | No | Yes |
| Agency Changes | No | Yes |
| Enhanced Listings | No | Yes |
| IDX | No | Yes |
| Seller Disclosure | No | Yes |
| Social Networking | Yes, Yes, Yes | Yes |

Indeed, our industry's response to the opportunities surrounding social networking and social media will definitely be influenced by how most agents perceive their value. Moreover, just as social networking will be employed based upon the intent of the user, the same is true for social media. There are hundreds, if not thousands, of social media definitions being bandied about or socialized, if you will, these days.

Interestingly, during the focus group meetings which Steve Hundley and I conducted across North America, when we asked for a definition of social networking, we would typically hear responses like the following: "It means connecting, interactivity, sharing, learning, building or joining communities, tribes, friends, fans, followers, etc." When we then asked for definitions of social media, our focus groups became remarkably more reticent. And when the responses did come, to either what social media or social networking represented, we almost, without exception, *did not hear the following*: "It's citizen journalism;" or "It's the democratization of information;" or "Social media represents content and social networking is the vehicle to connect content to communities." We also never heard that "Social media is either my, or our industry's, opportunity to reclaim real estate-information relevance and influence from the media conglomerates, and now we'll be able to directly influence consumers online with our more accurate and robust real estate content, because after all, we, the practitioners, are the real experts."

In terms of social media as opposed to social networking, it definitely appears that our industry is somewhat unable to articulate a clearly defined social media objective—one that properly employs technology and existing and future-formed online communities in order to disseminate rich and relevant real estate-related content to communities of interactive friends, fans, and followers.

However, Realtors can readily express that their chief goal is not to educate consumers, friends, fans, and followers, but instead to merely collect them. It makes one wonder if this professed premise is the equivalent of inviting a group of friends over for dinner and not feeding them? In *Twelfth Night*, Shakespeare (he of greater social media than social networking repute) had Duke Orsino say, "If music be the food of love, play on." One has to wonder, is social media serving as a synonym for either citizen journalism or the transformation of consumers from being *consumers* of content to being *publishers* of content, with content being the food that is necessary to fuel social networking in order to attain a far-higher degree of real estate transactions? If so, allow me to play on.

The reason why, in my view, we must deliver greater examples of thought leadership is not so we can remain at the center of the transaction, but rather to sustain our value before, during, and after a real estate transaction. Given the fact that the overwhelming majority of consumers, when they're looking to purchase a home, will utilize major listing/property aggregators—found by way of search engines and, thus, industry websites, for the most part—it is foolhardy to think that consumers need real estate agents in order to find listings. Real estate agents need to now attract and create strong relationships with consumers through social networking, social media, blogging, participating in online communities, etc.—or real estate social marketing, if you will—so that one's relationship with a prospective buyer or seller can withstand the monumental fact that *consumers do not need you* to get access to listing information, which you obviously already know.

Additionally, consumers who are thinking of selling their homes will most likely not say, "Let's go to John Doe's real estate blog." Instead, they are more likely to use other search alternatives. The key is to have consumers, even though they realize that there are hundreds of other access points to getting real estate-related information of all sorts, become materially impressed with you, as either a thought leader or as a published expert, as opposed to your only being seen as one of many real estate agents who have joined numerous online communities.

Many real estate bloggers recognize that their blogs may not become the first online destination for most home buyers. However, those who effectively leverage their links will command a much greater number of consumers who visit their websites, blogs, or blogs serving as their websites—once consumers realize that, due to the wonders of IDX, they can essentially realize content, classifieds, and interactive communication by visiting their agents' websites or blogs. Websites and blogs are only two examples of many social networking vehicles where content can influence loyalty. In order to obtain loyalty and become the agent of choice, regardless of where consumers stray for any and all real estate information, a real estate agent must demonstrate that he or she has differentiated him- or herself as a more positive, powerful, likeable, skillful, connected, and cut-above-the-rest thought leader. By way of illustration, we can learn a lot from how consumers behave during other retail experiences. And the following example is one that every reader can relate to, because you, too, are a consumer—hey, you purchased this book!

How many times have you visited a store for the express purpose of buying either a suit or a dress, and as you walked into the store, were greeted by a salesperson who aggressively inserted himself, prematurely, into your shopping experience, by enthusiastically asking if you needed any help? For many consumers, this represents, if not an ambush, a decidedly unwelcome overture. Yet, later on, after you've narrowed your search and require assistance, a salesperson is nowhere to be found. Naturally, you become irritated.

As a real estate social marketer, when you construct your strategy regarding how to best insert yourself as a real estate professional, always be conscious of the need to have a sense of *online appropriateness*. Otherwise, you might find yourself chatting to some folks online about how you like to travel, when what they really want from you is advice about real estate. Or, perhaps, you'll be posting a new listing while everybody else is discussing health care. Thus, one without the other—social networking without social media, or social media without social networking—can result in your becoming more popular but not more prodigious, or a great producer of content but not particularly popular. I say this because, remember, social media means *everybody* exchanging ideas rather than somebody trying to be the only voice—which you can do in some forums; however, in other forums, it means listening and learning more than conveying. Later on, we will talk about how social marketing helps you achieve the right balance.

Another distinction between social media and social networking also addresses the amount of attention that is devoted to the act of, what I would call, "irrelevant redundancy," as opposed to becoming one who, in an original fashion, truly inspires consumers regarding real estate. The irrelevant redundancy I speak of is when someone constantly tweets that he or she just got a new listing, so as to announce the news to consumers. Those consumers, however, are privately concluding, "Wow that's great, but so did 50 other agents today. Besides, I can see all of these listings in real time in one minute. I mean, if I am technologically evolved enough to be connected to you here online, then I certainly know how to navigate with ColdwellBanker.com or Prudential.com."

Besides being dismissed by consumers as being self-serving, another result of displaying that you are consumed with shallow and unremarkable announcements could be customer annoyance, which was amusingly demonstrated in a satirical headline I read online: "Get OFF Facebook and Sell My Friggin' House Already!" (By Janie Coffey, January 6, 2010; http://agentgenius.com/g-rants-insanity-more/real-estate/get-off-facebook-and-sell-my-friggin-house-already/) Therefore, chatting, celebrating, and calling attention to yourself because of your heroic act of securing a listing is a strategy that one needs to use selectively and intermittently. Strides must also be taken to make sure that your clients do not perceive that you're more interested in your new listings than you are in strategically promoting their properties.

Now, if you accept the definition of marketing as meaning, first determining the unmet needs in the market and then creating goods and services to respond to such needs, then what will automatically ensue will be the recognition that networking needs are very different from marketing needs. Aristotle—a top producer at Parthenon Properties—said, in *Politics, Book One*, that "Man is by nature a political [translated as *social*] animal." This is an important perspective because it suggests that social needs are satisfied in a different way than marketing needs are. And when this distinction is not clear, we may be serving the wrong needs and becoming a jack of all trades and a master of none. I make this distinction between networking, media, and consumers' marketing needs because real estate agents cannot afford to take years for the third phase, or Hegel's correction period, to play out.

To further illustrate my point, many real estate professionals are being seduced into thinking in terms of communities, tribes, and social networks, and this is necessary for two reasons: there's never been a real estate transaction that didn't involve people, otherwise known as friends, fans, and followers; and people are more likely to do business with those they know and trust. Therefore, social networking is critical and you can reach far more people online versus offline; however, this reality can also be significantly limiting. While you may want to—and *should*—belong to and participate in online communities, such as those existing for newlyweds, single parents, hikers, boaters, joggers, knitters, sports fans, political junkies, etc., let me ask you this, as I do elsewhere in the book: What FSBO community do you belong to? Or, do you know of an Expired Listing community or tribe? How about a First-Time Buyer community? Or where does one find the Short Sale tribe? These, my friends, are not tribes, communities, or networks. They're individuals who constitute *markets*. And, while the rest of the world can be satisfied with networks and communities as a means to an end, real estate agents need to know how to address networks, communities, and tribes, in order to aggregate markets, specifically First-Time Buyers, Downsizers, Developers, FSBOs, etc. To be able to do that requires a real estate social marketing system.

This profound distinction, at least in my view, is one that needs to be seized and acted upon by those real estate professionals seeking to exponentially increase their income—those who want to differentiate themselves from the dominance of the average. These are the real estate agents who can relate to the words of famed anthropologist, Margaret Mead, who said, "Life in the 20th century is like a parachute jump: you have to get it right the first time." Without question, college students and those not needing to leverage networks, media, and the marketplace for income purposes can afford to follow the crowd and blow with the wind, but most real estate agents, unless they have substantial trust funds, need to convert social networks into social markets.

A real estate social marketing system—meaning the way in which progressive real estate agents employ technologically powered social networking and social media activities—is a distinction that will not be lost on prospective home sellers. A real estate agent who discusses his or her social networking and social media involvement might be viewed by home sellers as being self-involved and self-serving. What does this information have to do with selling their home? Even their 12-year-old child tweets and has friends and followers online. The home sellers would more likely appreciate a real estate professional who has determined how to maximize the integration of social networking and social media as part of his or her personal real estate social marketing system.

Otherwise, we may find ourselves competing with the second generation of FSBOs, who will think that the key to selling real estate is merely mentioning a listing on Twitter or Facebook; they will understandably believe that they are capable of performing this perfunctory and routine type of behavior. However, if real estate agents speak in terms of their real estate social marketing systems, that will automatically convey a specialized skill set that relates to specific real estate marketing needs online.

Accordingly, I suggest that you begin to formulate, as a part of your overall online marketing strategy, your answers to the following questions:

1. What is my strategy for creating a social network of friends, fans, followers, blog traffic, etc.?
2. How will I use media (content) to feed and fortify my flock and achieve digital differentiation?
3. How will I use, converge, or integrate social networking and social media so that I can monetize them by responding to specific market needs and not just social networking and social media needs?
4. Considering that many consumers have multiple real estate agent friends offline, what can I do to create my own real estate social network, where my friends, fans, followers, etc. only belong to me? Specifically, how can I become a niche market for consumers versus consumers being a niche market for me?

One of the answers to question number 4 will become evident when one recognizes that, as presently constituted, online social networking does not satisfy an unmet consumer need. Most consumers would *not* say that, prior to the advent of social networking and its use by real estate agents, they recall a period of real estate agent-related famine, which led to their experiencing real estate agent-related withdrawals.

If you, too, agree that while unemployment rates are high but the availability of real estate agents is not low, then it informs us that our having followers will not necessarily result in our ideas and consumer-centric resolutions becoming viral. To that end, I must commend Steve Hundley for elevating his professional premise from encouraging real estate agents to participate in a "contact" management system to encouraging them to employ a "content" management system. Steve's point here, to me, is paradigmatic in nature. This will become apparent to you, as well, if you ask yourself whether consumers prefer that we contact them or that we provide them with access to relevant real estate content.

Not recognizing the difference will lead to the consumer view that those in the real estate industry are Internet social media interlopers whose community-engagement motive is to co-opt or subsume the more noble purpose of social networking, and that the way in which the real estate industry is using social media is a counter-productive and wasteful example of an industry solution chasing a consumer problem that never existed.

I am thrilled at the prospect of how we can all become more informationally vigilant regarding satisfying unmet consumer needs. In fact, it is my greatest motivation in writing this book. Becoming consumer-centric regarding content will require purging our informational perspective of the past. I remember reading in my real estate training program materials many years ago—a mere two weeks after learning that I had passed my Massachusetts Real Estate License test—that when buyers called and asked for information, we were to *give them* as little information as possible and attempt to get as much information *from them* as possible. And, to ensure that neophytes, like me at that time, did not misuse this opportunity to thwart the consumer, there were several examples like the one below for us, the unilluminated:

**Caller:** Does the home have four bedrooms?
**Agent:** Do you want four bedrooms?

Imagine if you went to a pizza place and asked, "Do you have pepperoni pizza?" and you were asked in return, "Do you want pepperoni pizza?" Little wonder that we rank so low in consumer satisfaction/respect polls. Consumers are fed up with the decades of us playing Three-Card Monte with them, just because they have the *nerve* to want information about real estate. I was never fully aware of consumers' dissatisfaction with our strategy until the day I heard a radio host ask his listeners to call in and share their top examples of frustrating behavior. Later that evening, I heard that the listeners chose *repeating someone's question*—a practice certainly not unknown within our industry's culture—as the number one technique that caused frustration.

# Linking Marketing with Social Media

*Regrettably, many in our industry were trained on how to repeat questions instead of answering them.*

**Home Sellers:** We have a friend in the business.
**Agent:** You have a friend in the business?

**Home Sellers:** We can't make a decision tonight.
**Agent:** You can't make a decision tonight?

**Home Sellers:** We're not going to pay [blank] percent commission.
**Agent:** You're not going to pay [blank] percent commission?

Here again, if there is not a clear understanding that, for decades, we have essentially denied consumers the information they have sought and required, then there may not be the necessary clarity going forward. By holding onto information that consumers wanted—property information, price, seller's disclosure (until recently)—and instead providing information they didn't want, i.e., our accomplishments along with *our high school pictures*, we did ourselves a great disservice.

Only when we are willing to acknowledge that the vast majority of real estate books are being written by those who are not real estate agents, brokers, owners, or industry leaders, but instead by real estate writers—who have only stepped foot in a real estate office as a consumer—will we begin to understand why we have a greater gravitational pull, as an industry, to the *networking* within social networking, as opposed to the *media* part of social media. And, if we don't gravitate to the media part of social media, not only will we not strengthen our social networking, we will also not achieve the convergence: real estate social marketing. Social media first begins with thoughts, as is the case with social networking. The following questions might help you sort out your thoughts regarding social media:

1. How often should you provide changing content on your website? Every day? Every week? Every month? Never?
2. How important is it for you to provide video of real estate content on your website?
3. How important is it for you to educate consumers about real estate on your blog?
4. Which of these content-related issues do you consider to be very important for you to convey to consumers? Information on:
    a. What to do if you have to sell your home before you buy another
    b. How to appeal your property taxes
    c. How to move up
    d. What to demand from a real estate agent who represents you
    e. What to do if your home hasn't sold
    f. FSBOs

g. Content provided in multiple languages
h. New construction
i. Vacation homes
j. Commercial real estate
k. FHA's Section 203(k) program
l. Foreclosures
m. Short sales

In summary, if you accept that social networking is creating contacts and communities, and that social media equates to the content that you provide to your communities, then what is your strategy—or real estate social marketing system—to ensure that both activities result in transactions?

# Chapter 4

# The Social Media Census -
## Executive Summary and Highlights

RISMedia's *2010 Dalton/Hundley Real Estate Social Media Census* was initiated in order to provide greater transparency regarding the impact that social media has had on our industry. The Census was distributed in an online format to over 500,000 real estate professionals during February and March 2010. Respondents represented all major sectors of the real estate industry, including Realtors (69%), Owners (10%), Team Leaders (3.2%), Marketing Directors (3.2%), and many others.

Some 3,362 professionals fully completed the Census between March 1, 2010 and April 5, 2010. These professionals have provided us with valuable and telling insights. This unprecedented industry-wide research enables us to offer greater clarity surrounding the subject of social media than has been available to date.

Among our key findings is that a significant majority of respondents reported that they consider the concepts of social networking and social media as essentially being one and the same.

That 80% of industry participants have arrived at this conclusion reinforces one of the central motivations and themes that run throughout *Leveraging Your Links*. This now-documented, industry-wide mindset suggests that if a real estate professional views both social networking and social media as interchangeable disciplines, then neither concept will ever be fully understood, appreciated, explored, and utilized in any way approaching optimum efficiency.

Moreover, this widespread teaching and acceptance of the interchangability of the terms social networking and social media also prevent proper integration and necessary cohesiveness, and, as I have written in this book, it is not possible to integrate sameness. Accordingly, Steve Hundley and I not only call attention to how social networking and social media have different purposes, but we also introduce a convergence of the two, leading to Real Estate Social Marketing.

Also remarkable in our Census is that while the majority of respondents acknowledge that, at present, they possess no social media plan, they also indicate that social media represents a very important part of their business going forward. Also of significance is that approximately 60% of respondents have not seized the opportunity—even in these economically challenging times—to employ social media practices as a way to cut expenses and 50% of respondents do not employ social media to market their properties.

Unsurprisingly, the Census uncovered that the number one certification or designation that respondents possess, given the correlation between Internet usage and real estate professionalism, was e-PRO. Also of note is that only 21.25% of respondents when asked, "Do you view social media as your responsibility to inform the public?" gave it the greatest importance ranking. This response begs the following question: If it is not the responsibility of real estate professionals to utilize social media to inform the public, then which other sector of society should we expect to assume this role?

This response also further validates additional research provided in the book that reveals that consumers only look to real estate professionals for real estate information or advice after first exhausting friends, family, neighbors and... financial planners (see survey in Chapter 2, Social Media to the Real Estate Rescue). This revelation has led this author to wonder if the reason so many real estate professionals who are engaged in Internet activity do not see it as their sacred responsibility to inform the public about real estate issues is due to the fact that these professionals have not yet realized that it is their responsibility to provide content online. Or, perhaps they lack confidence in ever being viewed by consumers as knowledgeable and trusted real estate advisors.

I am not willing to accept that the almost 80% of respondents who do not consider the use of social media to inform the public their highest responsibility reflects an indifference regarding responding to the informational needs of consumers.

Interestingly, and somewhat ironically, when it comes to receiving valuable information, 96.12% of our respondents, when asked, "Would you like to learn what other real estate professionals are doing in the industry regarding social media?" replied with a "Yes" answer. One of the objectives of *Leveraging Your Links* is to highlight how interested real estate professionals are in gaining information, tutelage, and coaching. Once that point is absorbed, it becomes easier to conclude that consumers, too, value real estate-related information as well.

The Census also revealed that not only is there much work to be done in regards to getting real estate professionals to first want to provide social media-related content to consumers and then doing so, but also that there is much room for improvement regarding the need to employ social media for the purposes of Real Estate Social Marketing, in order to target specific real estate markets such as short sales, expired listing home sellers, move-up buyers, etc. Specifically, the Census indicates that, stunningly, only 7.62% of respondents have created a social media/social networking strategy that targets these individual markets online.

These results also support a major premise of the book—that being that a principal explanation for why so few real estate agents, as reflected in our over-all research, can point to any significant increase in transactions due to social networking or social media is because they have not yet discovered how to shift their social media practices into real estate social marketing methods.

Another aspect of the Census that I found most instructive—and one that relates to my conclusion where I speak to the need for real estate professionals to upgrade their friends, fans, followers, communities, networks, and tribes by converting them and upgrading them to members of their personally branded "Real Estate Social Network" ("Become a member of the Jane Doe Real Estate Social Network")—is that less than 10% of respondents indicate that they have organized followers into a real estate network that they run. I am encouraged, though, that a much greater percentage of respondents have indicated that they would like suggestions...which they will find in this book.

In order to create one's own "Real Estate Social Network," which invites con-sumers to a more elevated, real estate-based relationship than merely one of friends, fans and followers, in my view, requires that "members" must have, if you will forgive me, "privileges or perks," which may mean ongoing infor-mation and advice presented online. This makes the Census question, "How frequently do you think you should refresh and update information on your website/blog?" an important one. To that end, less than 50% of respondents have the information on their website/blog refreshed every day.

Regarding the relationship between social media and mobile technology (see Chapter 25 in this book), nearly 50% of respondents manage social media applications on their mobile device. This level of participation shows how rap-idly the expanse of mobile applications is growing, as well as how real estate professionals are intelligently responding to this opportunity and consumer preference.

Our Census results also reinforce the need for very important work on Search Engine Optimization (SEO), which my colleague, Steve Hundley, has pioneered on behalf of the real estate industry. More than 50% of respondents replied that they do not know what SEO is or they are just now looking into its relevance in their social media strategy.

Of note, more than 30% of respondents were not aware that one is only al-lowed 140 characters or less in a tweet. A much greater example of social media sophistication was reflected, however, by the fact that 87.56% of respondents correctly defined RSS as meaning "Really Simple Syndication."

Another very interesting correlation that invites much greater industry-wide examination is that a whopping percentage (63%) of respondents' transactions are generated from their "center of influence." This data calls into question the strategic importance of keeping in touch with one's sphere of influence online, expanding one's sphere of influence through social media, and especially what will be required online in order to continue to sufficiently influence an agent's natural network in what is now and will continue to become an even greater and extremely competitive online marketplace. The reported importance of "center of influence" sparks the following question, which strategically oriented real estate agents must now ask themselves:

"To what degree will I be able to either sustain or significantly grow my sphere of influence online by either only essentially inserting myself in a networking fashion via social networking platforms, or by revealing myself as a thought leader online through the skillful deployment of media content as a part of a social media strategy? To what degree should I, or do I need to, represent the interests of my clients and/or the properties I market through my real estate social marketing practices?"

Clearly, real estate professionals need to consider how to best navigate all of these distinct challenges as part of an overall social media strategy. Those agents who principally seek to establish a greater social networking presence through their participation in various online communities and by aggregating as many friends, fans, and followers as possible might place the greatest emphasis on social networking.

Those real estate professionals who find real estate content to be at the center of how they seek to engage real estate consumers may become more devoted to robust blogging and have a greater commitment to providing links to highly relevant real estate content to their social network. Those professionals may wish to express this philosophy to a prospective home seller: *"Folks, my purpose in using Web 2.0 and what most call social networking or social media is not for me to create friends and fans and have people follow me online, but instead, to create a real estate marketing plan because my greater interest is to generate 'friends, fans, and followers' for your home. Folks, how does this sound to you?"*

Now, clearly, real estate professionals have to become proficient in how they leverage their social media links for all three purposes. This is also reflected in the fact that the Census indicates that there are numerous social networks that are heavily employed by real estate professionals, including many that serve the purpose of industry-centric idea sharing and networking.

Real Estate Social Marketing already plays a significant role in leveraging new business as evidenced by the 7,647 transactions that respondents have been able to trace back to their Real Estate Social Marketing efforts. Respondents indicated that 7.3% of their transactions came from social media efforts — a remarkable number given that only 15.4% of respondents have been using these techniques for more than three years. Let's compare this to the 10% of leads that are derived from local advertising to really gain perspective on the growing momentum of Real Estate Social Marketing.

The trends show that this number is likely on the low side and only represents new business derived from Real Estate Social Marketing. New business is only a part of Real Estate Social Marketing, as we know by now that social networking and social media are the perfect vehicles for staying in touch with people you already know. So, social media done correctly will also have an impact on how effective your "center of influence" marketing is.

Social media will become more prominent in the coming years, according to our respondents, no matter how the data is sliced. Obviously, there are some individual holdouts, but aggregated groups based upon geography, occupation, age, and years in the business all show an increase in the importance of social media in the next three years. This shift is most dramatically demonstrated by the fact that when asked the importance of social marketing to their business today, the average ranking across all respondents was 3.5 compared with a ranking of 4.3 in three years' time.

There is a lot of confusion about how to best utilize social media and many people are crying out for a plan. We would like to pull out several key metrics.

Most prominently is the fact that over 80% of the respondents felt that social networking is the same thing as social media. In addition, 60% of people are working without a plan, and 17% of those people with plans do not have the time or means to implement their plans. Finally, over 50% of respondents were self-taught using trial and error to navigate themselves through these previously uncharted waters.

The Census results are provided in their entirety on the following pages along with graphs of the results. We encourage you to visit us at www.social-mediacensus.org to participate in follow-up questions and read further analysis of the Census results.

## Methodology

The specific data for this analysis of RISMedia's *2010 Dalton/Hundley Real Estate Social Media Census* was administered via an online questionnaire during February and March 2010. SocialMediaCensus.org will continue to collect this vital information through 2010 and a new Census will begin in January 2011. To date, the Census site has received over 11,500 visitors and 3,362 professionals completed the Census; this analysis is based on their unique responses. Census respondents came from varied real estate-related backgrounds, with Realtors representing the bulk of the respondents. The Census was distributed via e-mail to over 500,000 real estate professionals and also promoted virally through Facebook and Twitter. Respondents were encouraged to participate in the Census and will receive an advance copy of the Census results in exchange for their participation.

## Geography Considerations:

The *2010 Dalton/Hundley Real Estate Social Media Census* was primarily targeted to real estate professionals in the United States. Some 98% of respondents were located in the United States with the remaining 2% coming from Canada and Europe. Every state was represented in the Census to some degree. The top five regions in which respondents were located were: California (20.6%), Florida (5.9%), Arizona (4.74%), Texas (4.58%), and New York (3.91%).

## Bias Considerations

It should be noted that the survey was distributed solely online; this means that there is an inherent bias toward respondents with some technological predispositions.

In addition, in an effort to provide information as accurate as possible, a normal technique of eliminating a percentage of the upper and lower outliers was followed when computing the results of the Census.

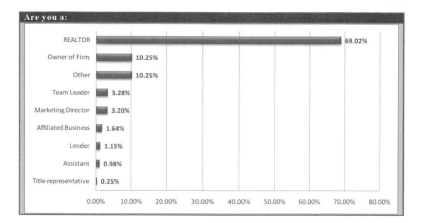

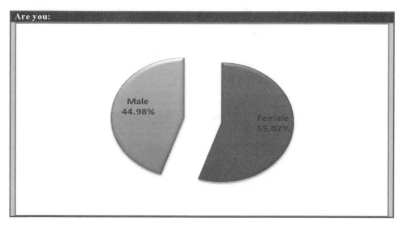

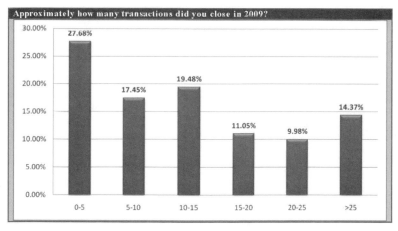

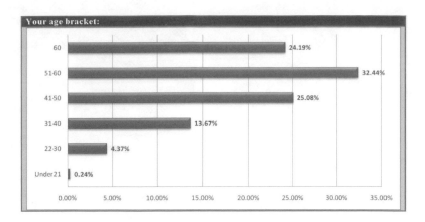

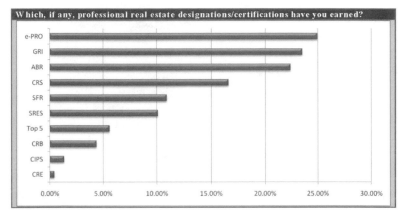

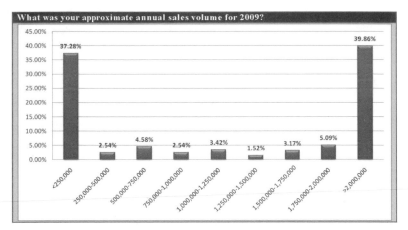

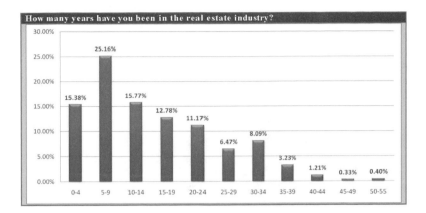

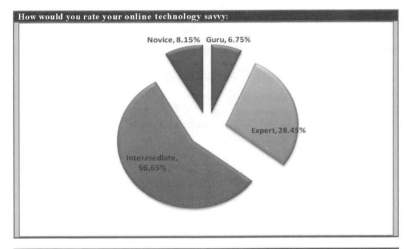

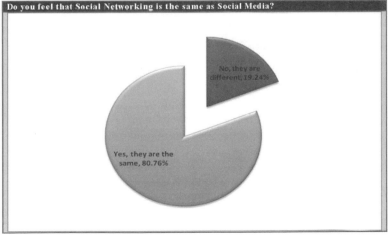

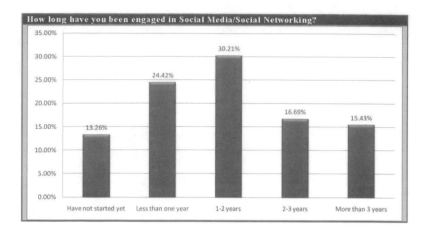

How long have you been engaged in Social Media/Social Networking?

- Have not started yet: 13.26%
- Less than one year: 24.42%
- 1-2 years: 30.21%
- 2-3 years: 16.69%
- More than 3 years: 15.43%

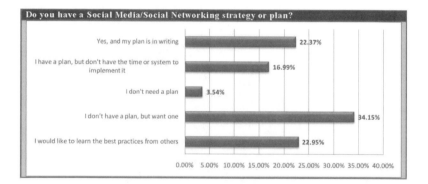

Do you have a Social Media/Social Networking strategy or plan?

- Yes, and my plan is in writing: 22.37%
- I have a plan, but don't have the time or system to implement it: 16.99%
- I don't need a plan: 3.54%
- I don't have a plan, but want one: 34.15%
- I would like to learn the best practices from others: 22.95%

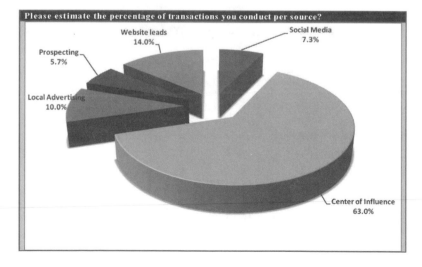

Please estimate the percentage of transactions you conduct per source?

- Website leads: 14.0%
- Social Media: 7.3%
- Prospecting: 5.7%
- Local Advertising: 10.0%
- Center of Influence: 63.0%

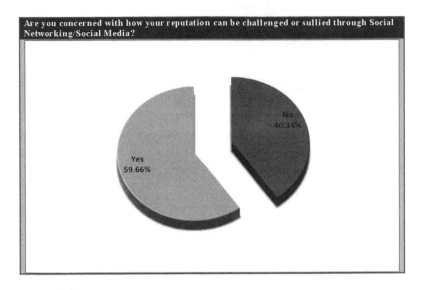

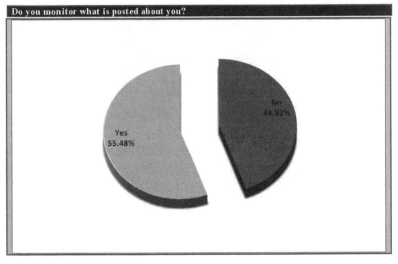

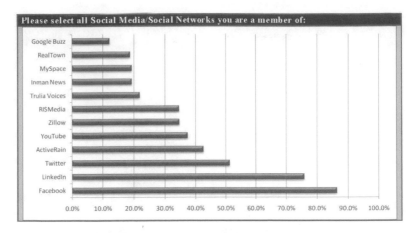

Please select all Social Media/Social Networks you are a member of:

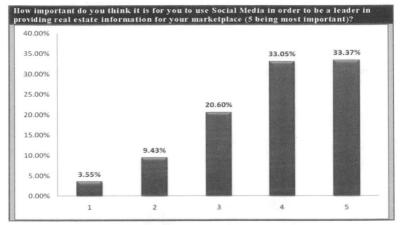

How important do you think it is for you to use Social Media in order to be a leader in providing real estate information for your marketplace (5 being most important)?

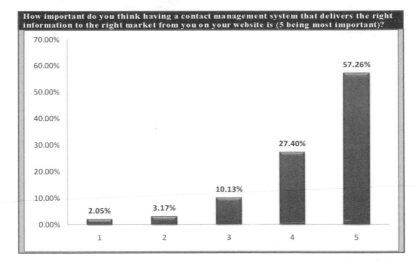

How important do you think having a contact management system that delivers the right information to the right market from you on your website is (5 being most important)?

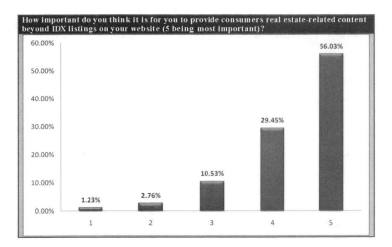

How important do you think it is for you to provide consumers real estate-related content beyond IDX listings on your website (5 being most important)?

| | | |
|---|---|---|
| 1 | 1.23% | |
| 2 | 2.76% | |
| 3 | 10.53% | |
| 4 | 29.45% | |
| 5 | 56.03% | |

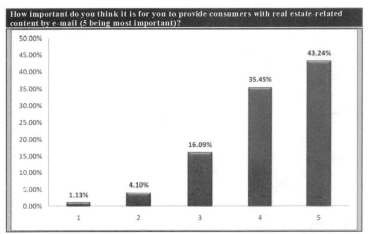

How important do you think it is for you to provide consumers with real estate-related content by e-mail (5 being most important)?

| | | |
|---|---|---|
| 1 | 1.13% | |
| 2 | 4.10% | |
| 3 | 16.09% | |
| 4 | 35.45% | |
| 5 | 43.24% | |

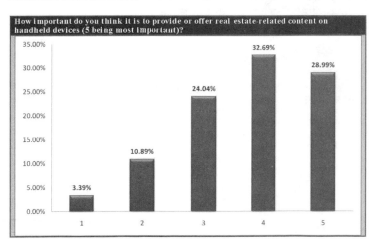

How important do you think it is to provide or offer real estate-related content on handheld devices (5 being most important)?

| | | |
|---|---|---|
| 1 | 3.39% | |
| 2 | 10.89% | |
| 3 | 24.04% | |
| 4 | 32.69% | |
| 5 | 28.99% | |

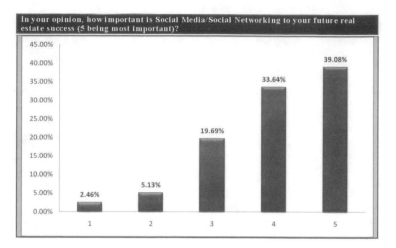

In your opinion, how important is Social Media/Social Networking to your future real estate success (5 being most important)?

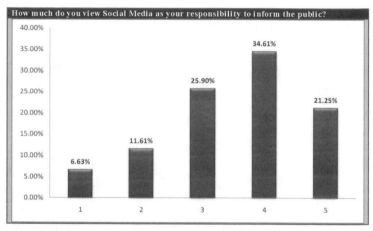

How much do you view Social Media as your responsibility to inform the public?

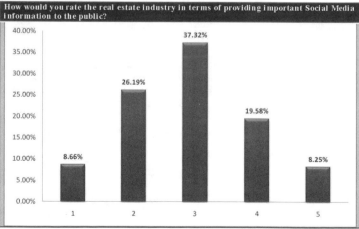

How would you rate the real estate industry in terms of providing important Social Media information to the public?

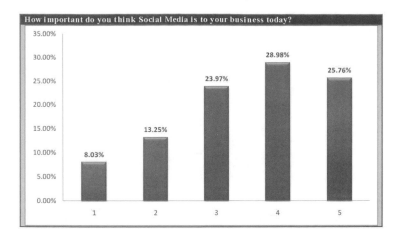

How important do you think Social Media is to your business today?

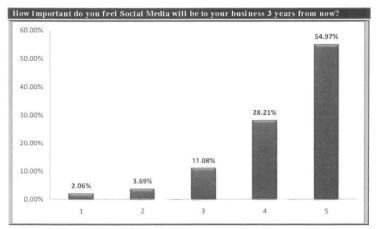

How important do you feel Social Media will be to your business 3 years from now?

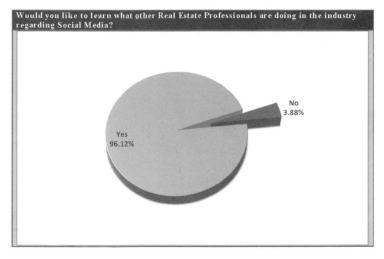

Would you like to learn what other Real Estate Professionals are doing in the industry regarding Social Media?

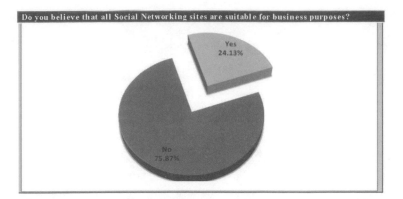

Do you believe that all Social Networking sites are suitable for business purposes?

Yes 24.13%

No 75.87%

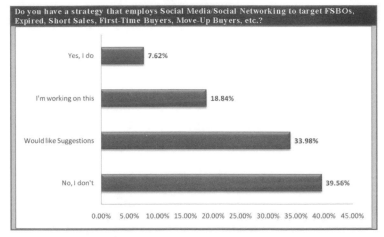

Do you have a strategy that employs Social Media/Social Networking to target FSBOs, Expired, Short Sales, First-Time Buyers, Move-Up Buyers, etc.?

Yes, I do — 7.62%

I'm working on this — 18.84%

Would like Suggestions — 33.98%

No, I don't — 39.56%

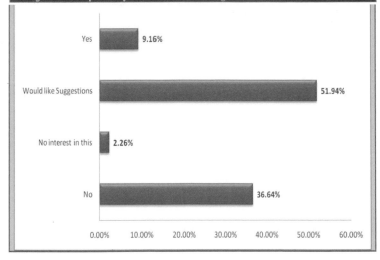

Have you organized your followers into a Real Estate Network that you run, rather than having them merely follow you on Social Networking/Social Media sites?

Yes — 9.16%

Would like Suggestions — 51.94%

No interest in this — 2.26%

No — 36.64%

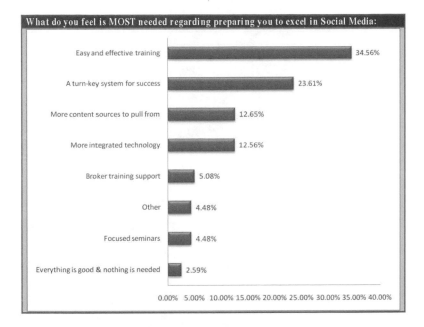

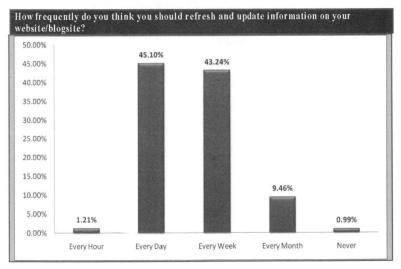

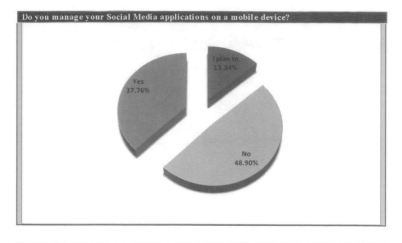

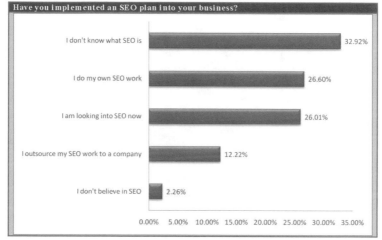

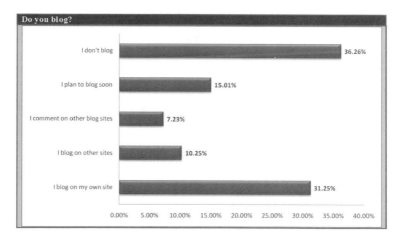

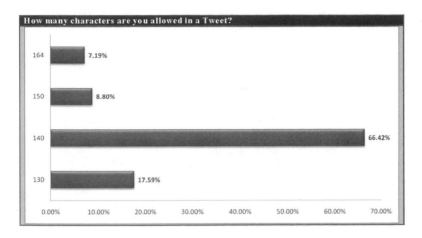

How many characters are you allowed in a Tweet?

| | |
|---|---|
| 164 | 7.19% |
| 150 | 8.80% |
| 140 | 66.42% |
| 130 | 17.59% |

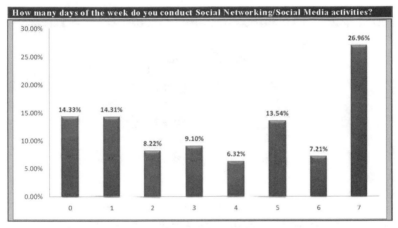

How many days of the week do you conduct Social Networking/Social Media activities?

0: 14.33%
1: 14.31%
2: 8.22%
3: 9.10%
4: 6.32%
5: 13.54%
6: 7.21%
7: 26.96%

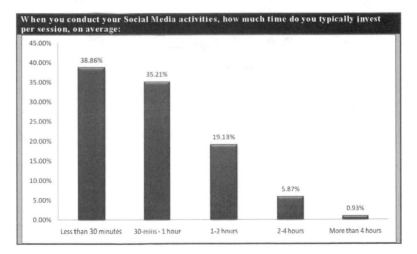

When you conduct your Social Media activities, how much time do you typically invest per session, on average:

| Less than 30 minutes | 30-mins - 1 hour | 1-2 hours | 2-4 hours | More than 4 hours |
|---|---|---|---|---|
| 38.86% | 35.21% | 19.13% | 5.87% | 0.93% |

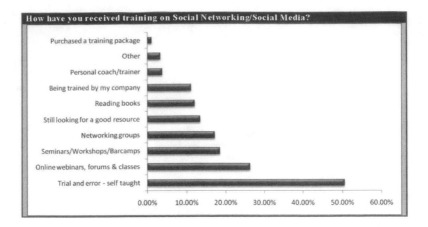

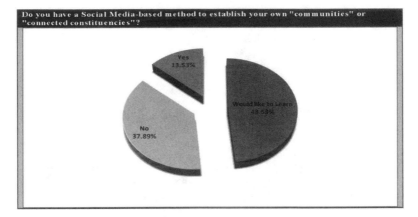

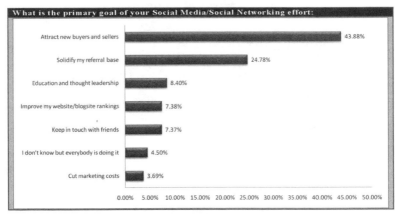

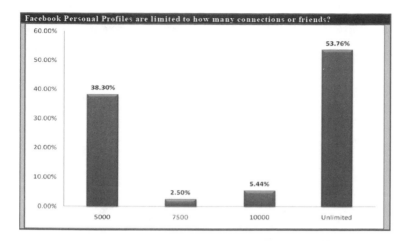

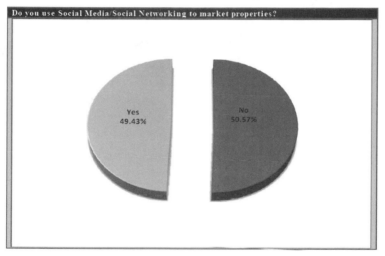

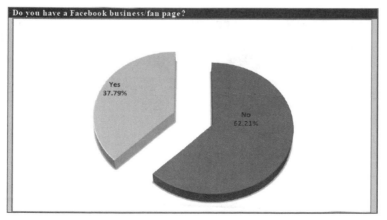

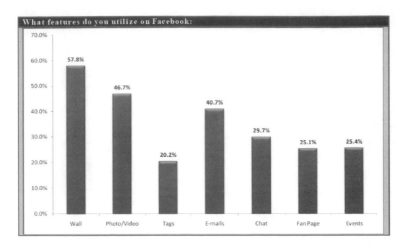

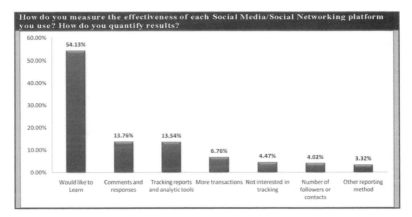

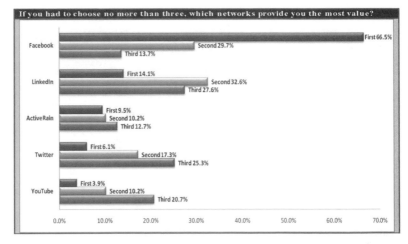

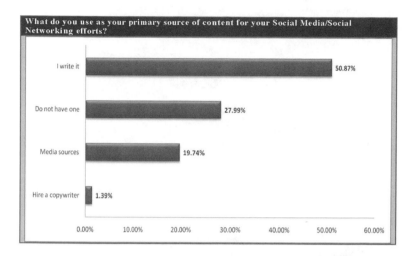

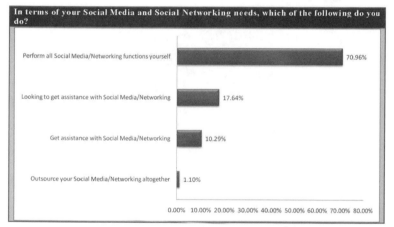

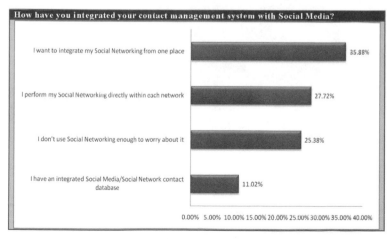

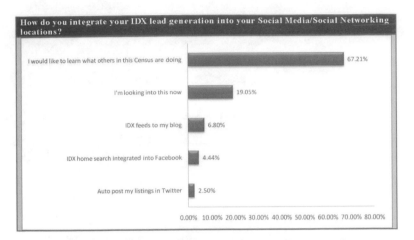

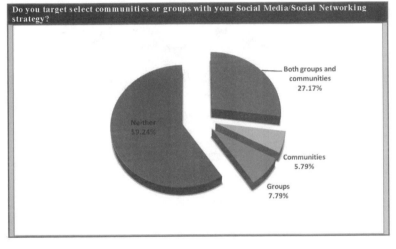

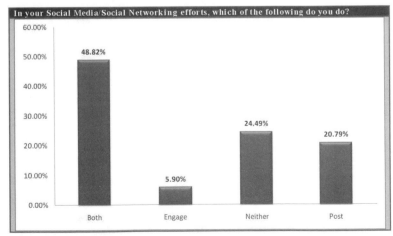

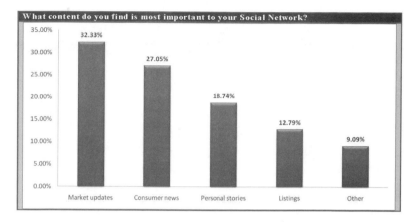

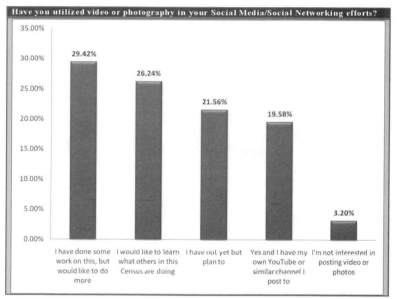

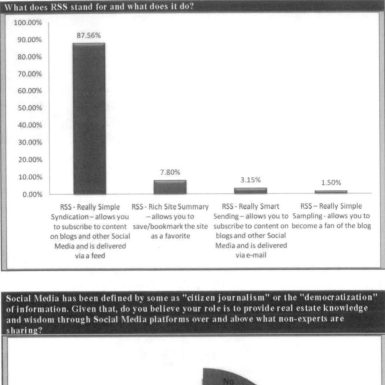

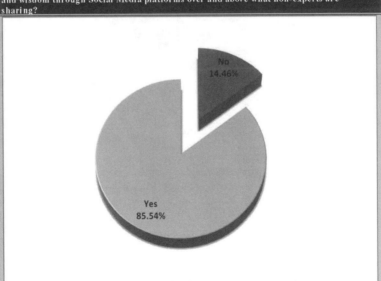

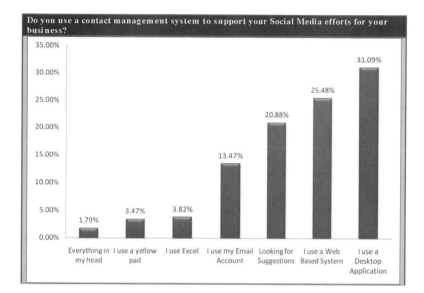

Do you use a contact management system to support your Social Media efforts for your business?

- Everything in my head: 1.79%
- I use a yellow pad: 3.47%
- I use Excel: 3.82%
- I use my Email Account: 13.47%
- Looking for Suggestions: 20.88%
- I use a Web Based System: 25.48%
- I use a Desktop Application: 31.09%

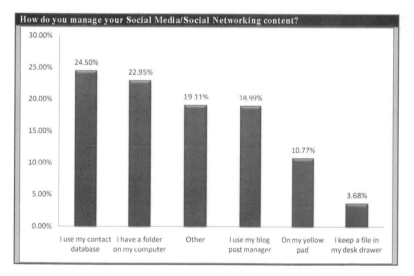

How do you manage your Social Media/Social Networking content?

- I use my contact database: 24.50%
- I have a folder on my computer: 22.95%
- Other: 19.11%
- I use my blog post manager: 18.99%
- On my yellow pad: 10.77%
- I keep a file in my desk drawer: 3.68%

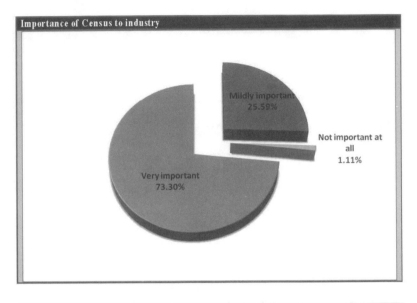

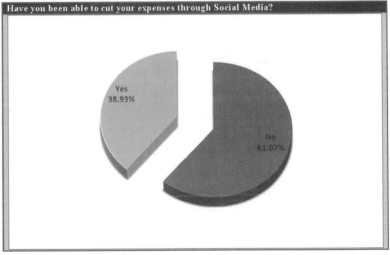

# The Social Media Mentors

*Insights, Inspiration, and the Individual Social Media Strategies of Real Estate Leaders Across the Country*

# Real Estate Chess, Not Checkers

## Krisstina Wise
Principal/Broker
The GoodLife Team, Austin , TX
Top 5 in Real Estate Member
**Serving:** Austin, TX
**Years in real estate:** 12 (two as broker/owner)
**www.goodlifeteam.com**

## Social Media Links:
www.glt.bz/fanpage
http://twitter.com/krisstinawise
www.facebook.com/goodlifeteam
www.linkedin.com/in/krisstinawise

**Allan Dalton:** Krisstina, you have spoken at numerous important real estate industry events on the subject of social networking. In fact, congratulations, Krisstina, on your recently winning Inman's prestigious "Innovator of the Year" award. Why don't we begin with your definition of social networking?

**Krisstina Wise:** Thanks, Allan, and to answer your question from my perspective, social networking is networking, the way we think of it in the traditional sense, but instead of only face-to-face interaction, it's networking that can be done, and is done, online. People now meet, mingle, socialize, and build communities, virtually.

**AD:** Obviously, if social networking and social media were the same thing there wouldn't be two different words after "social;" therefore, how do you define social media?

**KW:** At its core, social media is media, but instead of traditional forms of media, like newspaper advertising, magazine articles, and commercials, social media is transferred through social networks found on the Web. Today, people and businesses can publicize themselves, build their brands, communicate, coordinate, collaborate, organize, and advertise using social media tools that are inexpensive, easy to use, and viral in nature. Social media has dropped the cost to almost zero to expose a brand, build public identity, and build communities since there's no need to hire large media firms to produce the same intended outcomes. In addition, it offers more of an opportunity to communicate two ways—back and forth—which enables new relationships to form.

**AD: How would you define a real estate social marketing system?**
**KW:** A social marketing system is a constellation of activities across multiple social media platforms with a consistent brand and message. The intent behind every action is to build identity and trust, develop new relationships, deepen existing relationships, and eventually drive traffic to our website as the hub at the center of all social activities. Because of our commitment to provide only relevant and timely information, our real estate social marketing system is organic. We determine what to post organizationally and push out relevant and timely messages to our customers and to our agents' customers.

**AD: Krisstina, why did you begin social networking?**
**KW:** I could see where consumer behavior was shifting and wanted to be ahead of the curve.

**AD: Krisstina, which social networks do you belong to?**
**KW:** The social media tools we use specifically for social networking are Facebook, Twitter, LinkedIn, Gowalla, and Foursquare. In addition, we view our own website and blog as social networking sites because we actively engage with our consumers on them. The fact that they aren't static turns them from information tools into social networks. We use many other social media tools—for example, YouTube—but we do not use these tools for social networking.

**AD: Why did you choose these social networks?**
**KW:** We chose Facebook, Twitter, and LinkedIn when I noticed an increasing number of conversations about them. I invested my time to study and learn how to use them uncommonly. I put myself and my company on the sites in the beginning, before hardly any real estate agents were using them. I studied how people preferred to be communicated with and then I shaped my company's strategies. We remain on these sites because that's where our consumers are and that's where they want to be communicated with. Different consumers have different preferences—some only want to communicate through Facebook, some just want e-mails, others are on Twitter.

I am an early adopter of Foursquare and Gowalla for the same reasons. They will either take off or not, but if they take off, we will already be established brands in those communities and we will know how to use them effectively, i.e., we will be ahead of the curve.

**AD: Krisstina, how many friends and followers do you have on each?**
**KW: Facebook:** As of August, 2010, I personally have 2,607 friends. My GoodLife Team fan page has 1,534 fans. My agents and staff have an additional 5,233 friends. In addition, I have several other pages and groups (networks) that we have created. For example, we have a fan page/network for each of the developments we market; we have created other specific niche networks for communities, such as East Austin Businesses and Austin Women Entrepreneurs.

**Twitter:** As of August, 2010, I have 3,410 followers. I am the primary face of the GoodLife Team on Twitter. But, we do have a GoodLife Team Twitter page with 601 followers and we created a Pre-MLS Austin Twitter page for promoting our new listings and that page has 656 followers. In addition, I am featured on 126 Twitter lists.

**LinkedIn:** I don't actively build my social network on LinkedIn. It's primarily used for business referrals—for example, when I or someone in my network is in need of a reputable SEO company or is looking to hire someone. As of August, 2010, I have 559 connections on LinkedIn.

**AD: Is your interaction with your friends, followers, and fans social, professional or both?**
**KW:** Both.

**AD: Krisstina, what do you generally post about on your networks?**
**KW:** Allan, I use Gowalla and Foursquare to post where I am around Austin and as a way to highlight great service. If there is a business or waiter that goes out of their way to provide great service, I'll add that comment on my post. My Gowalla and Foursquare posts show up on Facebook. In addition, from a professional perspective, my team and I promote all of our events, market stats, and latest real estate news. From a personal perspective, I post about my kids, about my running adventures, and great events around Austin. I also make sure that I am consistently responding to other people's posts. From a personal perspective, I probably spend most of my

time commenting versus posting my own adventures.

Facebook reveals more of my personality and my personal and professional life combined. On Twitter, I tend to post more professional-only comments. My posts on Twitter include communication with my Twitter network, as well as posts about real estate-related content, driving people to our blogs, events, and other relevant information.

**AD:** What real estate activities do you post about?
**KW:** I post about market statistics and the latest real estate news, such as changes in regulations, new condo developments, etc. I also use the Facebook Marketplace to promote our listings and we promote our developments through individual posts and video posts.

**AD:** Krisstina, can you give me an example of a post you might make?
**KW:** Certainly. In fact, here are several:

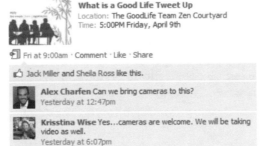

**Krisstina Wise** Our next GoodLife Happy Hour is on the calendar! All Austinites ... please join us in our Zen Garden for some networking & socializing with the background music of Nate Davenport live.

**What is a Good Life Tweet Up**
Location: The GoodLife Team Zen Courtyard
Time: 5:00PM Friday, April 9th

Fri at 9:00am · Comment · Like · Share

Jack Miller and Sheila Ross like this.

**Alex Charfen** Can we bring cameras to this?
Yesterday at 12:47pm

**Krisstina Wise** Yes...cameras are welcome. We will be taking video as well.
Yesterday at 6:07pm

Write a comment...

**Krisstina Wise** Sunday morning run with @Kelly White followed by Taco Deli!

**Tacodeli**
Krisstina checked in at Tacodeli.

2 hours ago via Gowalla · Comment · Like · Krisstina's Passport

**Krisstina Wise**

**I'm selling 9907 Woodlake Cove, Austin, TX 78733 for $385,000 in Facebook Marketplace**

Interested? Know anyone who might be?

Privacy abounds in this 4 bedroom, 3.5 bath home with loft/game room and study. Situated on a one acre beautifully maintained lot full of natural TX indigenous flora. Architecturally designed to "live large on a small footprint". -Master suite with amazing Hill Country...

See More

Thu at 5:28pm via Marketplace · Comment · Like · View Krisstina's Listing

Amanda Wernick likes this.

View all 6 comments

**Krisstina Wise** Sandra, this home is off of Cuernavaca.
Fri at 8:44am

**Krisstina Wise** Beautiful home on 1 acre wooded lot!
Fri at 8:44am

Write a comment...

**Krisstina Wise:** "★★★★★" For the location, price, views and very hip & trendy finish out -- there isn't a better buy in Austin!

**The Riverside Grove**

**AD:** Do you include social media-specific links to real estate content in your real estate posts on your social networks?

**KW:** Yes, we include video and photos in a lot of our posts. We link to news sources or our website.

**AD:** When did you start your website?

**KW:** I registered my GoodLifeTeam domain in 1999; my website beginnings started there. I was with a big box broker from 1999 through 2008, which limited my ability to custom design my site due to corporate policy. After leaving this brokerage and starting my own, we have designed and built a fully custom, consumer-oriented website within the past two years. We are in production of Version 3 of our GoodLifeTeam website. Version 2, our latest release in September 2009, turned our site into a fully interactive Web 2.0 platform for engaging with our consumers.

**AD:** What kind of content can be found on your website?

**KW:** We're the first in Austin to design a fully custom website around what the customer wants. Beyond search and information on what their home is worth, they want content...and not content that is about the Realtor or content that is static, but fresh, timely, and relevant content. We offer enriching content and a place where they can interact and have their questions answered quickly and professionally without their feeling obligated to us. Our website is evolving toward lead capture and having the tools and systems to follow up from the Web and build a relationship with the prospect during the 6-12 months before they buy or sell. We have built a content-rich and interactive site, not just an off-the-shelf template site.

Our website is very lifestyle-focused and is about what people need to live their good life. Real estate is a very relationally focused business that's about taking care of the customer—that begins by offering consumers a virtual experience to meet with us first, allowing them to experience what we offer. We're there in the background to offer the help they need initially through the site, so that when their virtual experience turns into an in-person experience, it's congruous. It's an online experience that matches the physical experience. The Good Life is an "experience," after all.

Specific content includes reasons why your home didn't sell, information on Austin schools, information on all of the Austin downtown communities (kept current and provided on a custom-built interactive map platform), information on our team members, etc. We are continually building our website to be lifestyle-focused. The next release of our website will include neighborhood-specific pages with blog content, new listings, neighborhood real estate stats, etc.

**AD: Do you have a blog?**
**KW:** Yes. We started blogging in early 2008. It is fully integrated into our website at www.goodlifeteam.com/blog. The bottom half of our home page provides specific, relevant blog feeds. The company produces a monthly market-statistics blog. I personally write articles educating the consumer on shifts that are happening in the market, such as the tax credit, the HVCC code, upcoming changes to FHA guidelines, etc.

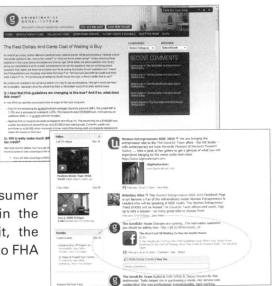

We only write articles that are relevant to the consumer, therefore, we probably do not blog as often as the typical blogger real estate agent.

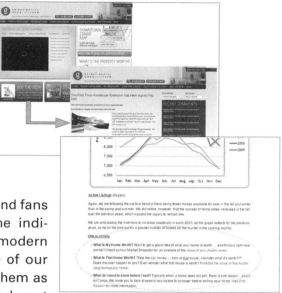

**AD:** Do you aggregate your followers and fans into demographic groups that you can individually target?

**KW:** We target our followers and fans by their interests. If someone indicates they are interested in modern architecture by attending one of our Modern Home tours, we flag them as such. If someone has attended past tweet-ups, we flag them with that interest. In addition, all leads are targeted as either buyer, seller, both, or investor.

**AD:** Krisstina, how often, then, do you send your friends, fans, and followers individualized messages with content or a link to your website?

**KW:** Allan, our "glife" e-newsletter goes out every 4-6 weeks. We use our network's tags in order to create dynamic content that will display information that is specific to an individual's interest. In addition, we only send specific event invitations to those who have indicated an interest in receiving notifications. This allows us to avoid spamming everyone else.

**AD:** Do you use multiple networks, i.e., Facebook, Twitter, MySpace, Google Buzz, to draw traffic to your website or blog?

**KW:** Yes. If we are on a social network, we are always using it to drive traffic to our website. For example, when we write a blog article, we promote the blog on Facebook, Twitter, and LinkedIn, with a short link to the blog.

**AD:** How do you draw traffic to your blog, i.e., do you have a link on your website or do you tweet about your blog?

**KW:** We tweet, we post on Facebook's individual pages, we post on our

GoodLife Team fan page, I post it on my LinkedIn page, we link to it on our developer pages, we blog about it, and we have signed up for several RSS feeds.

**AD: How do you draw traffic to your website, i.e., do you mention your website on Twitter, etc.?**
**KW:** Our blog content lives on our website, so the above blog strategy is used to drive people to our website. In addition, when we craft new narratives and offers (i.e., Top 5, *Why Your Home Didn't Sell*) we link to those pages in targeted campaigns. We are just getting ready to launch an entire campaign around appealing your property taxes, which will include links to our website from Facebook, Twitter, RSS feeds, press releases, etc.

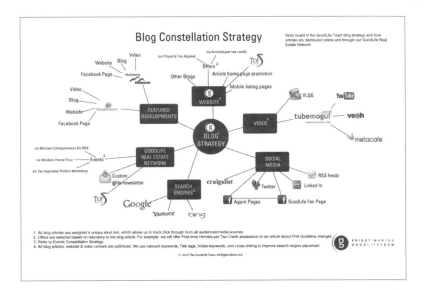

**AD: How have you effectively used Twitter? Please give an example.**
**KW: Example 1:** We monitor the Twitter stream for key phrases that people may tweet, like "selling my home," "buying a house," "real estate Austin," etc. Recently, we saw a post someone had placed looking for a recommendation of a real estate agent in Austin. We responded quickly and were able to secure a listing appointment with her.
   **Example 2:** We promoted a pre-grand opening for the developer of a

green energy project in town. The developer was hoping to have at least 100 people there for the event, and we decided to do an all-out social media campaign. No direct mail. As a result of promoting the pre-grand opening on Twitter, Facebook, and our blog, one week prior to the event we've had 250 people register (free on Eventbrite), and we've had a local television news station pick up the story. Once again, we've got 250 new names in our database of people that wanted to give us their information. You can't get that type of response using traditional marketing methods.

**AD: Krisstina, How do you measure ROI?**
**KW:** This is a great question. Because social networking involves mostly soft costs, and the tools are ones you are using throughout your day, measuring a precise ROI can be difficult. That being said, everyone added to our Good-Life Team Real Estate Network is sourced. We are able to see how many new relationships, leads, and closings come to us as a result of social networking. We review the sources of all media on a weekly and monthly basis. Our latest statistics show that Facebook is the third source of all traffic to our GoodLifeTeam.com website. With 30% of our total business coming from our website, we assess that Facebook produces real business, although we cannot directly attribute what percentage of that 30% comes directly from Facebook. In addition, it is difficult to measure the impact that Facebook has had on relationships established prior to Facebook when clients called us to list their homes or help them buy. We assess that the two-way communication offered by Facebook, which enables us to foster our relationships, was a deciding factor in those relationships calling us when they were ready to buy or sell.

**AD: What percentage of your income do you attribute to social networking and social media?**
**KW:** Over 30% of my business is generated through the Web and new online tools, such as social media.

**AD: How do you leverage your links?**
**KW:** We use our own custom short-link technology that not only allows us to track clicks, but extends and represents our brand (i.e., glt.bz/). We are always cross-linking between Facebook, Twitter, LinkedIn, and our website. In addition, we use short links on our direct mail campaigns in order to track campaign effectiveness. Short links are a powerful tool for tracking that

enable us to measure the success of every individual marketing campaign we promote. Tracking at this level was very costly, if not impossible, prior to these technologies.

**AD:** **How do you convert your friends, fans, and followers into buyers and sellers?**
**KW:** Our fundamental philosophy is consumer engagement. We work to engage our followers and friends in order to build new relationships, deepen existing relationships, and be interested in their lives. We work to be fun, yet professional, by creating polls, including videos of our customers, and hosting events. In addition, we only publish trustworthy, timely, and relevant real estate information that they can rely on to make their real estate decisions and/or to satisfy their real estate curiosity. In addition, our website is touted as a very useful tool and "the best real estate website" for anything real estate-related in Austin. We create a consistent identity of trust and value so that when they are ready to buy or sell, people contact us.

**AD:** **How do you incorporate Top 5 content into your social media strategy?**
**KW:** We include articles from the monthly *Real Estate Matters* in our glife e-newsletter. We have the Top 5 Real Estate news embedded in our website to provide our consumers with real-time information. We are actively using a customized version of the Expired Listings strategy from Top 5.

**AD:** **What is the most effective way you employ social media and social networking to differentiate yourself from other real estate agents?**
**KW:** First of all, we are disciplined, strategic, and rigorous about our use of social media and our customer engagement. I speculate that we put much more thought and concern into what we publish and don't publish, for the sake of being a trusted source of real estate knowledge and a credible brand in Austin. In addition, we use a consistent message and brand across all platforms. We provide relevant information about what the consumer cares about, which isn't the real estate agent, and we actively engage with them in conversations.

**AD:** **Krisstina, you have already determined the best and highest use of these platforms, and you're very comfortable with them. But, without question, many agents are struggling with social networking and social media, in terms of their not making as much money as they'd like to from**

its use. I believe that what separates those agents from agents like you is that they're playing checkers and you're playing chess. You're more strategic. You're running the marathon and they're running the 50-yard dash. You're not kidding yourself in terms of looking for instant gratification and, because you're not, you are not perceived as trolling the Internet for personal business. You are respectfully and respectably inserting yourself in a very appropriate way that gains confidence and builds trust.

**KW:** It's funny you used a chess analogy, because I've actually done a blog on that. That we're playing chess and other people are playing checkers.

**AD:** Thank you very much, Krisstina. You certainly are setting new standards for real estate professionalism, both offline and now online.

**KW:** Thank you, Allan. It is a privilege to be included in your groundbreaking book.

# Meet a Social Media Savant

## Valerie Fitzgerald
President of the Valerie Fitzgerald Group
Coldwell Banker Previews International
Top 5 in Real Estate Member
**Serving:** Beverly Hills, Bel Air, Brentwood, Malibu,
Santa Monica, Westside Los Angeles
**Years in real estate:** 20+

## Social Media Links:
http://valeriefitzgerald.com/blog/
http://losangelesrealestatetalk.com/
http://www.facebook.com/ValerieFitzgerald
http://www.facebook.com/ValerieFitzgeraldRealEstate
https://twitter.com/valrefitzgerald
http://www.youtube.com/user/ValerieFitzgerald
http://www.linkedin.com/in/beverlyhillshomesforsale
http://activerain.com/valeriefitzgerald

**Allan Dalton:** Hi Valerie, thank you for agreeing to contribute to this book. Before we get started, I'd like to provide my readers with some background information I obtained from your website, valeriefitzgerald.com:

> "Valerie Fitzgerald is the president of The Valerie Fitzgerald Group, a Beverly Hills Coldwell Banker real estate firm. Over the last 20 years, Valerie Fitzgerald has single-handedly managed to build a multi-million dollar real estate business. She has established her own charity foundation, spoken around the country at numerous business conventions, appeared on television shows like Entertainment Tonight and MTV's Cribs, ranks among Coldwell Banker's Top 10 agents nationwide, and has earned the attention of the *Los Angeles Business Journal* for highest sales volume in Los Angeles County for residential real estate in 2000."

And, Valerie, in May of 2009, Simon & Schuster published your book, *Heart and Sold: How to Survive and Build a Recession-Proof Business*. I am featuring you in my book because of your many and varied accomplishments. Well done!

## Meet a Social Media Savant

**Now, let's begin. What is your title?**
**Valerie Fitzgerald:** Previews Director, Coldwell Banker.

**AD: How long have you worked there?**
**VF:** I've been in real estate for 20 years and I've been with Coldwell Banker—well, we've changed company names a couple of times—but let's say 17 of those years.

**AD: How do you define social networking?**
**VF:** Social networking focuses on building online communities with people who share similar interests with you. For instance, I'm friends with a lot of Realtors on Facebook and Twitter because we share obvious commonalities, and that's where the conversation goes back and forth between us about an article or what's going on with interest rates. So it's having "like" interests.

**AD: Now, how do you define social media?**
**VF:** Social media is the medium. It's like Twitter, Facebook, LinkedIn. It's unlike what you would normally call "push" marketing. Social media is like a telephone. You put something out there and someone calls you back and continues the conversation. It's sort of an umbrella term that defines the various activities that integrate technology, interaction, the words, pictures, and, of course, video.

**AD: Thanks for your perspective, Valerie. I also like the definition that social media represents the "democratization of information" and "citizen journalism." With the upheaval of the media conglomerates, and with the social networking platforms that allow for connectivity and Web 2.0 interactivity, now social media is citizen journalism. So instead of having information from one to many, it allows *everybody* to be an embedded journalist.**
**VF:** Media is media. Media is a technology that's mixed in with, for example, the YouTube videos. That's media.

**AD: A common misperception is to call sites like Twitter and LinkedIn *social* media. Those are really social *networking* platforms. Because if you take away "social," media is media. Media has existed for hundreds of years. Social means everybody. It's how society communicates.**
**VF:** Right, so on Facebook, I can post a video.

**AD: But even if there wasn't Facebook, social media wouldn't be possible. It wouldn't be possible without these technological connectivity platforms. So, I see social networking as *connecting*. And social media is *content*. But let's get**

**back to you. When did you begin social networking?**
**VF:** Three years ago.

**AD: Why?**
**VF:** Because I could see that it was becoming more popular. And I could also see that a lot of the young people were using it to communicate—I have a young daughter so I could see the way she would use social networking to even communicate with me. I saw that this was going to be a very big possibility and a change of communication. I've got young clients that know how to e-mail and they post what they want to say to me on my Facebook inbox. It drives me a little crazy because it's another place I have to check regularly.

**AD: How many social networks do you belong to?**
**VF:** 49.

**AD: What are some of the major ones?**
**VF:** ActiveRain, ASMALLWORLD, BlogTalkRadio, Facebook, YouTube, Zillow, Entrepreneur.com; HomeSpace; ParentsConnect; MySpace; Plaxo; LinkedIn. I have some that are more client-based, more Realtor-based, and then I have some that are more women-based.

**AD: How do you selectively insert yourself professionally as a Realtor, or talk about business or try to attract buyers and sellers? Do you do it directly? Or do you think that because people know your brand and automatically associate you with real estate, that you can just be social in the same way as these different communities are and then, because you create top-of-mind awareness with people within these communities, that gets you more business? Do you try to influence them regarding real estate on these sites?**
**VF:** What I do differently is that I don't use my social networking sites to talk about myself—you know, "me, me, my, my." I bring them value. I bring them an opinion. I bring them an article. I bring them content.

**AD: So that's social media. Otherwise, it's just social networking—like a college student saying he's going skiing this weekend.**
**VF:** No, there's not one single thing you're going to find on any of my social networking sites about me personally.

**AD: Let me ask you this: How do you use our Top 5 content in terms of repurposing information?**
**VF:** I repurpose the articles that come out of RISMedia all the time. I think they're some of the most well-written, up-to-date, contemporary articles that

## Meet a Social Media Savant

I've seen. I do a newsletter, so I repurpose them often into my newsletters.

**AD: Now, how many friends and followers do you have on some of the major sites?**
**VF:** On my Facebook page, we were cut off at 5,000, so we went over to a fan page and I have another 1,200 or 1,400 people that are on those fan pages. I have another specific-to-my-company Facebook page—we hit the limit, so they make you create other pages—and there's 400 to 500 people on that. On Twitter, I've got a little under 3,000 followers. And on LinkedIn, I have about 600 connections. On Plaxo, I hit 1,000, so they stopped me, too, and I have about 400 people waiting.

**AD: Why do you think they stop you?**
**VF:** Isn't that the craziest thing in the world? I don't understand that, Allan. I don't have the answer because it doesn't make any sense to me. They're not getting revenue now, but maybe they're looking at the ways by which they'll eventually create revenue: "Hey, you stopped at 5,000, so now to keep all these fan pages, you've got to pay us this much a month." Maybe this is an experimental sort of thing that these companies are doing to see the people that really use them and really need them, and then they can start to figure out their revenue stream because right now they don't have any.

**AD: How much time do you spend maintaining your social networking sites, and do you have anyone who helps you keep up?**
**VF:** I have an employee who's virtual—she's in Arizona—and she helps me stay

up with it. I'll send her the articles that either I've written or I like. She posts all that stuff for me and she'll answer my wall things because some of it's just really simple things. But the inbox stuff I answer and I go on probably every two days and it takes 20 minutes for me to zip through a bunch of them.

**AD:** How current do you feel you have to keep your Twitter page? Are you posting things on Twitter every day, every two days, or every five days?
**VF:** No, we post every day on Twitter. I don't spend time doing that. We discuss the posts in advance.

**AD:** You post in advance, that's good. And, LinkedIn, you don't have to do anything? Right?
**VF:** No, you don't have to do anything.

**AD:** And then Facebook...how do you approach Facebook?
**VF:** We probably use Facebook the most.

**AD:** Give me an example. What are you posting?
**VF:** I post when something happens that I'm really excited about. I just read a couple of articles recently and we posted them to Facebook. Facebook is always *about* something; I'm sharing content with my followers. A lot of people react. They'll react to the article, they'll react to something, such as an opinion I have about the market.

**AD:** So, it's more about thought leadership on Facebook than it is on Twitter, correct?
**VF:** It is. It's totally about the *content* on Facebook.

**AD:** Do you have a blog?
**VF:** Of course I have a blog.

**AD:** So, you're driving people, leveraging your links from all of these other sites. Is your ultimate objective to get everybody to your blog?
**VF:** No, my ultimate objective is to get everybody to my *website*. The blog is on my website. But I have many more things on my website that I'd like people to see, so I like to drive that.

**AD:** What are some of the things you'll post on Twitter to get people to your website?
**VF:** Earlier this year, for example, we were talking about the Feds no longer backing the mortgage-backed bonds, and that by the end of March, the interest

rates would start to go up.

**AD: And what do you do then? Have a link to your website for more informa-tion?**
**VF:** Yes, then we might go back to Facebook. I link my tweet to an article about the subject, because I read so much and I keep all of the articles.

**AD: You're limited to 140 characters on Twitter, which can be used as link bait. Are you trying to get people from Twitter to Facebook or to your website? Do you want them to first go from Twitter to become friends of yours on Facebook and then visit your website?**
**VF:** Right. It usually goes Twitter to Facebook and then they pop over into my website. As an example, we posted on Facebook that I want to grow my team and now we've got three really good local applicants—people that are coming here with their resumes to join our team. I got two referrals, including one guy from South Carolina. Quite a few agents ask me if I have a property for their buyer, that type of thing. My book has been another big thing on Facebook. Women, people who have read it, radio shows—I do radio shows all the time— and all of those people who are listeners go to my Facebook page every time.

**AD: Valerie, you're the only real estate professional, Realtor, or broker I've known in all my years anywhere in the world that had a book published about their life story and real estate story by Simon & Schuster, or any other major publisher, but I must say, without any modesty here, that I was one of the few people you featured in the book. You interviewed me—how much impact did my interview in your book have on the book's success?**
**VF:** None whatsoever.

**AD: Okay, then. Let's move on. Regarding the communities you participate in, it never appears that you are imposing yourself, looking as if you're desperate for business, or that you're trolling for real estate business.**
**VF:** That's correct.

**AD: How do you reconcile business networking and social networking?**
**VF:** The style 20 years ago was always, "Hey, I'm great. I'm number one." No-body uses that in their ads anymore.

**AD: Do you post, "I just got a listing," like some other agents do?**
**VF:** No, I don't do that.

**AD: What I'm saying is, if you were posting anything on these non-professional**

sites that looked like you were trying to entice buyers and sellers directly, that wouldn't be effective. Is that what you're saying?
**VF:** Yes, I don't think it would be effective.

**AD:** But at the same time, you want them to connect you to real estate so it seems as though you're bringing attention—almost like the *LA Times*—to vital real estate-related transcendental issues. Therefore, because of that, no one is going to privately or personally think to themselves, "Gee, what's she doing here?" because your insertion of who you are is more high-minded.
**VF:** I want to build trust. I want people to know they can depend on me.

**AD:** Has anyone ever posted or tweeted, "Hey Valerie, this isn't supposed to be about real estate?"
**VF:** No.

**AD:** Do you post information about your community?
**VF:** No, I do not.

**AD:** Why don't you? Why wouldn't you?
**VF:** Because it's not about real estate; it's not about business. It's not what I want to be positioned and known for.

**AD:** It's great that you said that. In this book, I provide examples of "digital don'ts and do's." For example, I don't want to know that a great surgeon is also a great cook.
**VF:** Right, absolutely.

**AD:** So you don't want to give your friends, fans, and followers a glimpse into your social or personal life.
**VF:** It's not relevant.

**AD:** Even though you are heavily inserted into multiple social networking sites, you are never manifesting social or personal behavior. You are basically edifying these communities with your sophistication regarding real estate and trusted advice.
**VF:** Absolutely—100 percent. We haven't wavered from it.

**AD:** Give me examples of posts you might make.
**VF:** We did one about—because right now, it's critical since some buyers are still sitting on the sidelines—how interest rates will go up. They *will* go up. They're going to go up soon. So, we posted that. We post about the tax credit

that is supposed to be eliminated by August 30 [at press time] because that's a big deal. I'm going on Fox News tomorrow morning here, and I'm talking about three different points for buyers that I think they should be doing right away, and three points for sellers that they should be doing right away.

**AD: When did you start your website?**
**VF:** I think my website's about 12 years old. Well, no, excuse me. My website's brand new; I just put it up last year but I started my first website about 12-13 years ago.

**AD: What type of content would we find on your website?**
**VF:** I scaled it down. Because I used to have every topic—you could find out how to make a margarita.

**AD: So you're saying that your new website strictly features relevant information. If it's not there, it's not relevant.**
**VF:** Well, that's true. I've got my Projects page; I've got my property listings; I've got my newsroom page; and I've got a resource page.

**AD: What do you mean a newsroom page?**
**VF:** My newsroom page gives my readers a rundown on the sort of stuff I've been doing, such as a radio show they can download. I also do a mentoring program once a month and people call into my mentoring program from all around the country—they can also download that from my newsroom. People can get a really clear idea of what I do. I've also got a page on my site for my book.

**AD: Do you aggregate these friends, followers, and fans into demographic groups that you can individually target?**
**VF:** Yes, I do. I do that beginning with my newsletters, which are separate from my social media activities. But every time you accept friends on Facebook you can put them into groups, like Realtors, which we do. So right now, we're working on pulling those contacts that we have and putting them into more groups because I absolutely believe—and I've been doing this now for about two years—in my group-specific content and e-mails. As far as Facebook, it can be a little tricky, so we're working on that. But my friends, everybody on Facebook, have opted in, because you can opt out if you don't like my information that is sent to you—but nobody does.

**AD: How often do you send individualized messages with content, or a link to your website, to these different, specific groups?**

**VF:** We don't e-mail blast to the Facebook friends because there are about 5,000 of them. There's a lot of spam I receive every day and I don't want to be one of those people blasting untargeted messages.

**AD:** Do you use multiple networks like Facebook, Twitter, and MySpace to draw traffic to your website?
**VF:** Yes, of course. We like to call my website my "home base."

**AD:** Let's talk about how you use social networking and social media for real estate purposes.
**VF:** Oh, it's been a lot of fun. I got this one project, the beginning of last year—a high rise condominium, new building, and it was under construction—and they said, "Okay, let's get marketing this thing." You couldn't take pictures of it and I thought, "Gee, how am I going to get it out to people to understand what's going on and make it fun?" So I decided to do a video blog. I went out there with a hard hat on and went right through the noise; they were talking about the building and saying, "This is going to be this," and "That's going to be that," and "The paneling's going to be there." And at the very end, I would say, "Watch us progress." I did these every week. For the very last one,

when the building was completed in the front, I took my hard hat off and I threw it—and it landed in the trashcan. It was fun.  People could watch the construction progress and get the project name into their heads. That's how I started using the social medium for that particular project. I also use the videos as press releases, such as "Gee, we just had Bruce Willis move into the building." It populates everywhere and then the media comes back to me. So we're really using the online capabilities. I do everything online now. I'm up for an award from Bloomberg Television.

**AD: What's the award for?**
**VF:** It's for real estate agency marketing—a detailed, complete marketing campaign and examples of other marketing strategies.

**AD: How do you draw traffic to your blog?**
**VF:** We publish blog posts. The blog post alerts go to Twitter, Facebook, LinkedIn, and all the other ones. And then I have an RSS feed set up on my site so that they're populated automatically as soon as we publish a new blog post.

**AD: You're basically using Twitter to post real estate headlines to interest people into visiting your blog to read more robust content?**
**VF:** It's more of a headline, no doubt about it.

**AD: How do you measure your ROI?**
**VF:** By website traffic—we use Google Analytics. There's another program called HootSuite. For our newsletters, we use something called Constant Contact, so you can look at the back end and see who opened them, how many, who watched…and sometimes people do opt out, but not very many of them. We also use a program called BudURL, which tracks the leads that come in, time versus the investment, the media leads and the employment leads.

**AD: What percentage of your income do you attribute directly to social networking and social media?**
**VF:** I can't say that right now. It's not a big portion of it. The social media thing is two or three years old and to get it defined will take some more time.

**AD: I'm hearing that everywhere. Since you're the master, you need to measure in a way that isn't ROI. You can just sense that you're building your brand so you're connecting to more people.**
**VF:** We're headed in the right direction.

**AD:** Would the income you attribute directly to social networking and social media be less than five percent of your income?
**VF:** I'd say five percent would be accurate right now.

**AD:** How do you convert friends, fans, and followers into buyers and sellers?
**VF:** Let's go back to Top 5. Just yesterday (at press time), regarding your Census, we asked people to fill it out and we posted it on Facebook to 5,000 people. As I told you, many times we've repurposed *Real Estate* magazine articles and different news items on my blog posts. We take out sound bites and get tremendous reaction to some.

**AD:** That's great. What is the most effective way you employ social networking and social media so as to differentiate yourself from other agents?
**VF:** I don't think twice about differentiating myself from other agents because I don't really think about what they're doing. I've got the philosophy that I'm here to have up-to-date information and to help people.

**AD:** That's a wonderful attitude.

# Strategy that Links

## Hector Aguilar
Realtor, Team Leader
Coldwell Banker Town & Country
The ALMA Real Estate Group
**Serving:** Covina and the Los Angeles, California area
**Years in real estate:** 18
**www.HectorSellsHomes.com**

## Social Media Links:
www.HectorSellsHomes.com
www.Facebook.com/HectorAguilarRE
www.Twitter.com/HectorAguilarRE

**Allan Dalton:** How long have you had the pleasure of being associated with Coldwell Banker and the ALMA Real Estate Group?
**Hector Aguilar:** For more than two years. I've been in real estate for close to 18 years—eight as a mortgage broker/banker and the last 10 as a Realtor.

**AD:** How do you define social networking?
**HA:** I define social networking as an opportunity to touch base with various persons through different Internet social platforms.

**AD:** How do you define social media?
**HA:** Social media is an online platform that allows us to contribute and communicate with others.

**AD:** How would you define a real estate social marketing system?
**HA:** I define a real estate social marketing system as a system that incorporates blogs, social media, Internet, and websites. It would be on autopilot and would require a minimum of my time to maintain it. The system would generate inquiries and conversations, and ultimately increase traffic, and seller and buyer leads.

**AD:** Why did you begin social networking?
**HA:** I am an advocate for new technology when I believe it will help my business and my clients. I am also fascinated by integrating solutions into my busi-

ness so I can prospect better and deliver better service to my customers. My goal with social media is to ultimately figure out how to increase my number of clients and reduce my operational costs. The key for me is to move cautiously so that, for one, I don't become overwhelmed and, two, so I can clearly measure the results of my efforts.

**AD:** **What social networks do you belong to?**
**HA:** The main networks I use professionally include Facebook, LinkedIn, Twitter, and YouTube. I'm exploring others, but I am focused on these for the time being.

**AD:** **Why did you choose these social networks to belong to?**
**HA:** I chose these main four because it seems that these are the most talked-about platforms in social media.

**AD:** **How many friends and followers do you have on each?**
**HA:** This is probably the area I am the most sensitive to. *Whereas many of my colleagues are out trying to get as many friends and fans as possible, which mostly seem to be other Realtors, I am limiting my friends and followers to actual friends, prospects, and past clients.* This process, while time-consuming, allows me to provide thought leadership about the topic that my social network is interested in most—our real estate industry. Therefore, my aggregation of friends and followers is very selective. I may change this policy over time, but, for now, I am practicing with different techniques to determine what works best for me.

**Current Numbers**
**Facebook:** 346 friends. I'm selectively adding about 10 per month.
**Twitter:** 81 followers
**LinkedIn:** 65 connections
**YouTube:** Embedded in my website and blog site

**AD:** **How do you balance the way in which you engage your professional and personal contacts?**
**HA:** I try to practice a balance of both. On average, I spend about half my time posting and the other half commenting and interacting with others in my network. Out of my postings, I usually post about four business posts to one personal one. That way, I can connect to my network with mostly business information and the occasional personal post to share some human factor. The personal posts might talk about causes that I am in support of or activities I do in the community.

**AD:** What do you generally post about on your networks?

**HA:** I try to be a resource to my friends as much as possible. Starting with real estate news, I generally study news sites such as FOX, CNN, CNBC, MSNBC, ABCNews, RISMedia, and others, to find articles that pertain to real estate and the current market, positive or negative. I also set up Google news alerts for topics of interest that may be happening in my farm areas and local market. I am exploring conducting my own news channel online and want to connect with the local Chamber of Commerce in order to network with other business professionals via our respective social networks. Once I post, I evaluate interest via the comments from my network. Sometimes it's surprising what people respond to, so you have to mix it up a bit. Controversial items seem to get more action than news or market information.

**AD:** To what degree do you post about real estate activities?

**HA:** Real estate is my main topic, but rarely about my own services. It's hard to practice safe social networking as a Realtor because you just want to sell more homes and promote yourself like heck, but that's taboo in social networking best practices. I also don't post every listing I get, but the good ones or ones that have special terms may make it. But yes, real estate and related topics are prime for me. Here is an example of one of my posts:

# Strategy that Links

**AD:** When did you get your first website?

**HA:** I got my first website in 2000. Since then, I have been working on leveraging not only the website, but keeping up with the feedback and the needs of my clients and team.

**AD:** What kind of content can be found on your website?

**HA:** I try to keep the information simple, to the point, and useful. I know that most in our target audience are looking for homes and, in many cases today, they are looking for foreclosures and other value-provoking property opportunities, so I focus on providing a quick search to both of these types of properties. I've tried different lead capture systems over the years, but found my 1parkplace IDX lead capture tools to work best for me and my team, so I promote that system very actively and find good results from that.

**AD:** Do you have a blog?

**HA:** Honestly, blogging has been a difficult bridge for me to cross. I made several attempts over the last couple of years and I found that I was eating up a lot of time trying to get it dialed in, and I found myself not focusing on my core business. At this time, I'm researching what some of my successful blogger friends are doing. I expect to own a hyperlocal system like Gregg Neuman's in San Diego someday. I like the fact that it has integrated MLS data, ghost blogging services, and a turn-key management system that will ensure our team is capitalizing on blogging properly. Not to mention that Gregg is tearing up the search engines with his blog. I look forward to getting that implemented this year. In this market, our philosophy is that if you can't do it right, then don't waste the money.

**AD:** Do you aggregate your followers and fans into demographic groups that you can individually target?

**HA:** Absolutely. I think that is essential as you grow your friend base. I don't even have that many online friends, compared to others, but I've already learned that if you don't start out organized, then it gets ugly real quick when you try to send messages to key groups. I created groups for buyers, sellers, and past customers. I also have a group for investors, and one for my family, just in case I want to send a message to them and not necessarily announce a message to all.

**AD:** How often do you send your target groups individualized messages with content or a link to your website?

**HA:** I generally always include a link to a website. Most of the time my own, but often I will link to the website that provided me the information. It really depends on the content and the source of the content. What's key here is to promote others who you believe can provide reciprocal value back to you.

**AD: Do you use multiple networks, i.e., Facebook, Twitter, to draw traffic to your website?**
**HA:** There is only so much I can do within my own Facebook and Twitter posts for driving traffic. I am having reasonably good results with getting my friends back to my website. But, what I have found to be even more compelling for driving traffic is when I comment or post on other sites and on the walls of some of my friends. The main network for driving traffic is Facebook for me right now. I am really concentrating on doing a good job with Facebook. I figure that since there are 500 million+ people on that network, there has to be gold in there somewhere. I am going to dig until I find it.

Next for me is a Facebook website so I can expand the value to my social community. I would like to integrate an IDX search into it as well. I'm not sure if this is possible, though, but I'm looking into it now.

The key is always going to be the content you write or post about. People are not out there looking for sites to click on unless they believe there will be something of interest or value to them. Right now, the hot topic is REOs and investor properties—ones that can be purchased and rented out for more than the payment. They go quickly, so when we get those types of posts, people will click your link in high numbers. We still have a lot to learn here and will look to others to see what works best.

Traditionally, I focused on advertising and farming and I still do those, but I am now exploring social networking and am really trying to dial in our SEO (search engine optimization). We realize that the key to traffic is generating the *right* traffic. This is an area where quality is much more important than quantity. For this, I try to find credible sites like government sites and high-traffic real estate sites to conduct postings and comment on other posts. This has proven to drive traffic, but more importantly, I am working on the back links to my website, so that Google ultimately ranks my site high for the neighborhoods that I am focusing on marketing in when consumers are conducting their searches.

**AD: How have you effectively used Twitter?**
**HA:** I'm no expert here. I just try to keep my network informed about the latest activities. I don't feel that I have done anything revolutionary, but I just try to be consistent and not offend anyone. I will say that I have not seen the same reaction to postings from Twitter that I have seen from my actions on Facebook. I think there is so much going on in Twitter that I mostly see Realtors and not my clients using it.

**AD:** How do you measure ROI?

**HA:** This is a good question. I would *like* to measure ROI by the amount of true transactions that are generated directly by my social media marketing; however, there have not been many to date in comparison with my time investment. I'm looking at this like gardening and I have to be patient. But for now, my measurement is from the reaction I am getting from friends in my network.

**AD:** What percentage of your income do you attribute to social networking and social media?

**HA:** At this point, it's hard to tell. Since many of my transactions are from people I have in my social network, you would think that I can say most of my income comes from social networking. However, since I largely added people I already know to my network, there is no telling how much our social networking contributed to additional transactions. However, I will say that social networking has helped me communicate more regularly with those I already know; therefore, I attribute social networking to be an essential part of keeping me in the game and in front of those I know. I estimate that I obtained about a handful of transactions from people I met through social networking as a byproduct of referrals online, but I know that will increase significantly over time as I tap into the circles of my existing friends. It's enough of a light that I am going to turn every stone to get proficient at this. I am always looking for methods to improve my performance as well.

**AD:** How do you convert your friends, fans, and followers into buyers and sellers?

**HA:** This is another good question. In my case, they start out as potential buyers and sellers or as past customers. So, as far as prospecting goes, that is an area in which we are going to sharpen our skills.

**AD:** What is the most effective way you employ social media/social networking so as to differentiate yourself from other real estate agents?

**HA:** Honestly, I'm no role model here, but I think the biggest difference for me is the selectiveness of who I let come into my network. I pretty much know everybody outside of the computer as well, so even though my list may be small, it is effective for me from a networking side. I will usually add about 10-15 new friends per month as I meet people at open houses, during floor calls, etc. I am also taking a proactive step to work with other businesses in my area so we can share marketing ideas and networks of customers. There is so much to learn and I look forward to learning from others what is working and what is not. I just need to be able to have time for my family and myself. I want to make sure I don't get addicted.

# The Right Message for the Medium

## Rebecca "Becky" Boomsma

Licensed Sales Agent
Coldwell Banker Residential Brokerage
CRS, e-PRO, SRES
Top 5 in Real Estate Member
**Serving**: Bergen, Passaic, and Morris County, New Jersey
**Years in real estate**: 12
**www.BeckyBoomsma.com**

## Social Media Links:

http://www.facebook.com/BeckyBoomsma
http://twitter.com/BBoomsma
http://www.linkedin.com/in/beckyboomsma

**Allan Dalton: How do you define social networking?**
**Becky Boomsma:** Individuals or small groups who meet, socialize, and connect or engage with others for professional networking, friendships, or sharing of special interests.

**AD: How do you define social media?**
**BB:** Social media is a type of online media that facilitates sharing, ideas, conversation, and connection.

**AD: How would you define a real estate social marketing system?**
**BB:** A method of social outreach to convey that a company's product, service, and image is of exceptional and preferred worth.

**AD: Why did you become involved with social networking/social media?**
**BB:** I began because I wanted to be ahead of the curve with what I've heard you describe, Allan, as a positional advantage and be recognized and respected as an early, effective adopter of newer, strategic resources to communicate and share information.

## The Right Message for the Medium

**AD:** Which social networks do you belong to?
**BB:** Facebook, Twitter, LinkedIn, YouTube, Proxio, ActiveRain, Inman Communities, RealTown (and the Top 5 Community), Trulia, and groups within these networks.

**AD:** Why did you choose these particular social networks?
**BB:** Each of these had sound platforms for contributing to and participating in real estate industry topics and sharing.

**AD:** How many friends, followers, connections, etc. did you have on each as of March this year?
**BB:** Facebook: 1,023; Twitter: 2,100; LinkedIn: 195; Proxio: 61 and growing.

**AD:** How do you balance the way in which you engage your professional and personal contacts?
**BB:** By employing social networking strategies, where the emphasis has to be memorable on both fronts.

**AD:** What do you generally post about on your networks?
**BB:** Real estate, lifestyle, money/finance topics, events, personal experiences, and motivational quotes, along with most of the information I receive from RISMedia and Top 5 in Real Estate.

**AD:** Becky, what are a couple of your favorite motivational quotes you would like to share with our readers?
**BB:** "The simple act of paying positive attention to people has a great deal to do with productivity." - Tom Peters

"If your actions inspire others to dream more, learn more, do more and become more, you are a leader." - John Quincy Adams

"We must become the change we want to see." - Mahatma Gandhi

**AD:** Becky, what percentage of the time do you post about real estate activities?
**BB:** The key is to ensure that you are not business-based when the setting calls for you to be only social and not to be superficially social when the online engagement calls for a business response.

**AD:** What's an example of a post you might make?
**BB:** Local/regional absorption rates and how that might position buyers/sellers; incentives for buying now with article links; quick fixes for home enhancements/beautification/lifestyle changes with article links.

**AD:** Do you include social media, i.e., content, in most of your real estate posts on your social networks?
**BB:** I absolutely always create links to substantive real estate content, especially the relevant content and videos provided by RISMedia and the Top 5 in Real Estate Network®.

**AD:** When did you launch your website?
**BB:** In 2002.

**AD:** What kind of content can be found on your website?
**BB:** Featured homes, property listings, market snapshots, home valuations, community videos and regional resource links, newsletters, RSS feed, and buyer and seller articles and information.

**AD:** Do you aggregate your followers and fans into demographic groups that you can individually target and, therefore, better service?
**BB:** Not yet. I understand the importance, but I have not had the time or assistance to break this information down.

**AD:** Which social networks have you found predominantly beneficial?
**BB:** Facebook, Twitter, and LinkedIn.

**AD:** How do you draw traffic to your website?
**BB:** Through linking and commentary reference via a shortened URL.

## The Right Message for the Medium

**AD:** Well, that was certainly a shortened commentary reference, Becky! I have never developed, to the dismay of many, your gift of conciseness. Now speaking of those things shortened...given Twitter's 140-character limitation, how have you most effectively leveraged this social networking phenomenon?

**BB:** For promoting local/regional community events, philanthropic interests, real estate events, property promotion, buyer incentives, special green promotions. Example: CRS Education courses/meetings, RISMedia and Top 5 in Real Estate Network® events, Real Estate BarCamp event promotions—all with measurable linkage. When working this past year to help host the Real Estate BarCamp in New York City, I routinely posted the event information, registration, and flyer links via Twitter and other social media.

It became a great branding piece to immediately identify my important connections to real estate in the region, and show that I am aligned with innovative, cutting-edge technology, methods, information, and education, and that I am always striving to get others involved to participate, network, and learn.

I also used this technique and opportunity earlier in the year with RISMedia's Leadership Conference to accomplish the same branding aspects, raise the awareness and importance of Top 5, and also publicly thanked RISMedia and Top 5 for inviting me to share my knowledge and professional perspective by participating on one of their esteemed panels on social media during that conference.

This provided me the opportunity to demonstrate respect and appreciation for a great business and networking opportunity, raise awareness of the important affiliation, and also, brand myself as an exceptional and valued professional, presenter, and speaker on real estate matters. And, of course, I then leverage all of this to consumers via my social networking platforms. Incidentally, during this event, I also tweeted about the speakers and content of presentations to share the important topics and perspectives being presented, underscoring the importance and awareness of great ideas being shared at this illustrious RISMedia Leadership Conference.

**AD:** How do you measure ROI in terms of your commitment to social media?

**BB:** Specific inquiries; leads that turn into customers; opt-in requests for newsletters/information; attention given to a topic measured via bitly.com or ow.ly.com, and resulting sales. That said, I cannot exactly correlate the return on my investment as my investment is difficult to break down, both in terms of how much time I devote, as well as how difficult it is to separate prospecting, networking, and marketing in general from what I would be normally doing in these areas, even if these new social networking platforms did not exist.

**AD:** What percentage of your income do you attribute to social networking and social media?

**BB:** I would have to estimate that I can directly attribute approximately 10 percent of my income the past couple of years to my social media commitment and I expect that to grow.

**AD:** If you'll forgive me for asking a blatantly self-serving question, please tell me, how do you "leverage your links?"

**BB:** Allan, I love the book's title. What I do is incorporate links to my content and website. I can post/express more with less and have the opportunity to measure the attraction and engagement of the content I provide via monitoring the stats available through shortened URLs and linkage.

**AD:** How do you convert your friends, fans, and followers into buyers and sellers?

**BB:** By offering information or observations that stimulate consumers to either begin to contemplate the benefits of buying, selling, or investing in real estate, or better yet, to take immediate action when it is in their best interest. At the same time, it is imperative that I never provide the sense that I am only interested in accommodating the transactional needs of consumers, but rather that I remain dedicated and prepared to assist them in resolving any real estate-related question, concern or overall decision.

**AD:** How do you incorporate RISMedia and Top 5 content into your social media strategy?

**BB:** I have the Top 5 RSS feed/website content on the homepage of my website, which I value as the content is consistently topical and ever-changing each day; I incorporate the brochures and magazine articles into occasional posts as part of my "free reports."

This is something I first heard John Featherston advising real estate agents to do many years ago. I print out and mail and/or e-mail the valuable weekly newsletter and brochures to my network sphere and provide them as a take-away at open houses; and I post Top 5 events and content to bring awareness to the consumer, via social media outlets, of this elite organization, which I'm a part of, to help build its brand, and attract additional interest in Top 5 to help grow its membership.

## The Right Message for the Medium

**AD:** What is the most effective way you employ social media/social networking so as to differentiate yourself from other real estate agents?

**BB:** First of all, there is no differentiator that I respect more than the fact that I am a CRS. Consequently, *at every opportunity, I seek to stress the value to consumers that I am not only a Realtor, which I am extremely proud of, along with the Code of Ethics that is embodied in each Realtor's value proposition, but also that I have joined with a network of Realtors that I believe represents the highest level of professionalism within our industry, that being those who have the initials CRS next to their names.*

Beyond CRS and Top 5 as differentiators, I am also constantly reminding online consumers that I have a material edge over many in the industry in that I bring to real estate my vast experience in interior design and lifestyle-related art. I engage consumers with interesting articles and information on home improvements and home/lifestyle. I also bring awareness to and support my local regional lifestyle. Just as I also make myself memorable by publicizing occasional industry and community/regional events and my personal involvement in such to remind people all over the globe about where I live and work and what types of activities/issues I find interesting, worthy of thought, and potentially relevant in their world.

My providing market data and e-mailing my weekly newsletter is also well-received and memorable, especially for local/influential eyes. This approach is much more effective in branding, sharing my professional perspective in tandem with my personal side, rather than posting less engaging or thoughtless remarks about what's happening in my daily life, which most people have little interest in. This practice, along with posting professional events and commentary, has expanded my referral network and provided measurable referrals to me. And, of course, I immediately took advantage of the opportunity provided by RISMedia and Top 5 to be on the front cover of the illustrious *Real Estate* magazine, especially since the cover story superbly addresses for consumers the process they should go through when selecting a Realtor...which, obviously, subliminally would suggest that the Realtor to choose should be me, since my picture is on the cover. (The story Becky refers to is on page 75 of the magazine).

**AD:** Becky, last question: what advice would you give to somebody new to the real estate industry or reading this book, who is considering the very important and most honorable profession of Real Estate Brokerage as it relates to social media?
**BB:** Allan, I am pleased you are asking me this question because, like you, I, too, deeply believe that it's not just about what the real estate industry can do for me, but what I can do for the real estate industry.

**AD:** Becky, let me stop you right there. I cannot afford to have two people in this book directly or indirectly quoting President Kennedy. Therefore, would you please rephrase your answer and then continue?
**BB:** I understand. Let me say it this way...I am very proud and, therefore, very protective of our industry and, as a result, take interest in doing anything I can to encourage the best and the brightest of today's young people to not only consider law, medicine, engineering, information technology, etc., as their career of choice, but to place a career in real estate at the very top of their list as well.

This is where social media and social networking become most relevant. The information technology aspect of social media, combined with the opportunity to provide valuable content and consultative guidance to consumers, automatically elevates the career requirements, both perceived and real, of what it takes to be successful in real estate. Therefore, when you consider that very few decisions are as important to consumers as their real estate decisions are, and couple this with the role of information technology, real estate becomes one of the most sophisticated of all professional endeavors and, thus, our industry should be attracting only the best and the brightest of our young people.

In other words, when you take the traditional skills of prospecting, selling, marketing, and networking that real estate requires, and add in the current need to become proficient at both technology and the dissemination of advice and content, it becomes clear that only society's most capable individuals need apply. So, my message to the Gen Ys is that the way in which you would most likely approach a real estate career would enable you to leap frog over many in our industry who are not as inclined to leverage the technology that is second nature to you.

## The Right Message for the Medium

**AD:** Well Becky, while some in our business like to irrationally suggest that there is enough business to go around for everybody, quite frankly, there isn't. So, therefore, let me commend you on your efforts to encourage the best and the brightest to come into our industry and take some of your market share... now that's really giving back!

# Increasing Networking Power

## Eric John Elegado
Real Estate Specialist
Prudential California Realty
**Serving:** San Diego
**www.ericelegado.com**

**Allan Dalton:** Eric, thank you for your willingness to offer insight into your very successful real estate career. Steve Hundley recommended you for this interview, which to me is very telling as Steve has visibility into the real estate practices of thousands of leading Realtors.

**Eric Elegado:** It is my pleasure.

**AD: Eric, please begin by giving us some of your real estate background.**

**EE:** I have been working for Prudential California Realty since December 2009. Prior to Prudential California Realty, I had an independent company for 28-plus years. My best year in my career was in 2006. I closed 884 transactions between E Real Estate & Loans, Inc. (my real estate company) and E Real Mortgage, Inc. (my mortgage company).

**AD: How do you define social networking?**

**EE:** I define social networking as taking time away from the office and connecting with colleagues and other real estate agents, business owners, etc. on a business level.

**AD: How do you define social media?**

**EE:** Although I feel that I'm just getting started with this whole new world of opportunity, I define social media as a very simple way of staying connected with my center of influence—friends and family—all at the same time on a personal and business level through mostly Facebook and LinkedIn.

**AD: Why did you begin social networking?**

**EE:** I began social networking because, even though I can be a bit shy, I know that I need to get out around other people and network if I want to complete my goals of helping people buy and sell homes. I like to take advantage of all opportunities to represent myself as a successful real estate agent.

**AD:** What social networks do you belong to?
**EE:** Mastermind Group – Top Producers, Mastermind Group – Christian Men, Weekly Bible Studies, The Mike Ferry Organization, Facebook, LinkedIn, Twitter, MySpace.

**AD:** I can understand why you joined the iconic Mike Ferry Organization, as he has uniquely helped thousands of real estate agents make additional dollars in their careers, but why the others?
**EE:** I chose these networks because I felt they would be an asset to me as an individual and as a businessperson.

**AD:** How many friends and followers do you have on each social media platform?
**EE:** Facebook – 3,773
LinkedIn – 182
Twitter – 17
MySpace – 493

**AD:** Is your interaction with your friends, followers, and fans social, professional or both?
**EE:** Both.

**AD:** What do you generally post about on your networks?
**EE:** Motivational ideas and quotes, daily thoughts, beliefs, real estate updates, website updates. Most of my posts are related to real estate.

**AD:** Do you include social media, i.e., content, in any of your real estate posts on your social networks?
**EE:** Yes, we cross-promote all social media activities when we blog.

**AD:** When did you start your website?
**EE:** My first website was created nearly 10 years ago, and two years ago, I upgraded my site to a 1parkplace custom hybrid blog platform in order to introduce blogging and social media marketing to my marketing mix. The hybrid blog is really a website and blog site all in one solution.

**AD:** What kind of content can be found on your website?
**EE:** Real estate-related marketing information, community events and news, family-related posts, content from other informative sites, information from Google news alerts, etc.

**AD:** Do you have a blog?
**EE:** Yes.

**AD:** When did you start blogging?
**EE:** Approximately two years ago.

**AD:** Is your blog separate from your website?
**EE:** Yes, but they are integrated together.

**AD:** What kind of content can be found on your blog?
**EE:** Real estate listings and neighborhood information mostly.

**AD:** Do you aggregate your followers and fans into demographic groups that you can individually target?
**EE:** Not yet, but it is definitely a goal. I do e-mail news blasts and updates to my database of more than 7,000 people, and my website is always easily accessed and announced through these blasts.

This is a good question. We didn't start with the intent of creating demographic groups we could target, but now, we need to. We have over 3,000 friends on Facebook, so that will be quite a task for us.

**AD:** How often do you send your friends, followers, and fans messages with content or a link to your website?
**EE:** Every holiday and twice a week is the goal; the website is always linked. We post content to Facebook every day—mostly on real estate, but also fun and timely information. Three to four times a month, I send every one of my contacts an e-mail with either news, holiday reminders, or information on a service or event we are affiliated with in the community.

**AD:** Do you use multiple networks, i.e., Facebook, Twitter, MySpace, Google Buzz, to draw traffic to your website or blog?
**EE:** Yes, so far LinkedIn and Facebook have proven to be successful. We are finding that our Facebook friends are referring their friends to our blog site to look for homes and gather information. The primary solution for our consumers is our 1parkplace IDX home search, which ties in with our contact database, so we know who is coming and going. I heard that the Top 5 Network can help us with new and valuable content, so we look forward to learning more about it very soon.

## Increasing Networking Power

**AD:** How do you draw traffic to your blog, i.e., do you have a link on your web-site, or do you tweet about your blog?
**EE:** We have some staples in our marketing, such as print marketing, billboards, e-mail marketing, and social network marketing. We also try out new ideas to see how they work.

**AD:** How have you effectively used Twitter? Please give an example.
**EE:** Twitter is one component that we have not had a lot of success with. We cross-post our Facebook posts; however, we have found that a majority of our friends are not using Twitter.

**AD:** How do you measure ROI?
**EE:** We survey all prospects and clients to determine which marketing and promotion resources are providing value.

**AD:** What percentage of your income do you attribute to social networking and social media?
**EE:** 100% of my income is derived from social networking of some type. I don't consider the technology platform when describing social networking, since that part is new. To me, as mentioned earlier, social networking is building relationships with or without technology.

**AD:** How do you leverage your links?
**EE:** Today, all of our information is within our 1parkplace contact management system, and that has worked great to automate the process of follow-up, so I don't have to worry about it. However, we are always striving to leverage all of our existing data and contact resources. We feel that with the little amount of time we have dedicated, we have already seen results and look forward to achieving so much more in this area. We also want to learn from other Realtors about how to best leverage our links in ways that will significantly increase our business.

**AD:** How do you convert your friends, fans, and followers into buyers and sellers?
**EE:** This may sound a bit old-fashioned, but I always build personal relationships with my contacts first, before entering them into my Facebook or LinkedIn networks. I want to make sure that I know everybody first and establish an offline rapport before moving to online. Nearly every one of my Facebook friends is someone I got to know personally first.

**AD:** What is the most effective way you employ social media/social networking to differentiate yourself from other real estate agents?

**EE:** I think the key differentiation for us is that we are targeting real buyers and sellers, not prospecting people we never met. My online community is simply an extension of all the communication vehicles I have built my business on. I used to use personal mail messages; then came e-mail and now social networking. The key is consistency and providing information that has value, with the occasional personal touch. I hear many other agents out there claiming to have all these fans and followers, but 90% of those seem to be other agents or people they really don't know.

**AD:** Eric, as in every other interview conducted for this book, I realize we are only scratching the surface in uncovering the many depths of your commitment to real estate and your unquestioned greatness in what you do. Thankfully, due to the Internet and social networking, each reader of *Leveraging Your Links* can have far greater access to your business practices than this book covers. Thanks again for providing access into your career.

# An Information Archway

## Scott MacDonald
President, RE/MAX Gateway
The Results Realty Group
CDPE, CNHS, RCC, TRC
Top 5 in Real Estate Member
**Serving**: Northern Virginia
**Years in real estate**: 22

## Social Media Links:
www.TheResultsRealtyGroup.com
http://twitter.com/scottmacdonald
www.linkedin.com/in/scottamacdonald
www.youtube.com/scottmacdonald5
http://scottmacdonald.typepad.com/scottsupdate/

**Allan Dalton:** Scott, how long have you had the pleasure of being associated with RE/MAX Gateway?
**Scott MacDonald:** Allan, I started my company as part of RE/MAX just over nine years ago.

**AD:** Scott, you are considered one of the leaders in our industry because of your accomplishments and the excellence you display at all levels of brokerage, therefore, I am very interested in getting your definition of social networking?
**SM:** Allan, thanks for the compliment. To me, social networking represents a passive method of maintaining relationships with people in your database as well as, arguably, the most effective and efficient means to exponentially increase such numbers.

**AD:** Great answer, Scott. How about social media? What is your definition?
**SM:** The tools utilized in social networking.

**AD:** How would you define a real estate social marketing system?
**SM:** It would be a systematic and continuous approach to contacting those in your various networks for marketing purposes or to satisfy the needs within the market.

# An Information Archway

**AD:** I commend you on your very clear answer. Scott, definitions aside, why did you become involved with social networking and social media other than the fact that you and social media have the same initials?

**SM:** I thought you'd never notice! But seriously, we embraced social networking nearly five years ago. We recognized its potential in terms of representing a competitive advantage for our team. We concluded that being early adopters, while most agents and companies were not as yet engaged, would yield significant benefits to our team...and it has. Once arriving at the decision that we would assume the role of marketplace social media leaders, we began to educate our agents to the real estate-specific benefits of blogging, using YouTube and Facebook, etc,. to differentiate ourselves from our competition.

**AD:** Which social networks do you belong to?

**SM:** YouTube, TypePad, Facebook, LinkedIn, Twitter, Plaxo, ActiveRain, and Blogger.

**AD:** Why did you choose these particular social networks?

**SM:** These sites offer the most exposure, are the most recognizable to everyone, and they are more progressive and adult-oriented than MySpace and Tagged—they are also more USA-oriented.

**AD:** How many friends and followers do you have on each?

**SM:** I have 1,039 Facebook friends; 803 connections on LinkedIn; 782 connections on Plaxo; 340 followers on Twitter; and just a few hundred followers on YouTube and TypePad. My belief is that it is more important to have quality and not quantity in these categories. Another comment is that there are more people who are familiar with Facebook, LinkedIn, etc., and less aware of the impact of YouTube and blogging; therefore, we don't have as many followers in those categories.

**AD:** Is your interaction with your friends, followers, connections, and fans social, professional, or both?

**SM:** It is both personal and professional. My posts are 75 percent professional and 25 percent personal. It is important to show that you have a life outside of real estate and that you are a "real" person.

**AD:** Scott, what do you generally post about on your networks?

**SM:** I post my daily schedule, new listings, and articles of interest about our industry, my blog posts, when agents affiliate with the company, our company trainings, and press releases about our agents.

**AD:** What's an example of a post you might make?

**SM:** Allan, I might post videos of our agents, videos of our new listings, our training programs, invitations to our Real Estate Exchanges, blog posts about the market, and so much more. We have a director of social media who posts information throughout the day, as well.

**AD:** Do you include social media, i.e., content, in any of your real estate posts on your social networks?

**SM:** Yes, we do—we have to let our sphere know that we are active in the business, that we are getting results for our buyers and sellers, and that the company is growing, with new agents joining us regularly.

**AD:** What kind of content do you post?

**SM:** In keeping with some of what I have previously mentioned, we post information on our local market, interest rates, pricing strategies, information gathered from our mastermind groups, trainings, and Real Estate Exchanges. We are also going to start to do blogs on neighborhoods and schools as well.

**AD:** When did you launch your website?

**SM:** I had my first website in 1999, but I really got into it more about eight years ago.

**AD:** What kind of content can be found on your website?

**SM:** What can't be found is a better question! First and foremost, we provide a property search—the consumer demands it—our blog, an area to register to get listings sent to you automatically, Top 5 resources, "Join our Team," school and community information, and our "Find an Agent" area, just to name a few.

**AD:** Do you have a blog?
**SM:** Yes.

**AD:** When did you start blogging and may I offer a link to your blog in the book?

**SM:** By all means, Allan, and thank you. We started our blog about four or five years ago.

## An Information Archway

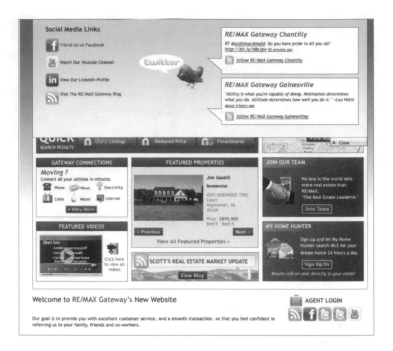

**AD:** It's very impressive, Scott, that you have been blogging that many years, but I shouldn't be surprised as RE/MAX Gateway and specifically "gateway" is perhaps as suggestive and symbolic of Internet relevance of any name that any real estate company possesses. I guess the opposite would be if there were a company named "RE/MAX Gatekeeper." Again, your company name is definitely in sync with the entire concept of providing online opportunities for consumers. That said, is your blog separate from your website?

**SM:** Yes, but it is linked to the website and is featured on our home page.

**AD:** What kind of content can be found on your blog?

**SM:** Market conditions, motivational content, updates on financing, how to choose an agent, short sales, foreclosures—all kinds of great information for agents and the public.

**AD:** Do you aggregate your followers and fans into demographic groups that you can individually target?

**SM:** No, we don't at this time.

**AD:** How do you draw traffic to your blog, i.e., do you have a link on your website, or do you tweet about your blog?

**SM:** Yes, I have links from Facebook and Twitter primarily, and we also have links in our e-mail signature and business cards that show all of our various sites.

**AD: How have you effectively used Twitter?**
**SM:** We have several posts and we retweet throughout the day, which keeps us out in front of people.

**AD: How do you measure ROI?**
**SM:** It is definitely hard to track, in my opinion, but we get feedback from clients that they read this or saw that on one of our sites. Agents also comment on how we are growing or that it was great that a certain person joined the company. It is definitely something people recognize—that we are "into" social media.

**AD: What percentage of your income do you attribute to social networking and social media?**
**SM:** Again, we don't specifically track it, but it has had a significant impact on the branding of my team as well as the company; we are recognized by what we do, how we do it and, in the end, it gets us results. Social networking is just another spoke in our marketing wheel that moves us down the road to success in real estate.

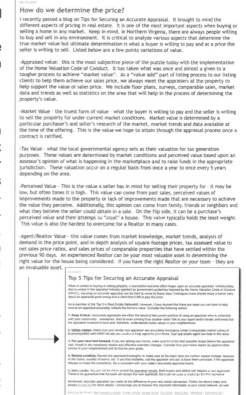

**AD: How do you leverage your links?**
**SM:** Our links are found on each of our sites, on our business cards, on our promotional materials, on our mailings, on our brochures, etc. We are constantly trying to get the word out about us and all that we do online.

**AD: How do you convert your friends, fans, and followers into buyers and sellers?**
**SM:** By showing our competence through our market knowledge and by post-

ing our successes—we sold a house; we found a property for another homeowner; we recruited an agent; and things along those lines. You have to show you are getting the results—not just talk about various things about real estate. People like to work with successful people.

**AD: How do you incorporate Top 5 content into your social media strategy?**
**SM:** Top 5 is a major provider of content and credibility. There is a link on our websites and in our e-mail signature; we post the Thursday Top 5 Social Networking System articles as blogs, and it is in our marketing materials that we hand to clients.

**AD: What is the most effective way you employ social media/social networking to differentiate yourself from other real estate agents?**
**SM:** We have a director of social media, who does training for our agents, and who consistently gets the word out about us and follows trends to ensure that we are ahead of the curve and not behind it.

**AD: Thank you Scott, for the overall leadership you provide within our industry and for being an industry pioneer in the social media space.**

# Being Digitally Discerning

## Normalina Martin
Real Estate Consultant
Prudential Florida Realty, Oviedo, Florida
ABR, e-PRO, SFR,
Top 5 in Real Estate Member
**Serving:** Central Florida including Orlando, Winter
Park and Oviedo
**Years in real estate:** 5

## Social Media Links:
www.OrlandoYourHome.com
http://normalinam.featuredblog.com
www.facebook.com/normalina.martin
www.trulia.com/profile/Normalina/

**Allan Dalton: How do you define social networking?**
**Normalina Martin:** A connection with one's sphere of influence, such as friends, family, neighbors, and past and present clients that I have created a bond with throughout my life.

**AD: How do you define social media?**
**NM:** I would define social media as a network created via social networking sites, to learn from one another, help each other out, and specifically to provide content that will help to sustain my social networks.

**AD: Why did you begin social networking?**
**NM:** My generation communicates better via social networking; I wanted that option available to people who need my services. I am responding to my niche market in the way they want to be responded to.

**AD: What social networks do you belong to?**
**NM:** Primarily, I am active on Facebook, LinkedIn, and Trulia. I also maintain an ActiveRain blog site that I need to work more on.

**AD: Why did you choose these social networks to belong to?**
**NM:** I joined Facebook because of its prominence and because it is the top so-

cial networking site—it is practically on every website and commercial. I joined LinkedIn as other Realtors in the industry asked me to connect with them there, so I responded to that. I have a blog site on Trulia so that people who want to get information on properties and Orlando-area information can connect with me. It is a great opportunity for me to respond to consumer questions. I have an ActiveRain site that I started at the suggestion and recommendation of several of my colleagues. One of the informal conditions of social networking is that you not only make recommendations to your friends and followers, but you should also be open to suggestions and recommendations of others.

---

**Normalina Martin**

Q Filters

**More Good News on the Home Front**

RISMEDIA, May 10, 2010—Things are continuing to look up in the real estate market. More and more indicators are turning positive. Still, there's at least one major threat to the housing recovery that should make us wary of irrational exuberance. Th...

57 minutes ago · Comment · Like · Share

**Normalina Martin**

**Budget-Friendly Backyard Makeovers**

By Barbara Pronin, RISMedia Columnist RISMEDIA, May 10, 2010—If a stay-at-home vacation is in your plans this summer, it's time to make the most of your backyard space. Th...

57 minutes ago · Comment · Like · Share

**Normalina Martin**

**Going Green May Help Cut Cost of Insurance Premiums**

RISMEDIA, May 10, 2010—Green energy, sustainable food, recycling, hybrid vehicles – environmental awareness is impacting the lives of Americans everyday. Many consumers are choosing to make both small and large changes to reduce their carbon footprint. If...

57 minutes ago · Comment · Like · Share

---

**AD: How many friends and followers do you have on Facebook?**
**NM:** As of May 4, I have 330 Facebook friends.

**AD: Do you have a process for deleting Facebook friends?**
**NM:** Yes, I am a God-fearing person, therefore, when I either notice or have a strong sense that anyone within my network or community is behaving in a way that is not consistent with my basic attitude regarding proper comportment or shows behavior that is the opposite of godliness, or someone that I do not want peering into my world, I may choose to delete them.

**AD: Normalina, I admire the fact that you have set standards or expectations regarding online communication. Is your interaction with your friends, followers, and fans social, professional, or both?**
**NM:** At first it was more social; then it became more professional. I did not want all personal business on my wall, so now I am putting out more profes-

sional information. I have cut down the personal comments but still maintain my personal persona. I want to portray that I am a real person but I am not going to put my personal business on Facebook. I was thinking about separating the two, but this is me and I do not need to be two different people.

**AD:** What do you generally post about on your networks?
**NM:** I have the RISMedia feed on my site, with different stories each day. REALTOR.com is also on my site. I post pictures of my daughter and me, and I share videos between friends. My messages also focus on my faith.

**AD:** Normalina, regarding real estate information, you've made it clear that you use real estate content, whether it be RISMedia for journalistic purposes, REALTOR.com for listings, your IDX feed for property content, and sites like Facebook and LinkedIn for professional connectivity and networking, but in terms of your overall personal connectivity, by way of social networking, there appears to be an underlying spiritual mission that you are seeking to accomplish. Is that a fair assessment?
**NM:** Yes, Allan, because beyond my religious beliefs and desire to connect with true friends, I also believe that by letting those who are connected with me know how deep my faith is, it also makes it totally unnecessary for me to ever have to try to convey that consumers or friends can trust me or that I possess integrity because issues like that become automatically addressed by my sharing my faith.

**AD:** Normalina, it seems as though just as there are certain people that you would rather not involve yourself with online because of their ethics, this also extends to some deep concerns you have regarding the lack of ethics of many in the business community. Is this what you are saying?
**NM:** Yes, absolutely.

**AD:** If that is the case, then you want to discern how social media/social networking can help you to more strategically focus your time and efforts so as to only work with those that you are most comfortable working with or serving. Is that your opinion?
**NM:** Yes, I like where you are going with that idea. I do not want to put out signs to attract just anyone.

**AD:** Normalina, it sounds to me that one way you might look to employ social networking is to more heavily insert yourself and participate within faith-based professional online networks. Have you done this or have you considered this?

**NM:** I would love to do that, Allan. In fact as soon as this interview is complete, I am going to Google faith-based professional social networks and other keywords that should help me arrive at a place where I can more effectively combine personal and professional connectivity.

**AD: Normalina, you are one of the few folks we have interviewed that is not on Twitter. Why did you decide not to include Twitter as a part of your social media constellation of sites?**
**NM:** First, because I don't want to undertake any social networking-assumed obligation if I am not truly going to keep up with it. Plus, the idea of asking people to follow me is also in opposition to my belief that none of us should think we are the center of the universe and that people should follow us. So that would be why Twitter does not have the same appeal to me as it seems to for so many other Realtors. It took me all of about five minutes to know that Twitter was not my cup of tea.

**AD: How do you drive traffic to your website?**
**NM:** It is on all of my promotional materials...print, and online.

**AD: When did you start your website?**
**NM:** 2005.

**AD: What kind of content can be found on your website?**
**NM:** Everything from an MLS search for free, Top 5 information—including information on short sales—videos, foreclosure lists, relocation information, information on the Orlando area, and a market snapshot.

**AD:** Do you have a blog?

**NM:** I have a blog on my website.

**AD:** Normalina, if instead of just settling for inviting consumers and friends to become friends, fans, followers, and users of your website online, have you considered joining several online faith-based professional social networks and then inviting those community participants to become members of "Normalina Martin's Real Estate Social Network" by posting a link to your website/blog? When they arrived, they would click on a link that was titled "Become a Member of Normalina's Real Estate Social Network...it's free." They would then learn what members receive, including all of the informational services you provide along with your expertise and how members—as opposed to just friends, fans, followers or visitors—could communicate with one another. Do you think this would help you create a greater and higher level of bonding than just aggregating friends, fans and followers and inviting people to your website?

**NM:** Allan, that is a brilliant idea, because I haven't seen any real estate agent really create a membership following. It is never that organized or formal. We are only now just doing the friends, fans, and followers thing. Buyers shop around...what incentive would the buyer have to stay with me as a member?

**AD:** Normalina, living in Orlando as you do, should immediately signal to you how much of the retail world strategically offers their prospective customers and clients membership benefits. For example, a tourist visiting Orlando, looking for a hotel, might be able to actually get a better room and rate from a hotel other than Marriott, but because they are a member of Marriott, and there is a Marriott Rewards program, they are now less likely to continuously shop around, even if another hotel would give them benefits beyond those of Marriott Rewards. This is because beyond the rewards, they feel more special checking in as a member than they do as simply a guest.

In terms of real estate, we are not offering rewards, and in many cases we cannot do so legally. Our rewards have to come before and after the transaction in order to create loyalty. Otherwise, if all we are doing is providing the *same* information and content to those we have classified as members, then the consumer recipient will not feel any loyalty to us because the information he or she received was expressed as a component of a real estate agent's prospecting for customers as opposed to responding to the implicit needs of members. The way in which all things are branded carry with them, profound consequences. When we inform people that they are consumers that means they have loyalty to nobody. When we inform them that they are merely friends, fans, and followers, that relationship is becoming trite, predictable, non-remarkable, and non-proprietary.

But by upgrading friends, fans, and followers to become members of your particular social network, it strongly suggests a distinctly different relationship carrying with it expectations. For those Realtors who feel up to meeting such expectations, especially informationally, membership now means privileges (with apologies to American Express ) not only to the consumer, but now for the real estate agent as well. Now, of course, Normalina, to address your point, a buyer's greater loyalty will be to a selfish opportunity more than to a particular relationship with a real estate agent, but hundreds of thousands of real estate agents have not as yet found a means of establishing loyalty for the millions of occasions when consumers have not as yet determined that there is a special deal out there for them. Normalina, forgive the industrial-length question, but let me summarize with an add-on question. Would you prefer to have 1,000 friends on Facebook, or 300 signed-in members of the Normalina Martin Real Estate Social Network?

**NM:** Now I get it. I definitely would prefer to have 300 signed-in members of my Normalina Martin Real Estate Social Network than to have thousands of people who are friends, fans, and followers.

**AD:** That's great because if consumers can become members of a social network for hikers, why can't they become members of a real estate social network and why not one that *you* have organized? One that has *your* name attached to it...one that is hosted on *your* website and blog and one that they have a private password to, where only they and other members can receive your most valuable content?

**NM:** How would this work with something like Top Producer? I have, for example, several thousand names in my database.

**AD:** Normalina, great question. When I was president of Move's real estate division, my job included responsibilities for Top Producer, although Errol Samuelson, at the time, managed that service 100 percent. That said, I will use Top Producer to make my point.

First, as a consumer, it gives me very little sense of loyalty to learn that I am one of the 5,000 names in your database. What does that mean? Does it mean being scrubbed, categorized, and contacted as I get to enjoy my incubation period? No thanks. I'd rather be given the opportunity to belong to your real estate social network where I am a member, and where I can go to your website to discover hundreds of real estate articles and topics that I choose than to have you presume to know what you should send me. In other words, ask yourself this: Do consumers want us to contact them as much as we want to contact them? I think you'll find the answer is no. What consumers have answered anthropologically and sociologically over the years is that they like to belong to groups and networks. I cannot belong to your database. The difference is that you use Top Producer or 1parkplace in order to invite consumers to come to your website where they can become members of your real estate social network so they can manage the relationship by their own navigational means as opposed to feeling as though they're in a perpetual state of being prospected to. That's the difference, Normalina. What are your thoughts?

**NM:** Allan, you are definitely right, that idea totally turns around the relationship structure that we have all been sold on for many, many years.

# In a New York Minute

## Pat Neville
Broker and Team Leader
Country Estates & Manors, Katonah, New York
CBR, CLHMS, PRS, RMN,
Top 5 in Real Estate Member
**Serving:** Westchester/Putnam Counties, New York
**Years in real estate:** 30

## Social Media Link:
www.patneville.com

**Allan Dalton:** Pat, how do you define social networking?
**Pat Neville:** Allan, to me, social networking means engaging in the more prominent social networking venues in order to more effectively and strategically reach, and hopefully expand, my sphere of influence.

**AD:** How do you define social media?
**PN:** Social media would seem to suggest that all of us, even we Realtors, have the opportunity to individually assume certain media functions because we can all be our own publisher due to the Web 2.0 evolution of the Internet. And this is right up my alley because if I weren't a totally dedicated real estate professional serving Westchester County, I probably would want to be either a real estate or lifestyle writer for Westchester County. I say this because a major part of my career involves constantly creating both content for and greater interest in all of the wonders of Westchester living. Now that I can do online what I have essentially been doing offline for 30 years, all the better. To me, that is what social media means.

**AD:** Pat, can you provide our readers with an example of how you extol the virtues of Westchester living virtually?
**PN:** Allan, I'd be happy to. I think it is important for people to understand why they would want to live in Westchester County. With the ability of my Westchester Living photo marketers, we have captured many of the illustrious images that best define our exquisitely beautiful and abundant region.

**AD:** Pat, in other words you are demonstrating not only to buyers why they should live in Westchester County, but also illustrating to prospective home sellers how you are constantly elevating the real and perceived value of Westchester County communities, which then elevates the desirability of *all* homes within the county?

**PN:** Allan, I don't know if I would ever say it as nicely as you just did, but that is exactly the reaction that home sellers—and, more specifically, all homeowners—seem to have. I cannot tell you how many times community residents have thanked me for what I do to promote their particular towns. It took me a while to get used to this because, in the early part of my career, residents would only thank me because I helped them buy or sell a property. Now, I have just as many, if not more, thanking me for how I am using social media and social networking venues on their behalf.

**AD:** Pat, what seems to be going on here is that while many other real estate agents are inviting community residents to follow them on Twitter, you are inviting the community—through the use of Twitter, Facebook, and LinkedIn—to follow their community almost as though it's a weekly serial and you are the well-known producer.

**PN:** Allan, that's an excellent way of putting it because, just as I mentioned our Westchester Living video and photo marketers, everything I do, I see as a professional production. I'm always trying to educate not only buyers but also residents of Westchester County and visitors about the many wonders of the area. It also amazes me how often I am approached by longtime residents of particular towns who excitedly tell me that they learned something new about their own community from me.

**AD: Pat, I am not fortunate enough to live in Westchester County, yet I have heard of your famous "365 Things to Do in Westchester County, NY" campaign. Please enlighten me further.**
**PN:** While I am the only one in my area, that I'm aware of, who is employing this campaign, I cannot take credit as being its originator. So, before I tell you about my particular version of this concept, I think it is important to point out that I would never have had access to this concept that benefits my beloved Westchester County if it were not for social media, and all it implies, because I first became aware of the concept earlier this year on the Facebook Fan Page, "Realtor Tips: Marketing Ideas Using New Media." Julie Ziemelis is responsible for the great content on this page and the idea was generated by the social media success story she posted, "365 Things To Do In Vancouver, Washington."

Now, regarding the campaign: Every day, all 365 of them, I post a relevant Westchester County gem or nugget of information, as well as an invitation to the community to participate.

**AD: Pat, I love what you are doing. It reminds me, as I mention in my book, of a program I created 20 years ago and named "Neighbors Know Best." I would invite neighbors to a marketed listing to provide me with narratives on what they liked about the neighborhood they were living in. Then I would publish them in a brochure to both market the property and to hand out at the open house. The entire neighborhood would rally behind this opportunity to speak on behalf of their property values.**
**PN:** That's brilliant. I am surprised that I haven't seen this since you did it 20 years ago.

**AD: Trust me, after this book comes out, I am sure you will see a number of "Neighbors Know Best" campaigns or more people, hopefully, employing ideas like your daily postings in "365 Things to Do in Westchester County, NY." But to switch topics, why did you begin social networking, Pat?**
**PN:** I got interested in social networking through RISMedia and the Top 5 in Real Estate Network®, and also by listening to you talk about the relationship

between content, social networking, and the community you serve. I also credit the many classes, courses, and individuals—like Stephen Fells from Agency-Logic.com—who really helped me understand some of the many specifics.

**AD: I am not surprised that Stephen was extremely contributory to your social media development as he is highly regarded in this area. What social networks do you belong to?**
**PN:** Facebook, LinkedIn, Twitter, YouTube, Flickr, and the Top 5 in Real Estate Network® community hosted by RealTown.

**AD: That's both great and unsurprising that you are attending the Ivy League of social networks. I am interested in knowing what each of these social networks provides to you, or, in other words, why you joined them.**
**PN:** I joined Facebook because it appears to be the most utilized forum for connecting through social networking. The reach is phenomenal, and how can I properly represent Westchester County and all of our great towns and properties if I don't introduce Westchester Living through the power of Facebook?

**AD: And how do you use LinkedIn?**
**PN:** I like LinkedIn more for professional networking and idea generation from other professionals within my industry. An example here is the Top 5 in Real Estate Network® on LinkedIn. When you think about it, Allan, what real estate professionals had to pay for in the past—in terms of purchasing books about buying, selling, marketing, and real estate practices in general—can now be found virtually *for free* online. Also, it is not as necessary to pay one person a lot of money to coach you on their ideas when you can receive thousands of ideas from hundreds of top producers through online communities and idea sharing.

**AD: Pat, I hope you are not telling me that I shouldn't charge for this book.**
**PN:** No, I didn't say that. I am thinking more about social media networks, and the return on investment where people have spent *time* on travel and to be educated; the investment now is about time.

**AD: Pat, you don't realize this, but the cost of the book is going to be $4,000 a copy.**
**PN:** From what I am gathering from your knowledge, it is undoubtedly worth it, Allan.

**AD: Getting back to reality, Pat, can we talk about how you employ YouTube?**
**PN:** The future of real estate seems to point to the power of video. YouTube,

which is the most familiar video-based venue, makes a great forum for the informative Top 5 videos and for videos personally created through our real estate channels. I am preparing to launch a major video campaign around Westchester Living topics. We are considering branding our video initiative "Come Home to Westchester" as we own the "Come Home to" URL, which we extend to communities within Westchester—for example, "Come Home to Pound Ridge.com," "Come Home to Bedford.com," "Come Home to South Salem.com," "Come Home to Mount Kisco.com," and others.

**AD: Pat, will you be using the music from "Won't You Come Home Bill Bailey" or will you be selecting something more contemporary?**
**PN:** It's funny you say that, Allan, because I am actually shopping for our music accompaniment, and, of course, I am shopping online.

**AD: Pat, has social media caused you to feel differently about your role as a real estate professional?**
**PN:** That is a great question, Allan, because the Internet and, now, social media have provided all real estate agents with an opportunity to use parts of our brains that we didn't use years ago—in the same way that the rest of the world has had to adapt to this new technology. Therefore, as a middle-aged person, I feel that technology and social media have totally rejuvenated my intellectual appetite and have created opportunities that did not exist in the past. I don't think there has been any development within the real estate industry over the past 30 years that has required my being as open-minded and responsive to change as has the social media movement. I never thought I would be exhilarated about having to learn something new at the same time that not only teenagers, but my five-year-old nieces and nephews, are...but I am. It's wonderful to continue learning in order to keep up with not only real estate, but with these youngsters as well, because it infuses me with greater energy—which an agent certainly needs, given the rigors of real estate.

**AD: What I am hearing you say, Pat, is that even though engaging in online social networking is not a *physical* activity, because so much *mental* energy is required, it actually stimulates and energizes everything you do in real estate.**
**PN:** Absolutely. Allan, I have never felt more vibrant and energized in my entire career because I have never before had a tool that allowed me to reach and help as many people as I can now. And, social networking also keeps the cobwebs from forming on my brain.

**AD: Pat, what you just said reminds me of a statement by a noted psychiatrist that I read years ago in *The New Yorker* magazine. This doctor said that while**

most people believe that the opposite of depression is happiness, in reality, the opposite of depression is *vitality*. He explained that because happiness is elusive, vitality, therefore, becomes something that represents happiness. So, it follows that we must be mentally engaged in order to become vital and, thus, happy. You have already discovered that engaging in social networking activities stimulates your mind and energizes you. However, as I show elsewhere in this book, social networking, if not properly managed, can also create stress.

**PN:** Allan, how can we condense this insight of yours into a tweet with a link to my blog?

**AD:** I'd be happy to create a tweet for you to use once you've posted my thoughts on your blog. How about, "Realtors' tweets can stave off depression: www.WestchesterNYHomeBlog.com?"

**PN:** That's perfect, Allan. Thank you.

**AD:** Pat, please share how your blog has impacted your real estate business.

**PN:** My blog connects the Westchester community with the daily news features and content of the Top 5 in Real Estate Network®. I have created a mental reminder for what my blog must always represent and it has to do with both my name and my blog's purpose.

**AD:** What do you mean, Pat?

**PN:** In today's world, the letters PC stand for Personal Computer or Politically Correct. I concluded that I wanted Pat's Computer Content to be Politically Correct so I extended PC to PCCC, meaning that Pat's Content within the blog must be relevant to the community, to consumers, and to my clients. Consequently, everything I do must serve the needs of at least one of those constituents, and many times all three.

**AD:** What a great way to monitor the essence or the spirit of intent of your blog.

**PN:** I'm glad you like it, Allan.

**AD:** Pat, how do you demonstrate, during a marketing presentation, that your social media initiatives benefit the home sellers and also better differentiate you from your very capable Westchester County competitors?

**PN:** It's a great question, Allan. I use a visual representation that is easily presented to the consumer just by opening my computer and showcasing the distinctive and customized online marketing plan that I would create, specific to their individual property. My marketing plan would rely heavily on using social networking sites to link to my website, which would present their property to the world. After all, Westchester County is a marketplace that is important to the world. I would further highlight the value of my social media commitment to my clients by engaging them through a series of questions that makes it inevitable that they will immediately seize upon the importance of online marketing.

**AD:** Pat, what kind of questions do you ask?

**PN:** For example, I might say, "Folks, if you were looking to purchase a property in Orange County, California or in London, how would you begin your home search?" Over the past few years, Allan, any time I ask home sellers this question, without fail, the answer is always, "By going online." This is a vital way to begin a marketing dialogue because it immediately causes them to focus on the importance and value of my specialty, which is online marketing. I would then ask this question, "How much do you think the value of your property is also connected to the perceived value of both your town and our county?" Here again, our sophisticated Westchester County home sellers immediately get the connection. In this way, I have now set the stage for explaining that I use the Internet and social media to gain greater exposure and appreciation for the property that I represent and also to constantly remind buyers of the value of the town and the community that the home is in. Home sellers love this explanation of how and why I embrace social media.

**AD:** What I love about your preliminary positioning is that it immediately suggests that you are more interested in employing social media to gain friends, fans, and followers of Westchester County—and each of its towns and every property you represent—than you are in accumulating friends, fans, and followers of your own.

**PN:** Allan, what you have just said is brilliant. *That is exactly what I am going to say to home sellers: I use social media more to create fans, friends, and followers of your property than for me.*

**AD:** Well think about it, Pat, if you were the home seller and I were your real estate agent, would you want either me or your property to be followed?

**PN:** My property, of course.

**AD:** Pat, about how much time do you spend monitoring your social networking venues?

**PN:** I monitor my *time* because it becomes all too consuming as part of my business plan. But I would say I devote approximately an hour a day, and sometimes more.

**AD: Pat, how do you measure ROI in regard to your social networking activities?**
**PN:** The investment is more in time than in dollars, and that has value, so I think it is not easily quantified. I recognize that I may never be able to say that I captured a lead specifically because I do social media, but I do know that I am communicating with so many more people than ever before.

**AD: In other words, Pat, what you are saying is that if someone comes out and surprises us and says that real estate is no longer a people business or that real estate is no longer a numbers game, then you will intuitively sense that if you increase the number of people you communicate with in your community, then you will increase your ROI.**
**PN:** Well said.

**AD: But clearly you, like every top-producing Realtor, need to be vigilant about your time management because you are always looking to not just market in general but to niche market. Therefore, you need to have some ability to assess how valuable your time is regarding your social media activities. So let me ask you for a quantitative answer by phrasing the question in this way: Pat, if you had to guess or estimate how much additional income, percentage-wise, you are making because of your personal social media transformation, what might that be?**
**PN:** First of all, if I were not doing this, I might as well retire my license. But, if I have to give an estimate, it would be at minimum 10 percent, but I expect a lot more in the future. It is quantifiable as I now know many more people in the community than ever before.

**AD: Last question, Pat. You mentioned your nieces and nephews earlier in this interview. Would you like to name them?**
**PN:** The computer geniuses in the younger generation of my family include, but are not limited to, Aurora, Brian, Caitlin, Ian, Kellyann, Kevin, Kylie, and Sean. There are more, but you told me we are out of time.

**AD: Well that means that I can now acknowledge my younger generation of computer wizards—my nieces and nephews—also in alphabetical order: Alex, Billy, Ciaron, Dalton, Danny, Kerrie, Keeley, and Megan. Now I know that I will have at least eight fans of *Leveraging Your Links* to offset the inevitable critics.**

# Becoming a Community Advocate

## Janet Taylor Reilly
Brokerage Manager
Sotheby's International Realty, Carmel, CA
CDPE, CRP
Top 5 in Real Estate Member
**Serving:** Monterey County, CA
**Years in real estate:** 30

## Social Media Links:
www.TeamReilly.com
http://help4montereyhomeowners.com
http://twitter.com/janetreilly1

**Allan Dalton:** Janet, how would you describe social networking?
**Janet Reilly:** Well, when I began my career, I would probably have defined it as a pleasant encounter with a glass of wine. Today, for me, it encompasses contacts that are face-to-face, by e-mail, or online.

**AD:** How do you define social media?
**JR:** I like Wikipedia's broad definition: media designed to be disseminated through social interaction. I think this encompasses a lot of the sites we think of as social media sites. A good example would be YouTube where I may see a video that I think is informative, cool, or funny and then share it with friends by e-mailing them the link or posting the link on another social media site, such as Facebook.

**AD:** How do you define a real estate social marketing system?
**JR:** I would call it any online venue that allows me to promote my services or brand through social networking. The first example coming to mind for me would be a Facebook fan page.

**AD:** Why did you begin social networking?
**JR:** I began by discovering Classmates. Since I had not been in touch with anyone from high school for years, I thought it would be an interesting way to find out where my former classmates were. Shortly after, someone invited me to connect with them on Plaxo. LinkedIn was next and it grew from there. It was all about being in touch with people.

**AD: What social networks do you belong to?**
**JR:** Classmates, Plaxo, LinkedIn, Facebook, Twitter. I have to say I belong to Twitter but am not active on it. There is only so much time and I find a lot of what comes out of Twitter to be pretty insipid. Industry-specific networks would be ActiveRain and CDPE. I also visit YouTube and a lot of industry-specific sites for information that then leads me to contact people.

**AD: Why did you choose these networks to belong to?**
**JR:** I was either invited to connect through them or I found them meaningful sources of information.

**AD: How many friends and followers do you have on each?**
**JR:** Classmates: there are 195 members from my graduating class. Plaxo, 2,190; LinkedIn, 616; Facebook, 322.

**AD: What do you generally post about on your networks?**
**JR:** Personal updates. I don't do a lot of posting. I tend more to read posts and comment. What is going on in the lives of other people is interesting to me. An interesting post would probably generate an e-mail or call from me rather than a comment on the website. Most of the posts I have done, if they weren't of a personal nature, have been about the foreclosure crisis as I have been very involved in helping homeowners avoid foreclosure.

**AD: Do you include social media, i.e., content, in any of your real estate posts on your social networks?**
**JR:** Yes—links to videos of interest or a site with an interesting blog post or information.

**AD: When did you start your website?**
**JR:** In 2001, when I began The Reilly Coaching Group. That site is no longer active. Now I have three websites. Two are related to homeowners avoiding foreclosure (www.help4montereyhomeowners.com). One is related to real estate sales:

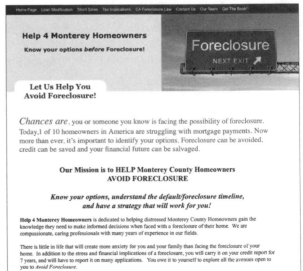

www.teamreilly.com. Soon the Team Reilly site will change and my team will take it over as I have moved from sales back into management and gave them the site as a gift. I will have a new website related to my position as the brokerage manager for Sotheby's International Realty within three months.

**AD: What kind of content can be found on your website?**
**JR:** Information on my listings, IDX search, short sale and foreclosure information, and a very comprehensive section on "Our Communities," which I wrote. I live in the most amazing place in the world. It was a pleasure to write about it.

**AD: How do you draw traffic to your website, i.e., do you mention your website on Twitter, etc.?**
**JR:** My listings draw traffic to the Team Reilly site. If you Google "avoid foreclosure in Monterey," I am number two and five on the organic search.

**AD: How have you effectively used Twitter?**
**JR:** I don't. I leave that to Demi and Ashton.

**AD: How do you measure ROI?**
**JR:** I can look at the number of deals I closed last year based on referrals through networks and sites. The CDPE network has been a great source of referrals and the best training out there on short sales.

**AD: How do you convert your friends, fans, and followers into buyers and sellers?**
**JR:** Ninety-five percent of my business in the last 18 months was by referral.

**AD: How do you incorporate Top 5 content into your social media strategy?**
**JR:** By using the outstanding content throughout my social media efforts.

**AD: Janet, how has social media changed, if it has at all, the way in which you view the practice of real estate brokerage from an agent's perspective?**
**JR:** I used to be in the relocation business, which is real estate done on a rari-

fied basis. You were not living transaction-to-transaction; you were in it for the long-term relationship...who you knew and how you networked. I belonged to the relocation networks. I look at it from that standpoint, from having been involved in that industry for so many years. For me, social networking/media provides the same opportunities that the relocation industry provided.

**AD: Janet, my sense is, knowing and observing your exemplary career all these years, when I think of you engaged in social networking, involved in relocation on an international level, I picture you as a very accomplished executive, even though you were extremely popular and well-known. Does that mean that you intuitively approach today's social networking opportunities as more professional opportunities, as opposed to others in the business?**
**JR:** I have been so busy, with so many opportunities; I have yet to take full advantage of all of the possibilities. It is rare for me to go on Facebook and post what I am doing or that I just had a latte at Starbucks. I would rather respond to what people are doing or wait until I really have something to say. It bothers me that people put their listings on their Facebook personal page as opposed to their fan pages.

**AD: That is a great perspective. What I am hearing you say, is that real estate professionals think they have star power like Ashton Kutcher and think that what they have to say is important. That leads me to ask, how do you use social networking sites?**
**JR:** I have used them to connect with people—so many people have friended me. LinkedIn is more effective for business networking; Plaxo is good for reminders, like birthdays. When it comes to online social networking, I am connecting with people I haven't connected with in a long time. For me, it gives me the ability to reach out on the phone and call them for something that I need. We are not using it effectively enough, however. It is more social and not business-oriented enough.

**AD: The word "social" can be a weakness; do you get distracted with the social aspect?**
**JR:** Facebook is powerful as it draws a big audience. Agents are led to believe that if they put themselves out there on social media sites, that people will flock to open houses. Those networks that are extremely specific to the business, like the Certified Distressed Property Expert (CDPE) network, work well for their online events. Everyone has one thing in common. They want to learn how to build their business from short sales; fellow members e-mail for help and it has been a great source of connections for me.

**AD:** Janet, that is more an industry network, rather than a consumer network, generating more agent traffic.

**JR:** I get referrals from the network. I got two this year. I helped them with a foreclosure.

**AD:** That is a great example of how the real estate industry continues to network professionally as is the case with people who are members of CRS, Star Power, etc. I think a lot of credit must be extended to Alex Charfen for creating the CDPE (Certified Distressed Property Expert) network, specifically for being essentially the only person who first conceived of and then created an industry-wide response to the momentous challenge millions of consumers are encountering regarding the financial circumstances surrounding the home they own.

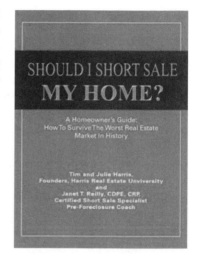

**JR:** Allan, speaking of responding to the short sale crisis, kudos to you and Top 5 for your writing *The 4 R's of Short Sales*. It's a one-of-a-kind educational piece. I take it in to seller appointments. It explains short sales in a way that a consumer understands and it is succinct. I also bring in my book, *Should I Short Sale My Home?* But they would rather read your brochure as it is much more succinct.

**AD:** One of the many reasons I am interested in your take and your experiential knowledge on social networking and social media is that I am wondering how a very distinctive marketplace like the Monterey Peninsula and Carmel, and the folks who live there in particular, respond to the practice of real estate agents seeking to engage them via this online methodology.

**JR:** What I hear you saying Allan is, how does social networking in an older, wealthy, and sophisticated demographic, like Carmel, work? Our agents are more likely to do more business due to LinkedIn than Facebook. Allan, the reason why I am also stressing a social network that is essentially based more on industry sharing and connections is because this opportunity is indispensable in building one's business. This is similar to my experience in the relocation business, which was all about best practices, business building, networking, and sharing. This is probably why I have a strong preference for LinkedIn; therefore, I could be wrong about which agents prefer LinkedIn over Facebook because of my professional bias. What you see on ActiveRain and not on Facebook, is an environment where you can work through a problem, get great ideas and find solutions. It used to take me weeks to get an answer over the phone. The Top 5 community on RealTown is another great example of how I can get an answer from my industry peers quickly.

**AD: Janet, tell us more about the book you mentioned earlier.**
**JR:** Thanks for asking, Allan. My book, *Should I Short Sale My Home?*, presented itself through Harris Real Estate University. I found them online looking for more short sale training. They provided me with the guts of the book and I was able to add things specific to my market. It was all about addressing consumer questions on whether short sales were the right option. It gave me a way to differentiate myself. The title, *Should I Short Sale My Home?*, was a great idea by Tim and Julie Harris the founders of Harris Real Estate University.

**AD: Janet, I have so much respect for your initiative regarding your overall response to the marketplace need of short sale information and guidance, and it makes me wonder, since there are well over one million real estate professionals in the U.S. alone, how many have also published a book for the benefit of consumers on this monumentally important subject?**
**JR:** I wouldn't know.

**AD: Janet, what do you think is the single greatest opportunity that social media provides real estate agents with that they are not capitalizing on?**
**JR:** A small percentage of agents are actually taking advantage of social networking. We are in the infancy of this. I honestly think the best use of this new medium is to network with other agents who can refer business to you.

**AD: So, what you're saying, Janet, is that the order of magnitude surrounding Internet searches for properties through Google and major company websites essentially draws the most consumer traffic regarding the buying and selling of real estate; therefore, you believe that the best use of social networking by real estate agents is for professional networking, best practices, and sharing of ideas and referrals.**
**JR:** Yes, Allan. What used to take so long—reaching people by phone or e-mail— can now all be efficiently managed online.

**AD: Janet, you manage three very successful Monterey County Real Estate offices. How much of a challenge is it for you to help your associates understand the proper balance between using Web 2.0 on behalf of their clients and their properties, and using it to advance their own educational interests? Based on our Census results, this message is still not clear to many real estate profes-**

sionals. Are you having success delivering this message to your associates?

**JR:** I don't think most of the associates in my office who are in the luxury market are excessively consumed by social networking because they are too busy physically out in the marketplace making things happen. Allan, you've got to remember that not only are Carmel and Monterey the best places to live in the world, but we also have the best real estate agents in the world and the most sophisticated ones. As a result, they instinctively gravitate to those elements of social media that are the most purposeful. Many of our top agents believe that, even though it may not sound technologically advanced, playing a round of golf with some of the most influential people imaginable will lead to more business, especially when it comes to high-end real estate, than mastering pithy commentary on Twitter.

**AD:** Now I know why I wasn't invited to play golf. I guess you have to be a real high net-worth individual, which leaves me out because my accountant told me this year, "Allan, you do not need any write-offs...you need some write-ons."

**JR:** If I have to choose between being online or being out with people, that is an easy choice.

**AD:** Janet, you have agreed to allow me to feature you as one of our social media mentors in my book, which leads me to ask you, of all the people that have influenced your career, who would you consider the most meaningful mentor?

**JR:** Bill Kiley who helped build and lead Hunneman and then Coldwell Banker Hunneman to become one of the 10 largest and most successful real estate companies in North America. What I learned from Bill was that one of the most uncommon characteristics of our industry is the need for individuals to be completely transparent, if not brutally honest, about what will or will not work in the business without fearing the consequences. Bill always made it clear what his true thoughts were, which was to the benefit of every person in the entire organization, because his honesty equated to complete company clarity.

**AD:** Janet, I totally agree with your characterization of Bill Kiley. I, too, consider him an industry giant and it's nice to see how much you continue to respect him. I feel the same way toward Joe Murphy who was my mentor for more than 20 years. Janet, would you give our readers the sense of how you integrate the importance of the Monterey lifestyle into your website and overall social media strategy?

**JR:** Great question. When I built the website, I was moving from the East Coast to be an agent. I wanted to provide relocation resources to buyers—to give a flavor of the area, which was so unique. So there is a section of the site about our communities that I wrote every word of, based on my research. I did it because I wanted people coming from out of the area to obtain information that you do not typically learn from a real estate website, such as nuanced photography and my carefully measured personal impressions of the areas.

**AD:** Janet, it seems that although you had moved from Bean Town to Carmel, by displaying Monterey so magnificently and visually on your website, it enabled you to become considered even more a part of the local landscape and, as a Realtor, more integral to the overall Monterey Peninsula experience than other agents who enjoyed longer-standing relationships with the area. Is that a fair analysis?

**JR:** Yes. Candidly, when someone is considering a move to another area, the agent is never part of the consideration, at least initially. The reality is, the lifestyle destination and all that it represents is what captivates consumers. Therefore, the way the Internet and social media helps me the most is that they provide me with the canvas on which I can paint the pictures of the community, with me being the artist...as opposed to my painting self-portraits.

**AD:** Janet, I am sure our readers are getting the picture that the only way that any of us have access to consumers is through their concerns. Everything you do regarding social media, from short sale publications to breathtaking photography, is in alignment with that principal. It's great to hear such clarity regarding your strategic use of social media. Since you have lived and been a real estate professional on both coasts, I cannot resist asking, are there contrasts you can make that might be of interest to our readers?

**JR:** What I have learned, Allan, from a real estate perspective, is that there are poor, good and great real estate agents and companies on both coasts and that if you treat people with respect, you will receive respect in return. There are some differences, however, that I find interesting. Real estate agents on the East Coast tend to be more direct, even blunt, while real estate agents in California tend to show a gentler disposition. I have greatly enjoyed being able to develop professional friendships from both experiences and consider myself to be very fortunate. The one thing, however, that does take getting used to in California brokerage is the incredible amount of forms and overall paperwork that is required to consummate a real estate transaction.

# Connecting with Connecticut Communities

## Julie Vanderblue

President, The Higgins Group, Fairfield, CT
CEO, The Vanderblue Team
2010 President of the Southern Fairfield County,
CT Chapter of the Women's Council of Realtors
Member of the Top 5 in Real Estate Network®
**Serving:** Fairfield County, Connecticut
**Years in real estate:** about 15 years
**www.VanderblueTeam.com**

## Social Media Links:

www.linkedin.com/pub/julie-vanderblue/11/26a/93
www.realtown.com/members/vanderblueteam/
www.trulia.com/profile/id/294737
http://activerain.com/jvander1

**Allan Dalton:** Julie, how long have you had the pleasure of being associated with The Higgins Group?
**Julie Vanderblue:** I have proudly been associated with Rick Higgins and The Higgins Real Estate organization for approximately six years and I have been in real estate brokerage for roughly 15 years.

**AD:** How do you define social networking?
**JV:** It is interesting because when you consider the two words, "social" and "networking," the words themselves would suggest networking for social purposes, yet I view and, therefore, define social networking as professional networking through the effective usage of online technology and platforms in order to create relationships with people via a myriad of resources available through the Internet, as well as over the phone, and face-to-face.

**AD:** How do you define social media?
**JV:** Examining the two words, "social" and "media," strongly suggests that it is media either generated by society at large or that is social in nature. But for my purposes, social media means becoming a personal distributor of media content digitally delivered. And, in terms of social media vehicles, I think of blogs, articles, and video.

## Connecting with Connecticut Communities

**AD:** How would you define a real estate social marketing system?
**JV:** To me, this means the integration of marketing solutions throughout social networking platforms.

**AD:** Why did you begin social networking?
**JV:** As a team leader, social networking necessitated my having to not only fully examine the popularity of how the new technology could better serve my existing and future clients, but also how I could be the catalyst that caused each of my valued team members to explore how the latest technology could lead to greater efficiency in their respective careers.

**AD:** Which social networks do you belong to?
**JV:** Facebook, Twitter, LinkedIn, ActiveRain, W.C.R., RealTown, and Flickr.

**AD:** Why did you select these social networks?
**JV:** I selected Facebook not only because it is essentially devoted to servicing an adult demographic but, also, because it enjoys such enormous brand equity within the demographic we want to serve. I joined Twitter because the rapid-fire, yet concise messaging format works perfectly for Realtors on the run with our handheld devices. Plus, even a micro-blogging site like Twitter offers me an opportunity to provide links to my website and blog. LinkedIn attracted me for three reasons: one, to cultivate career-seeking professionals for my team; two, because those seeking careers are also going through a real estate-relocation process; and three, for overall professional networking purposes. Of course, the more relevant you can make your LinkedIn profile by the proper use of key-words, the more effective your online networking becomes. I joined ActiveRain for SEO benefits because it enjoys enormous online visibility and thus connectivity and linkability.

**AD:** How many friends and followers do you have on each?
**JV:** Combined, in the thousands, and constantly growing.

**AD:** Is your interaction with your friends, fans, followers, and connections social, professional, or both?
**JV:** It's social until there is a professional need and then it's decidedly professional.

**AD:** What do you generally post on your networks?
**JV:** Links to Top 5 materials, links to videos of properties, links to various web-sites, and topical information. I tend to add interesting information to other people's posts more than I start my own, i.e., join a conversation and add tidbits of value. I see myself more as a counterpuncher—where I wait for the right op-

portunity to be additive—than as the puncher because, too often, when you are the puncher, the counterpunchers then have the greater opportunity to insert themselves on your own subject more comprehensively than you appear.

**AD:** **What's an example of a post you might make?**
**JV:** "Please join us at the Garden Expo this weekend to benefit the Mill River Project! Learn how to increase the value of your home through curb appeal, home energy audits, and going green! See link for invite!" Other examples are: "Congrats to Kim Vartuli from The Vanderblue Team for closing the highest sale price in Easton in two years! The market is back!" or "Introducing the newest Vanderblue Team office...We believe in Black Rock! Join us this weekend for your Grand Opening celebration!"

**AD:** **What kind of content do you post?**
**JV:** I often post Top 5 materials, such as the weekly articles provided, the Top 5 brochures, such as *The Four R's of Short Sales* and *What Every Home Seller Should Demand*, as well as articles from the Top 5 library, etc.

**AD:** **When did you launch your website?**
**JV:** About eight years ago.

**AD:** **What kind of content can be found on your website?**
**JV:** Top 5 articles and all Top 5 materials; IDX listings search; town information; statistics; team info, etc. Essentially, Allan, my content emphasis is to constantly be doing marketplace reconnaissance, which means that I always need to be aware—both for myself, my team and, in fact, the overall Higgins Group—what all other companies are providing by way of content. I also have to assess the most topical real estate issues that both sellers and buyers are being confronted with and are perplexed by, and then strategically insert relevant content by way of links throughout my social networking platforms. This is why I immediately seized upon the content you wrote, Allan, for expired-listing home sellers and for all parties involved in a short sale opportunity. The fact that my team members and I, like all other agents in our marketplace, already have a complete list of marketplace inventory through IDX, makes it critical that we differentiate

ourselves informationally and then promote—if you will forgive me—the living daylights out of the fact that we have all the answers. In a sense, I want the Vanderblue Team to be synonymous in our marketplace with concepts like "Ask Jeeves." But in this case, it's "Ask Vanderblue."

**AD: Do you have a blog?**
**JV:** Yes, I do, but I need to become more attentive to its potential. My emphasis has been more about being proactive through e-mailing content versus providing links to my blog because, quite frankly, I have been extremely busy putting together transactions for my clients and haven't yet had the time to blog about them. I realize, though, that these activities are not mutually exclusive and I plan on making my blog more informationally robust. But, I must stress that the real estate needs of my clients and the career development needs of my valued team members come before any other consideration.

**AD: What kind of content can be found on your blog?**
**JV:** My greatest emphasis on my blog is to respond directly to consumer inquiries versus providing stimulating, content-laden links that create traffic to my blog. Simply put, the content of my blog represents the answers to the questions consumers raise that come to either my website or blog.

**AD: Do you aggregate your followers and fans into demographic groups that you can individually target?**
**JV:** The answer is a resounding yes and here is why: The way in which I established the Vanderblue Team was pretty

much akin to how a medical practitioner establishes, let's say, a large practice, meaning that I have a team of specialists in a variety of areas, be it short sales, waterfront properties, 203ks, estates, equestrian properties, etc. Consequently, this has led me and our team of real estate specialists to reach out to a wide range of demographic interests, such as first-time buyers. The way in which we then coalesce these various and distinct niche markets is by employing social networking links to the ongoing public-based seminars and event marketing that we do. Otherwise, your expertise is very broad, but also very shallow. And, given the competitive landscape that online technology has created, this renders you ineffective.

**AD: How do you draw traffic to your website, i.e., do you mention your website on Twitter, etc.?**
**JV:** I link to the site from posts on social networking sites.

**AD: How have you effectively used Twitter?**
**JV:** I wish I had a remarkably original answer but essentially I follow others, ask to be followed, and judiciously, when it is appropriate, offer real estate-connected information and links to my website.

**AD: How do you measure ROI regarding your social media efforts?**
**JV:** If there was a section on one's tax return where you had to answer what percentage of your income is due to your social media endeavors, at this point, I confess I would need to request an extension. In fact, if there is anybody out there who has a magnificent spreadsheet that can quantify and total everything that goes into this analysis, from brand-building value to cost-per-click to converted inquiries to SEO-related page rankings, etc., and that collapses into a meaningful number, please send it to me and our team will be in your debt.

**AD: Julie, I hope you realize the IRS does expect you to know exactly how you expense the time you devote to Twitter as well as each and every one of your social media endeavors. I am amazed, since you're a person we've selected to participate in this book, that you don't have your exact number like the rest of us. What percentage of your income do you attribute to social networking and social media?**

Julie Vanderblue is one of the Fairfield Realtors to earn the new Top 5 Realtor designation, a title that recognizes the best agents in North America and Canada. (Photo by Ralph Petitti)

**JV:** All I can do is offer an estimate, but it's more qualitative that quantitative. I estimate I would be heading towards real estate extinction if I weren't significantly engaged in this digital expression of my real estate professionalism.

**AD: What is the most effective way you employ social media and social networking so as to differentiate yourself from other real estate agents?**
**JV:** By the content of our content, if you will forgive me. Allan, I once heard you say that the only way you have access to people is through their

concerns; therefore, the content I disseminate and display through all of my online channels differentiates me because it differentiates the consumer and the communities they reside in.

Specifically, while many real estate agents, teams, and companies continue to self-proclaim that they're all number one, and defy mathematical law and the process, our team's focus is on shifting the accolades and attention to the properties we represent and, therefore, the communities and towns in which they reside.

The Vanderblue Team strategically employs social media and cross-county marketing to robustly promote and leverage all of Fairfield County's distinctive towns and enclaves.

Our cross-county marketing methods are essential because, while some of the towns we market, like Greenwich, Darien, Westport, Fairfield, New Canaan, etc., are very coveted and recognizable to corporate transferees, Fairfield County is also blessed with a myriad of other compelling communities.

Virtually every day, we are able to help buyers, through social media and our overall marketing, to discover the distinctive richness of towns that were not even on their wish list. What makes Fairfield County number one is that all of our communities, in one way or another, are number one.

Social media is a great medium that helps consumers to better connect with our Connecticut communities. The word "connect," after all, is the first part of the word, "Connecticut."

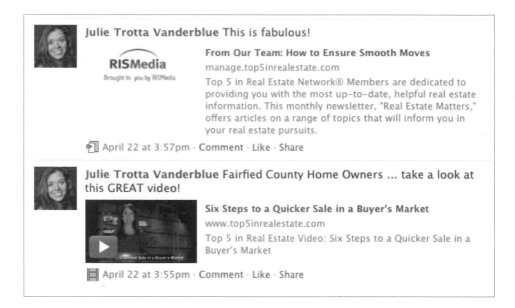

Julie Trotta Vanderblue This is fabulous!

**RISMedia**
Brought to you by RISMedia

**From Our Team: How to Ensure Smooth Moves**
manage.top5inrealestate.com

Top 5 in Real Estate Network® Members are dedicated to providing you with the most up-to-date, helpful real estate information. This monthly newsletter, "Real Estate Matters," offers articles on a range of topics that will inform you in your real estate pursuits.

April 22 at 3:57pm · Comment · Like · Share

Julie Trotta Vanderblue Fairfied County Home Owners ... take a look at this GREAT video!

**Six Steps to a Quicker Sale in a Buyer's Market**
www.top5inrealestate.com

Top 5 in Real Estate Video: Six Steps to a Quicker Sale in a Buyer's Market

April 22 at 3:55pm · Comment · Like · Share

# Creating Targeted Traffic

## Rosemary West
Broker and Relocation Specialist
RE/MAX Realty, Joliet, IL
ABR, CDPE, CLHMS, CRP, CRS
TOP 5 in Real Estate Member
**Serving:** Naperville, Plainfield, and Joliet, Illinois
**Years in real estate:** Over 30 years

## Social Media Links:
www.RosemaryWestTeam.com
www.facebook.com/rosemary.west
http://twitter.com/rosewestremax
www.linkedin.com/pub/rosemary-west-cdpe/6/904/724
http://activerain.com/rosemarywest
www.trulia.com/profile/RosemaryWestTeam/
www.youtube.com/user/rosemarywest1

**Allan Dalton:** How long have you had the pleasure of working for RE/MAX?
**Rosemary West:** Over 30 years.

**AD:** Rosemary, I respect how you have been with one company for your whole career. It speaks volumes about you and your company. I am going to ask you a question I wouldn't have asked you 30 years ago, although I am sure you would have come up with an answer to it, master communicator that you are. The question is, how do you define social networking?
**RW:** Allan, please don't remind me how long you've known me; but to answer your question, social networking, to me, is basically a channel of communication that enables individuals and, in my case, real estate professionals to actively engage in real-time communication with their friends, family, and, of course, the general public. For my business, I would define it further as an excellent and effective tool to connect to consumers and clients.

**AD:** How do you define social media?
**RW:** I must admit that until I heard you make a distinction between the two recently, I was always guilty of considering or mentioning social network-

ing and social media as being one in the same. Now that you've caused me to think about it, social media would mean using social networking sites for media or informational purposes.

**AD: How would you define what a real estate social marketing system might be?**
**RW:** Hey, I thought social networking and social media covered everything! But to answer your question, real estate social marketing must mean using the same technology more for marketing purposes and not just for media and networking purposes. Allan, is that where you are taking us?

**AD: What led you to become an early adopter of social networking?**
**RW:** Because I read some time ago that social networking is the number one online activity for consumers. As an example, the average consumer spends 7.5 hours on Facebook per month, in engagement and sharing.

**AD: Are you sure it is not 7.4 hours, Rosemary? Which social networks do you belong to?**
**RW:** Ha, ha...I will go back and check, but the networks I belong to, unsurprisingly, are Facebook, Facebook fan pages, LinkedIn, Plaxo, ActiveRain, YouTube, and Twitter.

**AD: Why did you choose these social networks to belong to?**
**RW:** Based on their popularity with consumers and since they are all free, why not?

**AD: How many friends and followers do you have on each?**
**RW:** Find out for yourself and become a fan!

**AD: Oh, you don't want me as a friend or follower, just a fan. Hold on a minute, I just did...I am now a Rosemary West fan and if you ever become more interesting, I might even follow you, too. Seriously though, Rosemary, is your interaction with your friends, followers, and fans more social, or professional in nature?**
**RW:** Both, and I wouldn't know the exact percentage, I hope that doesn't disqualify me from being in the book. Allan, you know how much social networking my husband, Roger, and I do that relates to our business. For years, we would host major functions on our boat that we had docked on Lake Michigan, as well as scores of other civic, social, and networking op-

portunities that ranged from NASCAR to various charities. We have taken our decades of offline connectivity and brought it all online.

**AD: What do you generally post about on your networks?**
**RW:** The latest industry news to educate the general public about current real estate trends and information. Also, I post about what is happening locally in the community. And I like to post items of interest that my friends, followers, and fans will enjoy as well. I also link from the banner advertising I do on REALTOR.com—which started with you, Allan, thank you very much—that focuses on short sales, foreclosures, etc. with links to my website where there is considerable relevant content on these subjects. I also post regarding current interest rates, government-lending programs, and open houses.

**AD: How often do you include links to social media content that appears on your website or blog when you post on various social networking sites?**
**RW:** I don't have an actual percentage, but it's every time that the information I am posting can be further expanded or where I have content that relates to it.

**AD: What content has provided the greatest ROI for you?**
**RW:** Helpful real estate advice and virtual tours of my properties.

**AD: When did you launch your website?**
**RW:** In 1998.

**AD: What content consistently appears on your website?**
**RW:** The Top 5 Resource Center with up-to-date news and videos for consumers, current listings, tools for buyers and sellers, and up-to-the-minute market reports, as well as links to my blog and to all of my social media profiles.

**AD:** When did you start blogging?
**RW:** In 2008.

**AD:** Is your blog separate from your website?
**RW:** Yes, but linked to my website. It's also in Blogger, WordPress, Trulia, ActiveRain, LinkedIn, and e-mail blasted through Top Producer and Facebook.

**AD:** Since you have a website and a blog are you looking to merge them into one hub?
**RW:** Yes.

**AD:** What kind of content can be found on your blog?
**RW:** Helpful real estate advice, industry news, up-to-date community information and links to all of my social media sites.

**AD:** Do you aggregate your followers and fans into demographic groups that you can individually target?
**RW:** Yes.

**AD:** How often do you send them individualized messages with content or a link to your website?
**RW:** Once a week with content from the Top 5 in Real Estate Network®.

**AD:** What are the different ways you draw traffic to your website?
**RW:** I have a comprehensive plan to acquire targeted traffic to my websites. This includes organic traffic, cost-per-click, tweets, banner advertising, extensive SEO, and several paid placements on popular websites like REALTOR.com and Trulia.

**AD:** How have you effectively used Twitter?
**RW:** By posting all listings and links to blogs as well as links to all Top 5 content and videos, and by interacting with all of my friends, followers, and fans.

**AD:** How do you measure ROI?
**RW:** By phone calls and leads.

**AD:** What percentage of your income do you attribute to social networking and social media?
**RW:** Social media and social networking are components of my overall marketing strategy and it is difficult to segment the income attributed to them.

**AD:** How do you leverage your links?
**RW:** By keeping them current and up-to-date with the latest information.

**AD:** How do you convert your friends, fans, and followers into buyers and sellers?
**RW:** Through the information sent to them via e-mail blasts and information posted on my blogs, as well as through advertising. Also, and most importantly, by staying engaged with my friends, followers, and fans so that I stay at the top of their minds when they make their real estate-related choices. One of the great benefits of Top 5 membership is that I use Top 5 content both off and online. I think real estate agents are overlooking how vital it is to provide information to consumers both digitally and physically.

**AD:** How do you further incorporate Top 5 content into your social media strategy?
**RW:** I consistently share Top 5 content with my sphere of influence through all of my marketing channels, including my offline Top 5 listing and short sale programs.

**AD:** What is the most effective way you employ social media and social networking so as to differentiate yourself from other real estate agents?
**RW:** By actively engaging and communicating with those I am connected to, using all of my available social networking resources to their fullest potential.

**AD:** Rosemary, you are one of, if not the most, modest, yet highly success-ful real estate agents I have ever known, which also has contributed to your likeability quotient being off the charts. One thing I need to express on your behalf, given your reticence regarding anything self-congratulatory, is that you not only have become one of North America's foremost relocation specialists because of your immense knowledge of the markets you serve and your overall proficiency, but you also make a great effort to become extremely knowledgeable—almost akin to a Wall Street analyst in terms of your knowledge and sensitivity to the companies and industries whose relocation needs you serve. Specifically, as one example, I marvel at how deep your knowledge is regarding the corporate cultures and relocation dynamics of the major oil/energy companies who fight to have you assist their transferring executives who are coming into greater Chicago.

**RW:** Allan, you are too kind, but I do believe that more real estate profes-sionals need to devote greater energy, no pun intended, to studying the relocation policies and programs of various corporations which, interest-ingly enough, can be learned both formally and informally through social media-related platforms that focus on specific fields.

**AD:** Rosemary, you have covered a lot of ground, almost as much as when we all toured New Orleans during the NAR convention after the Katrina devastation, which is a memory I'll never lose. I remember how you orga-nized our tour—just one small example of how you always seem to be in the middle of creating real estate networking opportunities that benefit others.

**RW:** Visiting New Orleans after Katrina was a memory I, too, will never for-get and I am so proud that NAR stepped up and became essentially the first major business to return to the great city, especially during the time directly after the tragedy.

**AD:** Thank you, Rosemary, for reminding all of us that individuals like you transcend technology, and not the reverse, and for your contributions to this book.

# An Interview with Steve Hundley

## Steve Hundley
CEO
1parkplace

**Allan Dalton:** Steve, before we talk about your immense contributions to the real estate industry, let's begin with how you first started in the industry.

**Steve Hundley:** I don't think a lot of people know this, but I was introduced to our great industry through my early passion for and involvement in NASCAR racing. My sponsor was Century 21. My car number was 21 and my sponsor talked me into giving real estate sales a try in the off-season. I was in Florida at the time and timeshare sales were the rage in the mid-1980s, so I threw my hat into the real estate ring, if you will. That trial period launched my real estate career, which I have thoroughly and continuously enjoyed to this day. In keeping with my automotive analogy, I haven't looked in the rearview mirror since. I still love car racing but, due to my record-breaking streak of wrecking cars, I found that I could not only provide greater value to the real estate industry and, therefore, to consumers, but I could also earn more money in real estate.

**AD:** So Steve, from all appearances and accounts, you have always been on the fast track. Is that an accurate assessment?

**SH:** Allan, that's a good way of putting it.

**AD:** What have you carried over from car racing to real estate?

**SH:** Well to start, working seven days a week—days and nights—is expected of drivers, so I was already accustomed to the regimen of real estate. Racing's dress code required us to suit up and so did real estate's; the only difference was that for real estate, I had to learn how to tie a tie. But most important to me was that I didn't have to leave behind my sense of competition, which is indispensable in car racing, because it is also a critical component of success in real estate. The real estate industry, as every reader of your book can well attest, is extremely competitive, which is ideal for me because I have always enjoyed the competition of selling, marketing, and now information technology. Allan, when I was 18, my approach then was to learn all I could so that I was providing valuable advice to my clients as opposed to merely trying to hone my prospecting and closing techniques. I had already discovered from my days with NASCAR that, as a driver, you have to first meet the needs of those other than yourself.

# An Interview with Steve Hundley

**AD:** Steve, can you give me an example of what you mean?
**SH:** In NASCAR, for example, you are constantly prospecting for and creating client sponsors who expect you to represent their value proposition to this niche market. This gave me exposure to the way the corporate world does consumer-related research and then executes proper messaging.

**AD**: Steve, what is your greatest and most lasting impression of your years in personal real estate brokerage?
**SH:** I would have to say it was both learning and developing sales and marketing systems as well as being mentored by some of the industry's most proficient real estate practitioners. In Florida, the timeshare sales team at that time was largely casual and did not dress professionally since they claimed they were selling vacations. My mentor—the absolute top salesperson in the organization—told me to wear a three-piece suit because this would enable me to immediately gain respect from the more formal buyers migrating from the Northeast, and because I was so young, it would help me compensate for my very youthful persona. From this advice, I learned a very valuable lesson—that even though I would have been much more comfortable in a Hawaiian shirt, especially in the dog days of summer in Florida, it was more important to project professionalism, especially because timeshare sales at that time raised credibility issues for some consumers.

In timeshare sales, however, they also engineered some of the best prospecting and technologically based sales and marketing systems in our overall industry. Because timeshare sales is so prospecting-intensive, you are actually taught that you can fail 90% of the time and still be hugely successful. Although my time spent with the world of timeshares was very brief and not really my cup of tea, the lasting impression it made on me was that—unlike many residential resale agents who are confined to a world of friends, family, and referrals—one can become very successful by venturing into far greater numbers of prospects, even if it naturally means that your ratio of closing sales is far less, because you are benefiting from a much bigger pie.

**AD:** Steve, what was your next career move?
**SH:** I joined a Coldwell Banker operation in the Almaden Valley of San Jose, California, and at 19 years of age, I was now excited to learn how to apply my sales training and systems from timeshares to what most would consider to be more conventional real estate. I remember that during my first few days at the office, I observed an interesting development: there were people who were in the office a lot and there were people who were in the office a little. The ones who were in the office a little actually had their names on the board the most for successful transactions. There was one agent in particular, whose name was

constantly on the top of the board. That generated great curiosity in me; I was determined to unravel the mystery behind his success.

**AD:** Steve, to your point about the more successful agents being less likely to gain squatters' rights within a real estate office, do you think this phenomenon might explain why it has been said that a real estate office is less like a real estate womb and more like a real estate tomb? I know that was the case throughout all of my offices.

**SH:** Allan, that's a great perspective and one of the principal reasons why I have devoted so much of my time these last 10 years to coaching real estate professionals on expanding their reach and influence—so that they are out of the office more often, putting transactions together.

**AD:** What else did you learn from your real estate brokerage career that remains memorable?

**SH:** The person that was most impressive to me at first was a Realtor named Phil Archer. Every day he'd come back with new properties to sell, new listings, and properties to market. I'm using my newfound vernacular that I learned from you, Allan. Phil projected a standoffish persona, but I was curious and wanted to learn what he was doing. He was kind enough to give me some time and his first suggestion was, "Hey kid, go out and get some glasses so you can make yourself look older." At the time, I thought my eyesight was just fine but out of respect for his success, I actually did what he said and sported eyeglasses. Later that week, I think as a reward for following his advice when he saw me run into the office wearing eyeglasses, he quickly said, "Now that you have your eyeglasses, you are ready to get expireds." Wow, did his advice and systems work well!

**AD:** Steve, I am always respectful of when a veteran goes out of his or her way to show the ropes to somebody new to the industry. This is important because sometimes new agents unknowingly receive disinformation from veteran agents who view them as representing unwelcome competition and go out of their way to inform the new agent that the company training is a joke, prospecting doesn't work because they have tried it, not to send direct mail to consumers because it is, after all, junk mail, and how they shouldn't make phone calls because people don't like to be bothered at home. So, again, it's always nice to hear examples of the many real estate professionals who reach out with a helping hand to the freshman class. In fact, I once wrote an article, "Don't Say Anything Good About REALTOR.com" because so many Realtors were telling me they loved REALTOR.com but were not willing to give testimonials because they did not want to tip off their competitors. Their philosophy was the same as that of a captain of a fishing boat, who, after returning from a private fishing spot with a boatload of fish will say to the competitors on shore, "They are not biting out by the reef."

**SH:** Allan, you're exactly right. Many real estate agents obviously recognize that they compete for some of the same business with some of their colleagues and, oftentimes, will not only not share what they know, but will actually discourage other agents. That's why I am especially thankful for how this particular superstar agent took me under his wing. In fact, Allan, I couldn't agree with you more about how top producers have to walk a fine line between sharing information and success strategies that might threaten their need for differentiation, while at the same time wishing to provide assistance to their colleagues. One example of this for me is that when 1parkplace offers $1,000 incentives to our most supportive, thankful, and enthusiastic clients if they will refer their colleagues to us, they always tell us, "I'd rather have the 1parkplace program for myself than the $1,000."

Out of respect, however, for Phil's unselfishness and graciousness, I made the decision that I would not compete directly or—to use your analogy, Allan— fish where Phil was fishing. Instead, I moved my sales territory to Los Gatos and Saratoga where I excitedly applied Phil's principals of success....new glasses and all, I might add.

The good news was that my expired-listing system worked great! I now needed a system to manage the results of my prospecting.

**AD: So, it looks as though you gravitated to the need for systems early on. Was there anyone else in your career or life that influenced you regarding the importance of systems?**

**SH:** Great question, Allan. Yes, I am the beneficiary of a number of memorable mentors, but most memorable and meaningful was my dad. My father not only constantly motivated me to strive for excellence and to be the best person I could be, but he also influenced me both directly and indirectly because he was a gifted and extremely accomplished computer engineer. Dad developed software for numerous mainframe computer systems during the early stages of computer development in the Silicon Valley region. Ironically, while he was very organized, these traits did not become prominent in my DNA, as I am the polar opposite when it comes to being either inherently or intuitively organized. While Dad was a detailed engineering type, I am more of an instinctive, run-and-gun type who doesn't always labor over organizational details. I just wanted to move on and try new things. When my father saw my organizational challenges, he stepped up and built me a computer system to manage my contacts, prospecting activities, and referral management. Just as some fathers will devote themselves to teaching a son or daughter the best way to hit a baseball, my Dad's sport of choice was the game of efficiency, organization, lifecycle methodologies, and, of course, systems.

**AD: Steve, what a blessing that your father wanted to pass on his gifts to you, his son, without knowing, perhaps, that some day, you would be passing on to the industry what he has taught you—or at the very least, has caused you to significantly focus on...systems for success.**

**SH:** Actually, my Dad had his life so organized that he was also my football coach and my racing coach. In fact, he was my crew chief. What's wild is that you have to remember that way back in the mid-'80s, there was no such thing as Microsoft Windows; the PC as we know it was not even invented yet and Top Producer was years away from being conceived. So, my Dad wrote me a management system in COBOL on the first generation of mini computers to help me manage my contacts, prospecting, advertising, and marketing activities.

**AD: So your dad actually created what might have been the first contact management system for real estate?**

**SH:** As I reflect back, I wish I would've thought of it, but I never thought about taking that product to the market back then; instead, I used it for my own business. Meanwhile, years later, companies like Top Producer, which I know you once oversaw, Allan, built their products and today, technology has taken over our industry. But it is safe to say that we were early pioneers in developing contact management systems for real estate. The 1parkplace system of today represents over 26 years of contact- and content-management history. On a personal note, Allan, I'm sad to say that my Dad passed away a few years back; however, his spirit is still involved with our product development today.

**AD: Please don't feel at all hesitant to remember your Dad in that way as a day does not pass that I do not recall my beloved parents, Robert and Rose Dalton, and all they did for me, my siblings, and their grandchildren. Steve, it's interesting how you characterize yourself as being disorganized. I say this because most people would assume that since you run an organization emblematic of efficiency and systems, that you would be inherently organized. It would appear as though the fact that you are not organized has led to your need to develop systems that organize you in spite of your natural resistance.**

**SH:** That's a great and accurate insight, Allan, and one that I have thought much about. You mentioned the word "need" and that's exactly what led to my systems approach to real estate brokerage because I discovered early on the need for contact management systems—there is no way this business scales unless you systematize the workload. One of the first things I had to do was figure out how to manage all the business I was generating. This meant developing systems for farming, client follow-up and referral management. Since I was generating a significant number of leads, it occurred to me that I, personally, could not be sufficiently attentive to the needs of all of these consumers and clients and, therefore, I gave three-quarters of them to my manager to refer to other agents in my office. The computer system I developed was necessary to track the evolution of these leads and to ensure that I was paid promptly and correctly. The system that truly was a tipping point in my career was the multifaceted and totally integrated Open House system I uniquely created for my marketplace. This system generated over 100 prospects a weekend for me and it was instrumental in providing me with the opportunity to double-end my transactions wherever possible. In fact, it's so much fun reflecting on the past, not only because the great volume that the system generated meant that I could also hire my mother to be my Chief Open House Administrator, but that it also represented a time in my career that was so abundant in so many ways that I find myself wondering at times if I should go back to these good old days, now armed with even more far-reaching technology and marketing systems intact. But then I remind myself of the great joy we at 1parkplace have in living vicariously through the success of our great clients.

**AD: Steve, while listening to you recapture some of your memorable real estate career, two words jump out to me as central to all you have accomplished— motion and systems. Would you agree?**
**SH:** Allan, I love how you put that. Yes, I live for motion! My life prior to car racing was motorcycle racing and at 1parkplace we built the first Internet-con-nected training center on wheels, named "1parkplace Mobile." I don't want to bore your readers with all of my history, but it is safe to say that I like to design systems and I enjoy going fast!

**AD: Steve, it looks as though after you figured out how to better organize your real estate career, you were then ready to put into "motion" a plan to better systematize the real estate careers of others.**
**SH:** Absolutely, and part of my culture—I guess the DNA that you mentioned— is that I'm always looking for a new, exciting challenge. So after 10 years of practicing real estate, I just kind of got ready for the next level. I was done with sellers telling me in the middle of the night that the cat got out, or that some other agent didn't turn the alarm on, or that someone drove over the sprinklers. I was ready for a new journey.

**AD: So what did you do next?**
**SH:** I wanted to develop marketing systems for the real estate industry. I start-ed as a consultant and I dreamed up this network that had brokerage, lenders,

new homes, title companies, construction, and all industry participants playing together in a central system designed to develop business and reach out to the consumer. This all came together right at the cusp of the Internet. Yes, there was life before the Internet. I thought I was going to use CD-ROMs for our delivery vehicle and then the Internet became a new and exciting frontier to leverage. All of a sudden, there was a whole new dimension and it seemed like organized real estate was ready to ascend to its next level.

And I thought, okay, that's me; I want to lead that crusade. So, I registered the name "1parkplace" on my birthday in 1995 and began my quest to build a network—a business network that would enable all the companies that participate in professional real estate to come together, to reach out to the consumer with an organized solution. That was my quest back in 1995.

**AD: Steve, what went into the selection of your company name, 1parkplace?**
**SH:** Two things. First, Monopoly is my favorite game and Park Place is my favorite space on the board, and second, instead of having just Park Place, I wanted to have a "1" preceding it, so that way, it looks like a real address...except this address is on the Internet. We use the motto, "Come Home to 1parkplace."

**AD: Okay, so early on, you were not only technologically and engineering-predisposed, but you also—even from your automotive days of getting Century 21 as a brand sponsor—possessed a deep appreciation for the value of branding.**
**SH:** Given my NASCAR experience, how could I not know that's what I was doing? Intuitively, I guess, I did have a knack for branding.

**AD: So, because 1parkplace is leveraging the brand equity of one of the most iconic brands in the world, Park Place in the Monopoly game, how important has 1parkplace been as a brand in helping you communicate your message?**
**SH:** I think we have done a good job of getting the brand name 1parkplace out there. However, having a great brand name is not enough, which means we are constantly committed to also conveying to real estate professionals and company brokers how our value proposition relates to their success. Since I'm an entrepreneur, it seems that it's hard to crystallize a brand when you are moving at the speed of light. We have developed a lot of award-winning solutions and systems over the years, for both brokerage firms and top agents. However, here in 2010/2011, it is my primary focus to dial in the brand and finally set our sights on pulling it all together with real estate social marketing as our anchor. It kind of ties everything we have ever done together.

**AD: Steve, how did you begin to effectively integrate the Realtors' need to capture and convert leads with their contact management efforts as part of their**

# An Interview with Steve Hundley

**website functionality?**

**SH:** That's a very important question, Allan. As a real estate agent, you know that we're constantly exposed to seminars and speakers and different techniques. There are listing cards, phone scripts, mail scripts, and all that stuff, and I thought: "Well, I've got this arsenal of content that I've purchased and used over the years for my selling, so I'd like to automate this. How can all this paper be automated?"

Don't get me wrong, while I am intrigued and drawn to emerging technology, admittedly I do not have a PhD in engineering from MIT or Cal Polytech. Fortunately, from my 25 years of experience in integrating real estate tasks with emerging technologies, I know enough about what I want to have built to collaborate with the necessary scientists. With 1parkplace, I built a company that focuses on integrating traditional marketing mediums with more modern Internet-based marketing mediums, and there are a lot of talented engineers who truly understand how to work with me to develop the necessary products and systems. For example, this means using the computer to take the content, merged with contacts, to automate the processes of sending out e-mails, processes reminding me of when I have to make the next call, and organizing what needs to happen in a checklist form. So, the computer was my crutch for being able to stay organized. The goal is having the computer become your 24-hour sales, marketing, management, networking, and content management system. Now you add Facebook, Twitter, and social networking management, and you have a real estate social marketing system, which RISMedia and 1parkplace, through you and me, are developing for the future.

At 1parkplace, before we agree to take on a new client, we must first gain a clear and comprehensive understanding of their business aspirations, their budget, and their willingness to make the necessary commitment to optimizing their online and offline marketing efficiency.

**AD: Steve, how does Web 2.0, where consumers and Realtors can now interact in real time, change, if at all, either the value or the functionality of contact management as we have known it?**

**SH:** Whew, that's a complex question. Let me answer it this way. Allan, you know as well as anyone that many agents today still struggle to fully grasp the value of even using a website, known as Web 1.0. So now you add another level, Web 2.0, and I think that the first thing we need to assess is what does that really mean? Simply put, it stands for "user-defined content." How that's different from the past is that, unlike the case where somebody simply presents marketing information within an online website (Web 1.0), with Web 2.0 there's an opportunity for someone to actually interact with the information in many different ways. For example: commenting on blog posts, submitting to bookmark sites, sharing information through feeds, and more. It's not for everyone, but those who are doing it well are finding Web 2.0 to be an exhilarating addition to their marketing mix. I expect your book, Allan, to uncover the techniques to do it more successfully.

**AD: Steve, how much of the 1parkplace contact management system relates to our Web 2.0-and-beyond environment?**
**SH:** There is a major step that needs to be addressed from where we started in pre-Internet days to our present Web 2.0 online environment. That's because there's a whole Web 1.0 crusade in the middle that must not be overlooked. This is why in my professional consultations, I advocate a mix of traditional marketing with electronic marketing. Let me suggest why I emphasize this middle step. It goes back to when I started in real estate and we were still using the MLS books.

Today, obviously there's a computer, which means that the relationship between real estate agents, consumers and information has been transformed. What has transpired between the days of printed listing data and now is that Realtors—who were totally in control of the information up until recent times—have witnessed their gatekeeping role become a thing of the past. Simply put, the consumer has now gained control of the information. This shift became even more pronounced due to IDX, followed by a host of sites the consumer could access to literally do the job of a Realtor, at least in their mind. I remember that Realtors were scared to death about their futures in real estate because some non-industry people professed that consumers could now buy or sell directly with other consumers, implying that professional real estate agents could be eliminated from the equation.

First of all, I never believed that could happen because the risk clearly outweighed the reward. Just the risk of lawsuits alone would eliminate any considerable gain from commission savings. Secondly, there is an expectation of a discount when buying or selling direct. Our position is to have our agent clients become experts in helping consumers understand how to make sense of the immense amount of information the consumer now has access to. The more information the agent provides, the more the consumer needs guidance. I know it sounds counter-intuitive, but this strategy really works, especially today with the introduction of Web 2.0, where consumers and agents can interact in nearly real time with tweets, comments, posts, and Facebook sharing. Agents today are able to preserve commission levels and close more transactions with the proper presentation of their real estate social marketing and Web 2.0 acumen.

So, all of a sudden, this Internet IDX went from being the enemy to the agent's best friend. Too many agents are looking for a silver bullet—and I don't want to direct any kind of disparaging remarks toward my own industry, but I've faced it myself with other agents, even in my own practice—whereby agents expect to go to that one seminar, come out, and all of a sudden have a book of business.

When you talk about Web 2.0 or Web 1.0, the key is knowing what your long-term strategy is. We recommend that agents connect their websites to their businesses as if they have 24-hour-a-day sales assistants who represent their businesses properly and provide the information their consumers are looking for. Too many agents, when they set up websites, set them up as information islands that are disconnected from their businesses and, therefore, they are not fully benefiting from the effort and dollars invested.

**AD: Steve, what impact did computerized technology have on real estate careers regarding contact management?**
**SH:** I think the first thing it did was to help agents organize their business better. As you know, Allan, out of the million-and-a-half professionals or members of the National Association of Realtors, a very small percentage of them are usually very successful; many are not able to earn a living and most treat it as a hobby. Our position is that agents who treat their business as a business—much like successful lawyers, dentists, or doctors—find that the value of their business is their contact database and not their furniture or glossy flyers. At the very minimum, computerized technology allowed professionals to measure their business better. We firmly believe in the principle that if you can't measure your business, you can't manage it.

**AD: Steve, what do you see as the future of contact management systems?**
**SH:** Allan, that is a great question. You know, today is no different than 26 years ago—you still hear agents say they get most of their business from referrals, from past customers, and contacts. With this in mind, you can understand the value of contact management; however, today, to be most successful and efficient, the monumental next level is really what I have coined as "content management." The key to the future of contact management is to merge your content sources with your contacts distributed via traditional e-mail and adding Twitter and Facebook as channels. The seminal challenge will be to find where to get the best content and a system that has all of your distribution channels built into it, along with tracking.

**AD: Steve, I know the industry will be most appreciative that you, as an individual, who is like Q was to James Bond, are busy at work providing the leading gadgetry and systems for our industry's leading operatives. Steve, specifically, how does content become king in an agent's overall marketing strategy?**
**SH:** This question has multiple answers depending on the goals of either the real estate agent or the company. I love that you are reinforcing, Allan, a concept that is widely accepted in the online space, that being that content is king.

As for content use, there are several forms of content for different purposes. For instance, sometimes we are working on website rankings and positioning to advance our SEO [search engine optimization]; other times, we want to create a direct response for lead capture, or we want to provide insightful information for branding and marketing. Many real estate agents contact our in-house consultants and ask if they can get all three in one and the answer is yes, it's possible. However, there are reasons why you don't always want to do that. There are numerous considerations that have to be strategically evaluated, each carrying its own particular issues and aspirations.

**AD: Steve, can you provide an example?**
**SH:** For instance, for Web positioning, we have to analyze our competition and develop what we have created and called the "Content Pyramid." 1parkplace's Content Pyramid was designed to strategically secure what is referred to within SEO circles as the "long tail" algorithmic-related approach. What this means is that real estate professionals who are seeking to improve their page ranking on Google, for example, must become knowledgeable and conversant regarding how a "long-tail" strategy differs from a "short-tail" approach.

In fact, Allan, I have submitted to Wikipedia a definition for both long- and short-tail regarding SEO and, hopefully, they will be adding my definitions. Website-positioning content must be crafted for proper Google indexing and keyword matching, and generally should be at least 300 words. For direct response, we tend to create short, quick-to-read, call-to-action messages. For branding and marketing, we tend to write about ourselves or what we do. Each serves a purpose and at 1parkplace, we define this as the "Content Pyramid."

**AD: Steve, your perspective on content is quite illuminating. How are you finding that agents are generating all this content?**
**SH:** The Content Pyramid will help to illustrate the categories and how we really have to break this down by purpose. For instance, our blog and search engine content largely comes from the combination of the excellent writing found in The Top 5 In Real Estate Business System℠ that you wrote, Allan, as well as from custom news feeds from RISMedia. The industry needs to give thanks for the tremendous content commitment

that John Featherston and Darryl MacPherson, and their expert team of journalists and real estate news reporters, have made. Because of this, we have creative license to localize this information for target marketing and search engine optimization purposes. This gives a busy agent involved with either 1parkplace, RISMedia/Top 5, or both, a huge head start in creating content. It's like having your own marketing and PR firm working for you, and for only around $2,500 per year. It is a major bargain. In the case study later in the book, I demonstrate how we used this content to help a top agent in San Diego target hundreds of keywords in Google for top placement. We also advocate utilizing Google alerts for topics that you are focusing on, as well as custom composition by you and your staff.

Another option—which I know some people reading this may not feel is "pure"—is ghost blogging. This is when writers compose blog posts on your behalf without your lifting a finger. At 1parkplace, we have a brisk ghost-blogging business where we write hundreds of blog posts per day on behalf of our members. Our big movement right now is hyperlocal blogging, meaning getting really deep into our community with blogging, with the goal of earning the top spots in Google for the search terms people will use to find homes in our community. In any case, the blog owner gets the author credit and we, as a service provider, ensure that it gets done—generally with the goal of securing high search-engine rankings for desired keywords. While our members still write their own posts once in a while, our writers write based on the personalities of our members. This way, it's turnkey and effective for the desired purpose.

For lead generation and direct response content, again, Top 5 has great information to use, but it is used in smaller portions for direct response, including tweets and Facebook posts. I feel it's very helpful to have resources because I'm not an accomplished writer and neither are many agents. Most would rather be prospecting and selling instead of sitting down and composing content. The busier the agent, the more he or she has to outsource this effort—not giving up creative direction, just composition. Another option is to have an assistant transcribe tape recordings. The key is to remember that marketing content needs to be short, sweet, and updated often in order to be effective.

Marketing and branding content does not have to be written as often; usually our recommendation is to have this content professionally written, or at least professionally edited if you desire to write it yourself. This information should showcase your services, encourage new agents to join your firm, or position your business against your competition. With this category, it is more important to explain your services than worry about SEO—however, gaining SEO benefits is highly achievable within this content category.

We have best-practice documents that we would be happy to provide to your readers if they request them.

**AD: I want to make sure our readers understand how SEO works and why it is important. Can you elaborate on how real estate social marketing and SEO integrate?**

**SH:** I will do the best I can in one brief answer, however, please realize that we have written entire books just on this question alone. Simply put, SEO translates into search engine rankings; the better the search engine likes your content, the better it will be positioned when people search using your targeted key phrases. We all know Google, Yahoo!, Bing, AOL, and others, and there's a crusade right now for agents and brokers, particularly, to be found on the "first page" of the Internet search engine.

Search engines look at trillions of different documents and decide how to rank those documents in relation to what people are searching for. So the question becomes, what has to happen strategically if you want to rank well, or, in other words, be found on the first page of Google? This is important, because that's all that matters. Google reports that 56 percent of the clicks happen on the number one position on page one from a search result and it goes down to 13 percent, 9 percent, 7 percent, and then, on the bottom of page one, it's like one-tenth of a percent; on page two, it's nothing. So our goal is to be number one at the top of page one for word phrases that we expect consumers to search by. But what words do we use to get there? This is where it gets to be very strategic and where we refer to the content pyramid and define tails—long and short.

For example, if we were to target "Boston real estate," we would have some very stiff competition; even if we ranked well, any leads generated would historically result in a longer incubation period to convert due to the generic "short-tail" search term. However, an easier search term to rank for would be "Lancaster Terrace Estates in Boston." As you can see, this is more descriptive, meaning a longer tail, and our history shows that this term would be searched less; however, the lead quality is higher due to a more specific search result carrying with it a much more intense interest, which also means a higher likelihood to close the deal sooner. Allan, I know that you are very knowledgeable on this particular issue, but this concept represents new territory for many real estate practitioners.

**AD: Yes, Steve, so what you're saying is that sometimes your keywords have to be longer and more descriptive, but the benefit is that you get a more refined outcome. So when it comes to SEO, at times, one needs to reverse the cliché from less is more to more is more.**

**SH:** Exactly, and the SEO team—folks who dedicate their career to managing search relevance at Google—will tell you themselves that the same search terms are only used 25 percent of the time. So that means you're chasing around 75 percent of the combinations of phrases people can use. When we talk about SEO, therefore, it's really a technique that must be treated with great seriousness. My advice to Realtors is that if they are considering using a company to help them out with an SEO strategy, they should search—if you'll pardon the pun—for a company that actually has successful real estate-selling experience—a firm that understands how to market real estate because SEO isn't about just knowing Google. SEO is all about knowing your content and how people are searching for your content on the Internet. It's a very different thing, Allan.

**AD: Very interesting, Steve. On another topic, what have been your findings, beyond our social media Census, regarding how real estate agents are leveraging social media and networking within their businesses?**
**SH:** Allan, this is a very good question, but it's difficult to provide a single answer and it really depends on the agent's goals and technology acumen. I certainly hope I don't offend anyone, but many agents are struggling with social networking. The chapter in your book on the *2010 Dalton/Hundley Real Estate Social Media Census* gets deep into this subject, but I will give your readers some additional points regarding what I have observed.

I believe social networking has been going on since the Stone Age, just without the computer. So, really, our industry has been leveraging social networking since its inception; however, I'm sure you are expecting this answer to be isolated to the new social media and networking technology platforms, so I will address your question with that in mind.

Obviously, social media right now has become a phenomenon and it's fascinating how quickly it's grown. *An interesting finding from our Dalton/Hundley Real Estate Social Media Census is that over 80 percent of agents are concerned that they have more Realtors than buyers and sellers as friends, fans, and followers.* This is due to poor targeting. What we also found is that, as of the 2010 Census, 6.61 percent of the transactions conducted by participants were a result of social networking. That's not bad for a start, but there's definitely room for improvement.

By the way, you might think it's the young people who are adopting social networking but our findings show that the fastest social networking adopters in real estate are in the 51- to 60-year-old age group. Why is that? Because it enables them to connect with their families, their grandkids, and the rest of the people they know. As a result, their mass adoption of this technology is making the entire real estate industry take notice and consider ways to take advantage of it.

I encourage all of the readers of your book, Allan, to study the findings in the chapter devoted to the RISMedia *2010 Dalton/Hundley Real Estate Social Media Census.*

**AD:** I appreciate your answers, Steve. When we talk in terms of a real estate social marketing system, what we are essentially conveying is that the integration of RISMedia and 1parkplace content, empowered by social networking and social media technologies, has led to the development of our Real Estate Social Marketing System. That said, it is important that we—considering our systematic approach to real estate social marketing—encourage our readers to develop their own customized and strategic real estate social marketing plans.

Steve, this is a process that you have deep experience in, as you have consulted with an extremely large number of sophisticated, forward-thinking real estate professionals who have developed such plans. Since we have devoted so much attention in this book to the subject of real estate social marketing but far less time to providing illustrations of same, perhaps this would be the appropriate time for you to provide an example of our concept.

With that, Steve, I would like to turn over the next chapter of this book to you so that you can provide our readers with this valuable information.

**SH:** Sounds good, Allan. In order to demonstrate how real estate professionals can integrate social networking and social media and create their own real estate social marketing system, I have selected Gregg Neuman, a top-producing Realtor here in San Diego, as an example. Gregg, I feel, represents the prototype of an individual real estate agent who has mastered the distinctions between social networking, social media, and real estate social marketing. But first, I will show readers how to develop their own social marketing game plan.

# Chapter 17

# Your Real Estate Social Marketing Landscape

*By Steve Hundley*

A s Allan has been repeating throughout this book, social marketing is not a new phenomenon. In fact, as he so eloquently elaborated in Chapter 1, social media, social networking, and social marketing have been around since the beginning of time. The only twist now is the addition of technology.

I love Allan's suggestion of removing the word "social"...what do you get? Media, networking, and marketing. All three have been a part of the real estate business, and any business for that matter, forever! However, when you add the word "social" to the mix, there is a perception that this is a whole new venture, when in fact, all we are doing is adjusting our marketing strategy to leverage a communication medium, not reinventing the real estate industry.

The challenge is that many so-called "social media consultants" tend to have their clients measure their results by how many friends, followers, or fans they are able to generate, when, in fact, the agent they are consulting should be measuring success by how many additional transactions he or she is closing. These are two completely different measurement objectives that have to be addressed at the beginning.

You have heard: "It's not about the quantity; it's about the quality." That sentiment cannot be truer than in the online world. My words of advice here are: stay focused and focus on your plan.

## Establishing Your Social Marketing Purpose
Through our experience, we have found that when it comes to social marketing, most agents jump in without a plan or purpose. In fact, to be successful at social marketing, you can't expect good results if you don't integrate your social marketing with traditional marketing.

The first thing we have to concentrate on when building a social following is how we are going to identify and find our target friends, fans, and followers.

In conducting the *2010 Dalton/Hundley Real Estate Social Media Census*, there was one sentiment that kept recurring: "I have a lot of followers and fans, but they're mostly Realtors...how am I going to get consumers?"

You can ask this question 100 different ways, but no matter how you ask it, this dilemma seems to be the consensus among our Realtor practitioners.

Why is this the case? Well, the answer is very simple; it starts with understanding where and how you are targeting your followers and fans. I'm confident that, after following the steps outlined in this chapter, you will find a huge shift in the methods top real estate professionals use to build their own social network.

Bear in mind that the very first step in developing your social marketing plan is to identify your purpose. For instance, is your purpose to:

A. Establish a network of *"local"* buyers and sellers?
B. Elevate your website page rank and search engine positioning on Google and Yahoo!?
C. Market your listings?
D. Stay in touch with past customers and friends?
E. Recruit agents and staff to your firm or team?
F. To maintain relevancy or "keep up with the Joneses?"

Taking a look at the purpose list, you may say, "I want to do all of the above." Great! You are in for an exciting journey. Each objective has its own set of requirements, budget, management, and accountability on your part. Our recommendation is to approach your social marketing strategy in steps, and to focus on the highest priority purpose first.

Let's say our highest priority is to establish a network of "local" buyers and sellers.

In this case, let's say I am an agent who wants to dominate a market area that I may or may not have already been targeting through traditional marketing. For this example, let's outline what I mean by "traditional marketing." The list below may not represent all traditional marketing, but it does cover a broad cross section:

A. Direct mail postcards or personal letters
B. Printed brochures and informational pamphlets
C. Yard signs in front of all of my listings
D. Local public relations—press releases, news appearances, etc.
E. Local advertising—i.e., newspapers, bus stops, shopping carts
F. Door hangers for my farm area
G. Cold calling and face-to-face prospecting
H. Participating in or conducting local events and workshops
I. Memberships with local organizations and charities

J. Leads from website or other online advertising

As we embark upon the social marketing journey to uncover the nuggets of new opportunity via social media and social networking, we want to make sure we are not abandoning what has already been working for us traditionally, but rather enhancing our traditional marketing by integrating new technology mediums.

I doubt I have to explain and define each of the traditional marketing mediums in detail so let's move on to the new mediums, which could also be termed "social mediums" or, as we referred to them before the word "social" came into the mix, "technology mediums."

However you know them, make sure they don't get confused with some phenomenon that is foreign to our real estate business. In fact, many practitioners make huge mistakes by becoming addicted to the technology and end up selling less real estate. Let's make sure not to make that mistake.

We are going to address our real estate social marketing system in three definitive sections: technology, content, and execution.

## Technology

Here is a list of the social media tools and networks representing the technology portion of the system. The following, in alphabetical order, will become your base technology as you prepare for the content and execution of your plan.

Each of the technologies listed below will have its own priority during your social marketing evolution. The combination works interactively as opposed to in linear order:

A. Blog – preferably hyperlocal
B. Cirrus Home Search – IDX lead capture and listing syndication
C. Contact management solution
D. Digg/StumbleUpon service
E. E-mail lists and management system
F. Facebook fan/business site
G. FeedBurner – account created and integrated into blog
H. Lead forms – call-to-action lead capture forms
I. LinkedIn – profile dialed in
J. Phone – for outbound follow-up
K. Twitter – account and background created
L. YouTube – video channel and distribution network

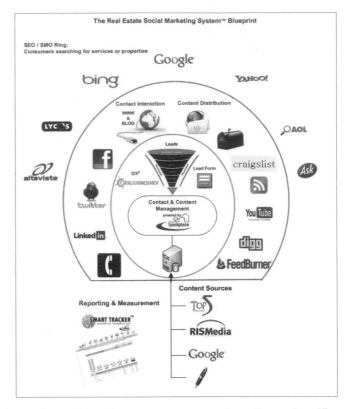

We are also going to introduce new terms such as "hyperlocal" and "webify" to the mix. Yes, this age of new mediums is also an age for new words and terms.

I'm going to give a brief definition and outline regarding the referenced terms on the previous page and then give a living example of how each of these items will be integrated into your Real Estate Social Marketing System.

While viewing a sample Real Estate Social Marketing System blueprint, we need to understand the overall concept as we clearly define each section in more detail.

In a nutshell, starting from the center (see illustration above), much like a pebble being tossed in the water, your social marketing plan should produce a continual ripple effect from the center, which is your hub of business, such as your contact manager, content manager, lead capture, and business process- ing. This is where all your information is organized and broadcast and results are collected.

Your content distribution methods and contact interaction reside in the sec- ond ring. This is where your contacts can view the information that you are broadcasting and interact with that information via your Twitter, Facebook or blog site, or even the phone. We don't want to leave any stone unturned.

All information, interaction, and activity are then made available to the search engines that hover in the outer ring. As you perform your day-to-day social marketing activities, the results of these activities should ultimately be indexed by the search engines. The better you concentrate on the key search phrases during your content creation and distribution as well as your contact interaction, the better the search engines will position your blog site, and the likelihood of your being discovered by new online client opportunities increases.

## Content

The key to success will be your content. In fact, according to the *2010 Dalton/ Hundley Real Estate Social Media Census*, 76.3% of practitioners ranked locating viable content sources as the largest barrier to social media success.

This is your social marketing foundation and, in my assessment, the most important part of your social marketing journey.

Before we go any further, I have to make sure we are all on the same page. According to the results of the *2010 Dalton/Hundley Real Estate Social Media Census*, 61.4% of participants did not know the definition of SEO. SEO stands for Search Engine Optimization and is a key term in social marketing. This is where the placement and producing of content on your site is positioned to help elevate your rankings within the search engines. There is an entire science here and there is no way I can cover every element of SEO; however, we do have specific writings on this topic located on our website and will be happy to answer any questions about this from our readers.

With this in mind, your Real Estate Social Marketing System should incorporate content from four sources. Though there are thousands of resources for content, I chose these four because, in my experience and exhaustive research, I find them to be the most dependable, unbiased, and useful sources of valid content pertaining to the real estate industry. The list includes:

1. RISMedia's Top 5 in Real Estate Network® (a member-only information network managed by RISMedia)
2. RISMedia
3. Google—through alerts and saved news feeds
4. Self-generated

## Execution

As content is composed and gathered from these sources for processing, it is piped into the center of the real estate content management system for distribution, publishing, and broadcasting.

The last, but not least item in the system is a reporting, measurement, and tracking solution. We often say, "If you can't measure it, you can't manage it."

# Your Real Estate Social Marketing Landscape

This is where we validate that our efforts are paying off, or identify what adjustments we need to make, or obstacles we are encountering during our day-to-day engagement of social marketing. Many agents tell me that they measure their marketing by how many closings they have, and while that method seems monetarily feasible, it does not give any details as to the results of long-term client development and does not offer any analytics to support the results of lead generation, content interests, worldwide reach, or online positioning in the search engines.

## Understanding the Mediums

Just to make sure everyone is on the same page as to responding to each component, and what its purpose is, I will give you an official definition and clear details on each.

The following definitions were all captured from Wikipedia. I will discuss how they interact with your social media blueprint.

### Blog
*Definition:*
*A blog (a contraction of the term "web log") is a type of website, usually maintained by an individual with regular entries of commentary, descriptions of events, or other material such as graphics or video. Entries are commonly displayed in reverse-chronological order. "Blog" can also be used as a verb, meaning to maintain or add content to a blog. Many blogs provide commentary or news on a particular subject; others function as more personal online diaries. A typical blog combines text, images, and links to other blogs, web-pages, and other media related to its topic. The ability of readers to leave comments in an interactive format is an important part of many blogs. Most blogs are primarily textual, although some focus on art (art blog), photographs (photo blog), videos (video blog), music (MP3 blog), and audio (podcast). Microblogging is another type of blogging, featuring very short posts.*

*Why it matters to you:*
By now, you have definitely heard of blogs, however, not all blogs are created equal. In real estate, your local market domination needs to be centered on what we call a "hyperlocal blog." These are not your run-of-the-mill blog systems, but rather a high-performance, locally focused, MLS listing-integrated, content-rich supersite for your desired farm or local market area.

What we will learn from the market domination example that we will review in the coming chapters is that the blog site will become the anchor for all marketing activities, both traditional and technological.

### Contact Management System
*Definition:*
*Contact Management System (CMS) is an integrated office solution that allows organiza-*

*tions and individuals to record relationships and interactions with customers and suppliers. This information includes all e-mails, documents, jobs, faxes, calendar and more. This type of solution is gaining more and more popularity as companies want to be able to control all this information from a single, integrated application, instead of having different proprietary applications, each with their own data collection systems.*

**Why it matters to you:**

For real estate, the contact management system has to also become your "content" management system. The key to successful marketing, both traditional and social, is the proper application of your content to your contacts. This means your content becomes the most valuable part of your marketing mission. Essentially this becomes the center of your universe.

### Digg/StumbleUpon

**Definition:**

*Digg is a social news website made for people to discover and share content from anywhere on the Internet, by submitting links and stories, and voting and commenting on submitted links and stories. Voting stories up and down is the site's cornerstone function, respectively called "digging" and "burying."*

**Why it matters to you:**

In this case, we selected Digg since it appears to have been the most popular content-sharing site utilized by our Census participants. There are several others as well that have similar features, i.e., StumbleUpon and Technorati. These sites play a role in distributing your content, much like FeedBurner does, except people can actually rate and promote your content as opposed to just sending it out into cyberspace. The benefit to your business is the forging of very important back links to your blog or website, thus increasing its credibility and ranking within the search engines. We all know that the higher your site ranks, the better your opportunity to generate new leads and contacts.

### E-mail

**Definition:**

*Electronic mail, most commonly abbreviated e-mail, is a method of exchanging digital messages.*

**Why it matters to you:**

Obviously, we all know what e-mail is and it really does not need a lot of explanation. However, what we will learn from our social marketing strategy is that e-mail is the third-most effective means of communication, only preceded by a face-to-face interaction and then the good old-fashioned phone. The key to e-mail is to always have your lists current and organized properly by target audience.

# Your Real Estate Social Marketing Landscape

## Facebook
*Definition:*

*Facebook is a social networking website that is operated and privately owned by Facebook, Inc. Since September 2006, anyone over the age of 13 with a valid e-mail address (and not residing in one of the countries where it is banned) can become a Facebook user. Users can add friends and send them messages, and update their personal profiles to notify friends about themselves. Additionally, users can join networks organized by city, workplace, and school, or college.*

*Why it matters to you:*

Now, we all know that Facebook is the "mac daddy" of all social networks today. Boasting over 400 million users, when people think social networking, they think Facebook. We will cover a lot of ground on marketing via Facebook and if you don't already possess a fundamental understanding of Facebook, I will lead you to some resources that are exceptional for learning and getting properly set up. The key to Facebook is the variety of features and tools that people and businesses can leverage for enhanced relationship building and business development.

## FeedBurner
*Definition:*

*FeedBurner is a typical Web 2.0 service, providing Web service application programming interfaces (APIs) to allow other software to interact with it. As of October 5, 2007, Feed-Burner hosted over a million feeds for 584,832 publishers, including 142,534 podcast and videocast feeds. Published feeds are modified in several ways, including automatic links to Digg and Delicious, and "splicing" information from multiple feeds.*

*Why it matters to you:*

As mentioned in the section on Digg, FeedBurner is a system, owned by Google, which distributes your blog-post content to channels throughout the Internet. We will expand on this area over time, but for now, we just need to get the account set up and we'll describe that in a help video connected with this section.

## LinkedIn
*Definition:*

*LinkedIn is a business-oriented social networking site. Founded in December 2002 and launched in May 2003, it is mainly used for professional networking. As of February 11, 2010, LinkedIn had more than 60 million registered users, spanning more than 200 countries and territories worldwide.*

*Why it matters to you:*

LinkedIn is much like the Facebook platform, except LinkedIn is mostly used for professional networking. This is an excellent platform for Realtors seeking professional clientele. Also, our Census participants rank this site number 2 behind Facebook as the most valuable network for social interaction.

## Phone
*Definition:*

*The telephone is a telecommunications device that transmits and receives sound, most commonly the human voice. It is one of the most common household appliances in the developed world, and has long been considered indispensable to business, industry and government.*

*Why it matters to you:*

I had to add this because this indispensable social networking tool cannot be overlooked. Did you know that this social networking platform is the widest used of them all?

## Twitter
*Definition:*

*Twitter is a social networking and microblogging service that enables its users to send and read messages known as" tweets." Tweets are text-based posts of up to 140 characters displayed on the author's profile page and delivered to the author's subscribers who are known as followers. Senders can restrict delivery to those in their circle of friends or, by default, allow open access. Since late 2009, users can follow lists of authors instead of following individual authors. All users can send and receive tweets via the Twitter website, Short Message Service (SMS) or external applications.*

*Why it matters to you:*

Twitter provides our industry with a valuable tool when it comes to sending out quick alerts and updates in less than 140 characters. The proper use of Twitter within the real estate brokerage community is growing. So far, studies show that about 60% of Facebook users also have a Twitter account, and with mainstream news and the entertainment industry advocating its use, consumers are adopting at a record pace. We'll explain later how we have added Twitter into the overall Real Estate Social Marketing System.

## Webify – Not in Wikipedia…yet
*Definition:*

*Webify is not yet in Wikipedia, however, used often as a "Hundleyism" to describe the porting or conversion of print or other pre-existing content to HTML (Hyper Text Markup Language) in order to present on the World Wide Web within websites, blog sites, mobile devices or any other platform that accepts HTML as its native language. The act of webifying content is known as "Webification."*

*Why it matters to you:*

You are going to hear a lot about this as we pour through the library of Allan Dalton's self-created works of marketing and literary content. The key to any successful Real Estate Social Marketing System is the webification of thought-provoking, consumer-focused content, blended and integrated with an automated technology platform.

### YouTube
*Definition:*

*YouTube is a video-sharing website on which users can upload and share videos. The company uses Adobe Flash Video technology to display a wide variety of user-generated content, video content, including movie clips, TV clips, and music videos, as well as amateur content such as video blogging and short original videos.*

*Why it matters to you:*

YouTube has become an essential component in any successful social marketing arsenal. Video is a powerful tool because, when implemented and produced properly, it provides viewers with a multi-dimensional perspective on a topic. Since video is able to combine moving pictures with sound and media, the viewer can be engaged in a topic and learn in minutes what may take hours to read. The additional benefit of YouTube.com is the ability to share and syndicate your video through the Net in order to gain valuable backlinks to your website or blog, thus potentially increasing your rankings in the search engines.

### Hyperlocal Sites
*Definition:*

*Hyperlocal sites, also referred to as local-local or microsites, focus on a very narrow geographical area—a suburb, a small town or perhaps a rural county—that is not currently well-served by existing media outlets. We have already seen similar efforts by print newspapers that publish separate "Neighbors" editions for different areas and by local television news stations that do "round-ups" of stories from suburbs surrounding the main metro area. But online, these efforts can be taken even further.*

*Why it matters to you:*

The ultimate Real Estate Social Marketing System consists of high-performance, hyperlocal blogging platforms. The key here is to have a local public web/blog site that focuses on the community or farm area. This solution, when properly developed and maintained can not only provide your consumers with the latest, up-to-date, and focused information and news, but with the right technology and execution, it will ensure that your information will dominate the search engines for the highest ranking key phrases you are targeting, thus translating into new opportunities and elevated presence with potential clients.

Now that we've explained the social marketing technology landscape, let's begin to cover how to put all of this together.

# Chapter 18

# Putting It All Together—
# Your Social Marketing Plan

**Allan Dalton:** I appreciate your detailed background on the social marketing blueprint, Steve. Now take us through the steps of putting all of this together.

**Steve Hundley:** Sounds good, Allan. First off, at our company, we have checklists for every function we are performing and, specifically, we have to select the right set of checklists for the solution we are trying to implement. The following is our checklist library:

**1parkplace Checklist Library**
**Contact Manager Setup**
- Integrating content and contacts
- Branding design checklist—e-mail and website
- Integrate all lead-capture sources
  - Web
  - Blog
  - Facebook
  - Twitter
  - Other
- Set-up tracking
- Organize dashboards
- Real estate team—set-up and training
- Real estate broker—set-up and training
- Agent training checklist
- Admin training checklist

**Facebook business site: __Site Name__**
- Facebook website design
- Integrated listings
- Lead-capture forms
- Launch and promotion from all sites

**Twitter page set-up:**
- Background

## Putting It All Together—Your Social Marketing Plan

- ▸▸ Profile
- ▸▸ Adding followers
- ▸▸ Additional resources
- ▸▸ Dashboard set-up

### Blog set-up:
- ▸▸ Domain selection
- ▸▸ Topic definition
- ▸▸ Competition review
- ▸▸ Categories and content
- ▸▸ Management schedule
- ▸▸ Reporting and tracking

### SEO plan:
- ▸▸ Keyword research and definition
- ▸▸ Positioning
- ▸▸ Goals
- ▸▸ Management

### Marketing set-up:
- ▸▸ Marketing strategy and schedule
- ▸▸ Content topic lists
- ▸▸ E-mail list management/organization
- ▸▸ News feeds set-up
- ▸▸ Print materials coordinated
- ▸▸ Ads scheduled and created
- ▸▸ Personnel roles and responsibilities/policy
- ▸▸ Overall marketing schedule

### Marketing management:
- ▸▸ Web tracking
- ▸▸ Solution tracking
- ▸▸ Keyword tracking
- ▸▸ Lead accountability monitoring

### Social marketing checklist:
- ▸▸ Network checklist with passwords
- ▸▸ Tweet schedule—weekly
- ▸▸ Blog post schedules
- ▸▸ Facebook update schedules
- ▸▸ E-mail lists

**AD:** Steve, you have worked with many clients. Who is doing real estate social marketing the right way with proven results? What does success look like?
**SH:** To illustrate what a successful system looks like, I chose to showcase Gregg Neuman of Prudential California Realty in San Diego, California. I selected Gregg for several reasons:

1. Gregg has averaged 159 homes sold per year for the past 28 years! That equates to one new sale every 2.29 days for the past 28 years.

2. Gregg does not like to be second best.

3. Gregg is not afraid to try new ideas or stretch the envelope.

4. With Gregg's solid team, he has the resources and systems to manage increased business from our social marketing efforts.

5. Gregg wants to offer his clients the very best information.

6. Gregg wants to project his social marketing expertise without having to personally touch the keyboard.

7. Gregg has a successful working model that can be duplicated for any other market in the USA and, quite arguably, the world.

### Gregg's Mission
To dominate the downtown San Diego real estate market…period! In other words, generate more listings and buyer transactions than any other agent in downtown San Diego; dominate the search engines for downtown real estate; and be a recognized thought leader to property owners in his marketplace.

### Gregg's Strategy
Find a partner to produce and implement a customized version of his real estate social marketing system so the program runs on autopilot.

### Gregg's Evaluation Steps
1. Analyze all online competition—knowing that consumers are using the Web to research and pre-qualify agents, your Web presence must offer the following:
   a. Top positioning within desired keyword searching
   b. Informative and up-to-date real estate news content, both locally and nationwide—shows commitment and informative knowledge
   c. Easy and accurate home searching system
   d. Integrated lead capture and contact management; for teams or brokers, you also need lead distribution and accountability systems

2. Evaluate all existing off-line marketing—for the purpose of determining its performance in relation to leveraging linking of social media with social networks and business blog sites:
   a. Advertisements
   b. Direct mail pieces and flyers
   c. Team branding and communication

3. Assemble a blueprint that links all social marketing and traditional marketing together:
   a. New blog site for maximum SEO
   b. Update all marketing materials with proper call to action
   c. Organize all contacts into a single location for marketing
   d. Implement an automated social marketing system—primarily, Facebook, LinkedIn, and Twitter to start
   e. Train sales staff and admin staff on best practices

## Results from Initial Analysis

Along with Gregg, we discovered the search engine competition for downtown San Diego real estate is extremely stiff. There seems to be a plethora of agents who have lots of time on their hands to spend tweaking their sites for search engine purposes. We realized we were also going to have our hands full in regards to offline traditional marketing. Gregg had a definitive edge, however, with his combination of an already established monthly newsletter and stealth website. The following was our plan of action.

## The Neuman & Neuman Plan

1. Develop a high performance hyperlocal blog system to target over 400 keyword phrases we want to show up in Google.

2. Join Top 5 in Real Estate Network® for content and PR support. This content will be used for blog posts, Facebook posts and tweets.

3. Set up a custom, outsourced system with integrated contacts and Top 5 in Real Estate content for drip e-mails.

4. Develop a Facebook business website and start a new "San Diego Downtown Real Estate" Facebook community for his target audience to join (www.FacebookBusinessWebsites.com).

5. Create a customized Twitter page for proper branding and professional appeal.

6. Engage 1parkplace's ghost blogging and social marketing virtual assistance programs for turnkey and consistent social marketing.

7. Modify all direct mail pieces to promote hyperlocal stealth websites for each target market.

8. Implement the 1parkplace listing marketing system with Craigslist publishing and auto listing syndication for free property exposure, increased lead capture, and better conversion to transactions.

9. Train buyer agents and admin team on proper follow-up and client interaction by using phone scripts, e-mail and social media.

10. Establish a monthly reporting and review session with Neuman Team leadership together with 1parkplace account management to refine process and further improve systems.

I bet you want to see what all this looks like, Allan!

First of all, let's start with the content. With any successful solution, the content is the key to attracting eyeballs, and the eyeballs of buyers and sellers are our top priority for more transactions. Content becomes the foundation of our system. As you say, Allan, "Content is king!"

For this, I'm going to reflect back to the Real Estate Social Marketing blueprint where I list four specific content sources:

1. Top 5 in Real Estate
2. RISMedia
3. Local Google news feeds
4. Self-created content

The reason I'm starting with content is because I'm sure many readers may already have a website or blog and they want to improve their content resources. Your Top 5 content is not exclusive to one type of site; however, if your goals are to have maximum search engine rankings at the same time as providing good content, then your site structure becomes very important.

**Content Sources in Detail**

Now Allan, I'm going to give my perspective on Top 5, knowing that you are obviously the brainchild behind its creation and content. I'm expecting you to outline the specifics in more detail somewhere in your book, but I will share my view.

Allan, this is where you hit it out of the park! Anybody can follow the steps it takes to get all the technology set-up, however, when it comes to content, I have to say, this is where I get the most excited in working with you.

You have done a masterful job of authoring the clear, concise and compelling content for the Top 5 in Real Estate Network®; in fact, that was the catalyst for us to meet and work together. I wanted to take your content and integrate it into our 1parkplace contact management system.

I love the fact you came up with the term "contact management is now content management," because without good content, we are just twisting in the wind, wasting precious time and effort to generate lackluster results.

The Top 5 in Real Estate Network® is a membership to an exclusive and powerful library of content. The most compelling content is authored personally by Allan Dalton. I tell agents who are devising their strategy for market domination that there is nothing better than having a marketing and PR expert like Allan Dalton on your team...especially when you can get the marketing and PR expertise of this industry legend for such a remarkable bargain.

Below are some examples of how we implemented the Top 5 in Real Estate membership content for Gregg Neuman:

1. **Website lead capture** on www.SellSanDiego.com — we positioned the marketing icons for the Top 5 in Real Estate brochures right on the home page. This was a custom installation that any agent can do once they are a member. Gregg outsourced the work to 1parkplace.

    The result of clicking on *The Four R's of Short Sales* takes you to the short sale category on the blog site with a further call to action and a carefully designed lead-capture form that provides the Neuman team a solid lead. Meanwhile, the client will automatically receive a series of carefully written e-mail letters delivered from the 1parkplace "Ultimate Top 5 BOSS" contact manager. This customization of the Top 5 content also provides Gregg with additional search engine content for keyword targeting of "short sales" within his market.

2. **Direct e-mail campaigns**

The screen below shows how we integrated *The Four R's of Short Sales* into 15 individual e-mails that will be delivered over a 45-day period. The 1parkplace BOSS allows us to personalize the e-mails to the client with a merged first name, making the e-mails appear individualized. Here you see the custom branded e-mail template developed for all of the Neuman Team agents to use in order to promote a consistent brand to clients.

3. **Blog and Facebook posts**

As I outlined in the previous section, the Top 5 in Real Estate information is portable and reusable for lead capture and in e-mail campaigns. We can also use the Top 5 in Real Estate content as blog posts. I figured it would be good to explain the best practices of blog post creation, especially since we intend to use each post on Facebook and Twitter.

The driving force behind every properly created blog post is the keyword-rich content constantly being added to it. Each post should serve a search engine purpose by properly organizing keywords to elevate rankings. We like to take the Top 5 information and modify some of the wording to provide the keyword goals we are seeking. For maximum search engine ranking benefit, each post exists on your blog site forever.

The perfect blog post has a keyword-rich title and tells the viewers the purpose of the article they are about to read. If the blog post is focusing on short sale real estate in downtown San Diego, make sure to utilize "short sales," "real estate," and "downtown San Diego" in the blog title and, for sure, within the body copy.

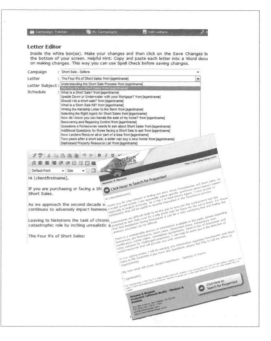

This will also benefit the reader because people like to scan a title prior to reading an entire post to see if the article will interest or inform them. In short, wordy or clever titles will never work as well as one that is keyword-rich and straight to the point.

Make sure the same keywords are used consistently in the post while also linking to a few other sites that will provide more information on the topic. Remember to also link back to previous posts that are relevant to the blog post topic. Keep the most important points of the article closer to the top—this is where you will capture the readers' interest and where search engines place the greatest value.

Close all blog posts with a strong call to action and encourage visitors to keep reading upcoming posts and to contact you for more information.

Once you have finalized your blog post, the next step is to set up a post on Facebook and Twitter telling your friends and followers about your new article. Set up a hyperlink that will direct them back to the post and include a short excerpt from the article. Works like a charm!

## 4. Tweets that generate business

The following tweet examples from *The Four R's of Short Sales* are designed to link a follower or fan to your blog site to view the full information or get the answer to a question. With a customized Top 5 in Real Estate membership and a 1parkplace Ultimate Top 5 BOSS, these tweets and posts are ready to integrate into your marketing. Expect similar formatting and content handling for each Top 5 brochure—all under 140 characters and with a hyperlink shortening tool. Every tweet drives traffic to your blog site.

- Learn the tax implications of a San Diego short sale here.
- What is the Mortgage Forgiveness Debt Relief Act of 2010?
- What effect will a short sale have on my immediate and long-term credit?
- How do I know if my property may be considered for a short sale?
- If a lender agrees to the short sale option on my property, can the bank still proceed with a foreclosure?
- How would I initiate the short sale process?
- If I'm considering a short sale, when should I contact a real estate agent?
- If I decide on a short sale, should I contact an attorney?
- How would multiple liens on my property impact short sale approval?
- Am I responsible to continue making mortgage payments if I have intentions of applying for a short sale on my property?

## 5. Utilizing RISMedia content

RISMedia.com is the leader in real estate information and provides Top 5 members with an exclusive link to news feeds that members can then modify, localize, and customize for their use on blogs, Facebook, and for local media press releases.

RISMedia also hosts educational conferences and provides ongoing best practices for marketing your real estate business. The RISMedia editorial staff reports on the latest news and provides information that you can then le-

verage in your own business.

Another good content source is Google News & Google Alerts.

Google Alerts are extremely valuable for their variety of content. The beauty of Google Alerts is the ability to pick just about any sequence of keywords, topics, or phrases which you can save as RSS feeds. Then you can decide if you want to post the information you uncover directly or take the time to rewrite the story in your own words.

Let me show you an example of how to set this up:

1. Visit: **http://news.google.com/**

2. See results:

3. Determine feed info:

4. Save search —That's it! Create away—make a list for events, news, or anything you are interested in staying on top of for your market.

| Your Google Alerts | | | | Sending HTML emails. Sv |
| --- | --- | --- | --- | --- |
| Search terms | Type | How often | Email length | Deliver to |
| ☐ San Diego Real Estate | News | as-it-happens | up to 10 results | Feed 🔊 View in Google Reader |

**Creating Content from Scratch:**

When leveraging your social networking/marketing links, it is vital that you have a mix of original content that you are broadcasting.

Self-created content is by far the most authentic and needs to project your personality and business style. This is where your followers and fans will connect with you the most. The other content sections provide valuable market or business information, which is informative and useful, but when it comes down to it, the real estate business is about forging strong relationships and having your relationships lead to future relationships. Mixing personality and perspective into your social marketing strategy is the key for optimal results.

Our recommendation is 5x business to 1x personal. The best way for this to happen is to create and share personal stories and activities you are involved in: you volunteer for a charity or have a special community service you provide or even if you just want to share your fun and personal experiences, so long as they are politically correct and not too personal. Gregg Neuman does not care to broadcast what he had for breakfast, but he will share his recent purchase of an electric car.

You can also create your own opinions based on the Google News or RISMedia news you are following by rewriting an article in your own words.

The only caution here is to monitor your time. Creating content from scratch is difficult to outsource, so this category requires you as the writer; every other section can be done on your behalf.

I like to recommend at least one personal story per month. The rest can be ghosted for you. This, by some accounts is not considered to be the most pure of processes, but the most successful of practitioners have found that delegating the larger part of their social marketing functions will provide the desired results while they increase the number of homes they close.

*This does not have to take much time; in fact we'll outline a plan that can get you dialed in in less than 15 minutes per day.*

# Chapter 19

# The Real Estate Social Marketing System™: A Case Study

*By Steve Hundley*

I n the previous chapter, I shared Gregg Neuman's home page in order to demonstrate how he integrates content. Now I'd like to dig into the real estate social marketing aspects of the system Gregg uses once the various sources of content are composed and incorporated into the system.

**The Gregg Neuman Real Estate Social Marketing System, powered by 1parkplace**

**Real Estate Social Marketing Components:**

1. Hyperlocal blog site
2. Stealth community landing pages
3. 1parkplace SMART BOSS— ultimate team system
4. Cirrus lead-capture system
5. Facebook website
6. Twitter integration
7. SMART Tracker analytics

## How Does Google Love Thee? Let Me Count the Ways.

I welcome you to the SellSanDiego.com website. The reason why this site is important is because of its Web 3.0, Semantic **hyperlocal SMART Blogger** design. What that means specifically is that this site is not just a website—it's also designed to be a highly organic, highly indexable, and high-ranking Google search engine machine. Here, we're going to explain how this site achieves the proper Google positioning. That's what really matters when we talk about hyperlocal.

As defined earlier, hyperlocal means providing information that is laser-focused to an area. Our purpose is to ultimately "dominate" the search engines with all the desired keywords for the location Gregg is targeting in order to create his own "net" and to bring as many unique visitors to his site as possible. Once on his site, we are working to get visitors to one of Gregg's lead-capture solutions. The ultimate goal is to convert his traffic into opportunities, meaning live contacts and prospects for his buyer's agents and more transactions.

In Gregg's case, we are targeting eight downtown districts of San Diego that represent the greater part of the 92101 ZIP code. This downtown San Diego region is home to about 80 or so high-rise condominium developments. The 1parkplace Hyperlocal System™ was designed to auto create a custom landing page and searchable category for each of the high-rise condo buildings. The system implements MLS/IDX data mixed with local content that is carefully arranged to maximize Google friendliness. Once composed, the system uses the 1parkplace SMART technology to look at every listing and auto creates an indexable blog post to submit into the site. This automatic activity takes place 24 hours a day, giving the search engines the signal that there are real people writing dozens of blog posts for this custom blog site daily.

The hierarchy of the structure is to first create a list of districts that aggregate the total number of properties available per district with a small amount of keyword-rich text to begin the search engine feeding process. This section needs to be updated when listings are added, changed, sold, etc. As you can see in the Little Italy example below, there are 13 condominium developments with 75 available properties for sale, 29 recent solds, and nine for-rent listings. This information is fed to the search engines as it is automatically modified. Once clicked, the user is taken to the district landing page explained next.

**Little Italy District** (13 condominiums or townhomes)

VIEW MORE

For Sale: 75    Sold: 29    For Rent: 9

The Northern most section of Downtown San Diego is the location of the historic Little Italy Condos Neighborhood. A unique eth with culture and history. Finding this neighborhood in Downtown San Diego is easy with the "Little Italy" sign prominently a India Street.

The influence of the Italian families who originally migrated to San Diego to take advantage of its profitable Tuna trade in th throughout this neighborhood. The many cafes, coffee houses, bistros, pubs and neighborhood businesses on India Street shops with business owners who may be part of the families of the original residents of this historic, unique neighborhood. visitors to San Diego and locals as well. Festivals and parades celebrating Italian Heritage are hosted by the residents of Littl San Diego Artwalk and Fiesta.

Modern condominiums and Victorian or Craftsman style homes are a few of the diverse architectural styles that add to th Diego's Little Italy neighborhood. A unique neighborhood, rich with history and culture yet conveniently located in San Dieg many people from different walks of life.

**Cortez District** (8 condominiums or townhomes)

VIEW MORE

For Sale: 73    Sold: 56    For Rent: 14

Named after one of San Diego's most historic landmarks, the El Cortez Hotel, the neighborhood of Cortez Hill Condos reseml those found in San Francisco. Sitting high atop a hill the original Victorian Style homes, high-rise luxury towers, row homes, buildings reflect the charm and diversity of this neighborhood. Beautiful views of San Diego's Bay as well as views of the owning a home in Cortez Hill.

# The Real Estate Social Marketing System™: A Case Study

For our example, we will click on the Little Italy District and arrive at the landing page explained in the next section.

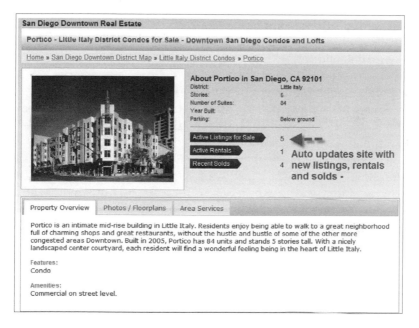

The figure above demonstrates the categorization of condo developments in the Little Italy district, for example. You can see that all of the buildings in this district are organized so that they list alphabetically as well as on the map. Without getting too technical, the system then auto creates the correct structural formatting so that the search engines properly index the keywords of the site to predict the most popular search terms that consumers may use when searching online.

The better the match, the higher the page will rank in the search results when consumers are searching. The key is to arrive at the Number 1 position.

Next, let's assume we want to see the Portico building, which will take us to the screen below:

# The Real Estate Social Marketing System™: A Case Study

The design of this site provides consumers with a custom written overview of each condo community with photos that Gregg had professionally taken for each building along with scanned-in floor plans when we were able to get them. FYI, floor plans are a hot search term. If you can get them, it will be worth it if they're properly indexed. From here, clients will be directed to the listing detail page of each property that is for sale, for rent, or has been sold.

This information not only helps the rankings of the site, but provides consumers lots of "sticky" information to keep them on the site and, ultimately, lead them into one of Gregg's lead-capture tools. The most compelling lead-capture tool is Gregg's IDX2, 1parkplace Cirrus Home Search system discussed below. For more information on Cirrus, visit http://Cirrus.1parkplace.com.

## 1parkplace Cirrus Home Search System

All lead-capture sections feed into a single, 1parkplace BOSS contact management system for eventual client development and ultimately a transaction. Bear in mind that leads generated on the Internet typically take longer to close than those that come in from a sign or advertisement, so it is vital to have a system in place to incubate those leads. Otherwise, you may easily be dropping your leads down the drain.

Please remember that our Internet marketing is not only for buyers; in fact, more than ever, sellers are also doing their research online and they're using the Internet to see who's doing the best job. It has become very relevant and extremely important to cater to sellers and owners as well as buyers.

And just a little FYI, Google reports that only 25% of the searches that are conducted through Google are repeated. In other words, 75% of the searches are literally unpredictable. So be sure to have balance and enough variables in your keyword selection.

## The Real Estate Social Marketing System™ Integration

I want to now explain how we tied in the rest of Gregg's real estate social media components, starting with Facebook. Boasting over 500 million members, more than the entire population of the USA, Facebook has developed into an interesting and strategic piece of the puzzle. Realizing that all social media and networking sites are in constant flux, we are going to address what we are doing at the time of this writing, which will address a solid fundamental structure; our fine tuning of this strategy will be reported at a special location for our readers. For more information, point your browser to: www.1parkplace.com/RealEstateSocialMarketing.

We followed Allan Dalton's direction to establish a personal social community and figured that Facebook would be a good platform to promote the "Gregg Neuman Downtown San Diego Real Estate Community." The first thing we did was create a custom Facebook website, by using the proprietary Facebook

# The Real Estate Social Marketing System™: A Case Study

Markup Language (FBML) and designing a real estate website within Facebook to leverage the Neuman Team branding, colors, style and, most importantly, lead capture within Facebook. On an ongoing basis, Gregg now has a real estate social platform to connect with downtown property owners, investors, and buyers on topics and key issues that pertain to them. This connectivity gives Gregg an opportunity to lead thoughts on topics and issues that can help bring value to his downtown San Diego real estate community. His online community can interact about concerns regarding HOA and property-management challenges, community clean-up, and any number of issues that affect downtown lifestyle and property values. We found that this unique niche created a tighter bond between Gregg and his market than even his blog site has done; however, he utilizes his blog site to promote the value of joining his real estate social network; they go hand in hand for a powerful combination.

Now let's tie Twitter into the strategy. With Twitter, we are able to send quick updates for each new blog post or Facebook post. The key here is to have relevant and important information. Don't waste tweets on frivolous information. Your community does not care what you had for breakfast or what TV show you are watching. Gregg, for instance, has his Twitter account tied into his blog and Facebook account, which means automatic tweets are generated every time new content is published on either of these sites.

Twitter also allows you to brand your background, which I say is a must. It is not expensive to do and this provides a very professional presentation of your positioning.

For instance, let's take a look at the before and after of Gregg Neuman's Twitter account: http://Twitter.com/SellSanDiego and you can clearly see the tie-in with Gregg's website, blog site, Facebook account and off-line marketing.

*Twitter Before*

# The Real Estate Social Marketing System™: A Case Study

*Twitter After*

If you have questions on how to create your own custom Twitter backgrounds or Facebook websites, please contact us at 1parkplace so we can give you a hand.

If you are using video, you can also incorporate branding within your You-Tube.com channel to complete your social marketing "staging."

I'm sure you've noticed that we also leverage the power of Gregg's Top 5 membership and affiliation throughout his social marketing as well. The magazine cover is impressive and, therefore, has now become a common theme for Gregg in all of his marketing.

This complete package provides Gregg with a formidable arsenal for competing against other agents for property listings and home buyers in his downtown San Diego marketplace.

## Driving Traffic to Your Social Media Sites

Creating a strategy to drive traffic to your social media marketing is where the gap between traditional marketing and online marketing is bridged. For instance, Gregg still has an active direct mail strategy to position himself as the expert in downtown real estate. This is important since it guarantees that he will be in front of his target audience in order to promote his online services. The example below demonstrates one of Gregg's many custom newsletters that are personalized for each condo community downtown.

Notice the promotion of Gregg's Facebook community as well as the customized landing page (www.ParkPlaceSD.com in this case) that owners can visit for specific online information and more detail regarding their building.

# The Real Estate Social Marketing System™: A Case Study

*Front and back pages*

*Inside newsletter*

These newsletters are mailed to each owner every month and have proven to be one of the most effective marketing solutions to drive targeted consumers to one or several of Gregg's many landing pages.

# The Real Estate Social Marketing System™: A Case Study

## Increasing Leads and Improving Search Engine Rankings

This next section is important if you have listings. Listings are gold to us in terms of generating qualified leads. You cannot take your listings for granted. Whether you work for a large national brand or a small boutique brokerage, you should leverage every angle to market your listings yourself; don't count on others. Besides generating more leads and improving web rankings, you may even sell the home faster!

The following three solutions are all built into Gregg's 1parkplace BOSS Real Estate Social Marketing System™.

1. **Listing syndication.** I know many agents may be doing this either through a national syndicator or through their company. The challenge with both of these methods is that they can potentially disconnect the possible leads and buyer opportunities from your back-office lead management network. When this begins to happen, it often creates what I call a "leaky bucket," meaning leads that fall out of the pipeline. Many agents don't know this is happening. Once you lock down your system and take control, you will have peace of mind from knowing that you are not unwittingly losing business.

2. **Craigslist publishing.** Craigslist and other sites that allow you to publish your listings are great ways to not only drive traffic to your lead-capture system, but also create very important backlinks for SEO purposes. This is another area that many agents take for granted. I think solutions like Postlets and vFlyer do nice jobs of presenting listings on Craigslist, however, they lack the vital social marketing integration and lead-capture capabilities that are part of Gregg's 1parkplace marketing system.

3. **E-mail blast of listings.** Much like mailing "Just Listed" and "Just Sold" cards, sending e-mails of new listings to your client database, and even other agents, will keep you connected with your audience while attempting to market your listings. Your contact database should have all of your contacts separated into groups. For instance, agents, past customers, chambers of commerce, etc. should all be grouped so that you can control your content distribution properly.

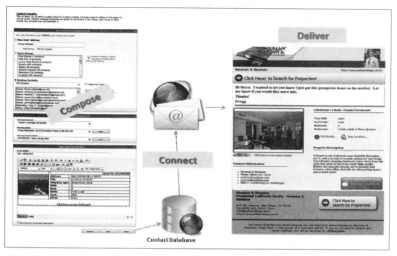

*Example of blast e-mail process*

On a side note, I often get asked if agents should post every listing on Facebook, Twitter and other social networks...and my answer is no! Clients are not expecting to see every listing posted on your wall. If you have a special property that has unique market characteristics, interesting history, or special financing, perhaps, then once in a while is fine. But as a regular practice, I don't recommend posting every listing on your wall unless you want to turn off your real estate social community. It would be better to integrate your IDX home search system into your Facebook so that your visitors can perform their own search and find specifically what they are looking for, thus, putting your community in charge.

**Measurement is the Foundation to All Management.**
Now that we have outlined the many methods we utilize in real estate social marketing to generate traffic—with the expectation that we are going to translate traffic into leads and leads into transactions—it is vital that we have the proper measurement technology to track our activities and thereby improve results.

As you can imagine, there are multiple programs available to measure your activities; however, the key is to measure the information that is going to make you money. Knowing how much traffic you're receiving is one thing, but how that translates into dollars in your pocket elevates the complexity quite a bit.

At 1parkplace, we have researched many different measurement methods and tools over the years and have since developed a proprietary method of measurement that is exclusive to real estate marketing. This is important because in real estate, the client development cycle, often referred to as "client incubation," can encompass many months, if not years, from the time a visitor originally begins a search to the time he or she closes a transaction. Studies show that consumers will generally start their Internet search a year or more before they conduct a transaction, unlike sign call leads, where the conversion time can be a mere few days. Armed with this information, we must have a solution to keep us in front of clients during the entire duration of their development cycle and, at the same time, keep us in the loop as to their ongoing activity, even though we may not be interacting directly with our prospects for weeks or months at a time.

All of this underscores the need for your real estate social marketing system to include integrated measurement tools that provide a deep look into your Internet-based prospects and future transactions. The system we leverage provides four fundamental areas of measurement:

**1. Website positioning and ranking,** including traffic and how and what methods or keywords visitors used to find your website or blog. This also measures links back to your site from other sites as well as the search terms a visitor used on the search engines to find your site. The example below shows the recent jump in traffic to Gregg's new 1parkplace hyperlocal blog system. On January 15th 2010, we rolled out Gregg's new 1parkplace hyperlocal blog system to target over 440 desired Google key words. As documented below, before launch, the site had only two of those keywords in the top 200. Within one month, nearly all keywords were in the top 100 and 187 were in the top 10. This translated into a huge increase in traffic and over 300 new leads generated in just 60 days. The numbers show a steady stream of traffic up until the day his new site deployed, then practically overnight his traffic increased by over five times as shown by our 1parkplace SMART Tracker report system.

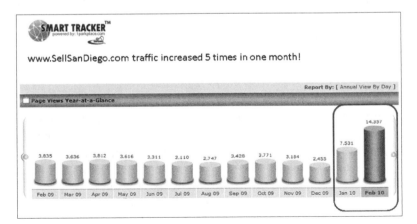

*Increased traffic to site one month after going live – corresponds with increased rankings.*

2. **Next, we track information and layout of each page** to determine the structural integrity of your site and verify that the call to action you created is doing its job in terms of converting the traffic you work so hard to generate into qualified leads and prospects. This is done through a technologically advanced map-overlay solution that measures every click on your webpage and records it so we can refer to it at any time for measurement and monitoring purposes.

3. **The 1parkplace Active Prospector measures the motivation of a client** who is using your site and auto ranks each prospect in your database with a star rating of 1 to 4 stars. The purpose of this measurement is to save busy agents like Gregg hours of time by organizing follow-up activities for those contacts that are most actively searching and returning to your website, as opposed to those that are idle. There are multiple sorting filters to choose from, but knowing your prospect's online activity is paramount to successful interaction. Now an agent can follow up with a client, knowing specifically which homes they have looked at online, what searches they have performed, and the number of times they have returned to the site so that the agent can take a proactive lead in provid-

ing accurate and timely consultation. This type of solution puts the agent in a unique position to earn the client's trust and confidence.

4. **Accountability measurement.** Never has accountability ranked higher in my mind than with Internet marketing...especially if you are the owner of a real estate brokerage or run a team where you pass leads to buyer's agents. This is probably the area that often has the largest "leaks in the lead bucket." Unfortunately, many agents are conditioned to the "spin to win" theory, where they classify a lead that doesn't close in 30 days as a junk lead, when in fact, studies show that Internet leads are not fast closers. When it comes to accountability, there are a few levels of measurement that must occur in order to be effective:

a. **Direct lead accountability** – In other words, being accountable to follow-up and staying on top of leads or contacts that are self-generated or those that were passed to an agent from their team leader or brokerage firm. Here, we track returns to the site, saved searches, saved favorites and, of course, showing requests and value requests. Each of these has a level of motivation that gives an agent an opportunity to proactively stay in touch. If they have an idle lead for three months and all of a sudden the system shows that the lead has returned and is now saving favorites, then the agent will want to know and may even reach out with a phone call to check in. The client does not have to know everything you know about their online activity (so you don't scare them with your "big brother" type of monitoring), but the coincidence between their visit and your call will be memorable to your prospect and, most often, they will appreciate your service.

b. **Leads you route** – In the case of a team or brokerage, if you refer leads to a colleague for follow-up and conversion, you must have a system in place to determine that the follow-up is actually happening as you monitor notes and interaction. This type of accountability tracking is invaluable, as it is the nature of many agents to take a shortcut or drop the ball on an opportunity if it doesn't represent an immediate transaction. Don't get me wrong, I'm not saying every sales agent operates in this manner, however, as a team leader or brokerage owner, you cannot afford to find out the hard way who is on top of your leads and who isn't by relying on the honor system. This is where technology is vital and in Gregg Neuman's case has become the foundation of weekly meetings and justifying lead assignments between him and his teammates—no proper follow-up, no more leads…it's that simple. In January 2010, out of the 20 or so transactions Gregg closed that month, 60-plus percent were from the Internet and only one was less than 90 days in the system. Most were over a year old and one was generated in 2004. Yes, that's six years of "client development" with his automated systems and on-board tracking. This piece of information is vital for high-producing agents and brokerage firms.

Last but not least is management accountability. Anybody reading this with a responsibility to manage multiple offices and oversee the activities of sales managers at branch offices will want to have a system in place to hold managers accountable for Internet marketing and recruiting activity between corporate and the branch. This area continues to prove to be a weak link in the multi-office brokerage firm chain. It's ironic how many brokerages want to focus on lead capture, but then don't have a system in place to verify the quality follow-up required to close the leads they generate. This is an area that can improve overall Internet and real estate social marketing activities by over 300% when implemented properly.

In the following Chapter, I introduce you to a publication we created at 1parkplace called "The 5 P's of Social Marketing." I invite you to use this information, which includes important checklists and worksheets, to help create and implement your real estate social marketing plan.

# Chapter 20

# The 5 P's of Real Estate Social Marketing
## *A Social Marketing Workbook*

*Produced by: Steve Hundley and the 1parkplace Team*
*Copyright 2010 ©1parkplace, Inc.*

## Overview

Successful real estate social marketing for business requires a coordinated and succinct implementation of our 1parkplace 5 P's formula. Everyone has heard of the 4 P's of Marketing and we felt that Real Estate Social Marketing needs its own set of P's since it is so unique in terms of traditional marketing; in social marketing you are really marketing with value and thought leadership as opposed to straight promotion, which is key to success when composing content and interacting with friends, fans and followers.

This approach to the overall social marketing strategy will ensure a properly executed system that creates value for your audience as well as revenue in your pocket. The 5 P's consist of the following: Purpose; People; Parts; Profile; and Process. As we embark upon our 5 P journey, there are two critical things to keep in mind: consistency and patience (which could in fact be a 6th P).

The following is the blueprint for a complete Real Estate Social Marketing System™.

## The First P is "Purpose"

Before anything else, you should fully understand why you are embarking on a real estate social marketing program and what you expect to gain from the program. This is by far the most important step as it defines your plan, determines your commitment, and establishes the baseline for accountability.

The following will assist with defining your purpose. Whatever your purpose is, make sure you are ready to embrace it completely. If not, you will find yourself wasting your time or not having any framework to measure your success.

## The 5 P's of Real Estate Social Marketing

**Common examples of Purpose include:**
- ▸▸ Awareness/branding
- ▸▸ Target buyers and sellers
- ▸▸ Lead capture
- ▸▸ Market your listings
- ▸▸ Establish a local network of buyers/sellers
- ▸▸ Elevate website ranking and SEO
- ▸▸ Networking
- ▸▸ Recruiting
- ▸▸ Promote/sale of a product or service
- ▸▸ Establish yourself as a topic thought leader

**What do you want to accomplish** with your social marketing plan? List your purpose(s) below:

**List your expected results – Identify your measurement(s) of success:** (i.e., increase market share by x %, decrease marketing costs by x %, close x more transactions, earn x more $$. Whatever you select, make sure it is quantifiable with measurement or reports.)

### The Second P is "People"

The key to a successful social marketing plan is to fully embrace the concept that social networking for business is all about providing value first, then building relationships and trust, which leads to sales opportunity.

The first **People** consideration is to identify your target audience and discover what places they frequent online. The next step to success with social networks is to listen and observe. This will allow you to discover what and how to engage with the audience so you can provide valuable content and engage in the conversation. Finally, you will want to attract friends, followers, connections, and subscribers as appropriate to the platform.

The second **People** consideration is to identify who will be executing your social marketing plan. Are you going to do this by yourself, delegate it to an assistant, or outsource some of the tasks for maintaining your online presence?

The following questions will assist you in defining your target audience, your perfect customers, and people resources to implement your plan:

| |
|---|
| *Who is your target audience?* |
| *What are your target markets? Niche or specialty areas?* |
| *Define your perfect customer.* |
| *What social networking sites are they using? (Conduct an informal or formal survey of your existing clients.)* |
| *Who is going to maintain your social marketing strategy? (Write and upload blog posts; status updates; post content to your targeted social networks.)* |
| *Do you have the time and personnel to sustain your strategy?* |

### The Third P is "Parts"

This phase is where you begin to gather all the networks, platforms, and content sources that will make up your real estate social marketing system. There are many variables in this section depending on your purpose and goals. For

# The 5 P's of Real Estate Social Marketing

instance, you may only want to use Facebook to interact with close friends. In this case, Facebook will be the only "part." However, if your purpose is a more elaborate one in which you expect to prospect via social networks, create your own social community, integrate video into your social networking, and focus on SEO as a derivative, you will have many more places to consider. You will also need to consider a time, and possibly dollar, commitment to reap your expected success and meet your original purpose.

A sample list of available parts is outlined below. Check off the social marketing parts you need and ensure that you have an account and optimized profile on those that you choose:

| Category/Product | Need it? | Subscribed? |
| --- | --- | --- |
| **Personal Social Marketing** | | |
| ▸▸ Professional blog | | |
| ▸▸ Marketing website | | |
| ▸▸ Google profile | | |
| ▸▸ Keyword research worksheet | | |
| ▸▸ Social Profile template | | |
| ▸▸ Blogging worksheet | | |
| **Real Estate Social Networks** | | |
| ▸▸ ActiveRain | | |
| ▸▸ RealTown | | |
| ▸▸ Trulia Voices | | |
| ▸▸ Zillow | | |
| **Consumer/Professional Social Networks** | | |
| ▸▸ Facebook | | |
| ▸▸ LinkedIn | | |
| ▸▸ Twitter | | |
| **Social Media Content Networks** | | |
| ▸▸ Craigslist | | |
| ▸▸ YouTube | | |
| ▸▸ SlideShare | | |
| ▸▸ Flickr | | |
| ▸▸ Delicious | | |
| ▸▸ DIGG | | |

| | | |
|---|---|---|
| ⇉ StumbleUpon | | |
| **Business Directories & Review Sites** | | |
| ⇉ Google Local Business Center | | |
| ⇉ Yahoo! Local | | |
| ⇉ ZoomInfo | | |
| ⇉ Yelp | | |
| ⇉ Angie's List | | |
| ⇉ Real Estate Agent Review Sites | | |
| **Brand & Reputation Monitoring** | | |
| ⇉ Google Alerts | | |
| ⇉ RSS Feeds | | |
| ⇉ Yahoo! Alerts | | |
| ⇉ Discussion Boards | | |
| ⇉ Twitter Search | | |
| ⇉ Blog Comments | | |

## The Fourth P is "Profile"

All social networking sites start with a Profile. The profile is your opportunity to make a first impression with others and to convey your message and value proposition, and provide your contact information.

### Here are some tips to building better online profiles:

- ⇉ Select a User Name that brands you or your company.
- ⇉ Create a Social Network Account Template to keep track of your login information.
- ⇉ Create a document that contains all the information you will need to build your profile so you can easily cut and paste.
- ⇉ Here are the major areas to start gathering information for your Profile Template:

| **Your Contact Info** | |
|---|---|
| ⇉ Phone #s | |
| ⇉ E-mail | |
| ⇉ Websites | |
| ⇉ Blog(s) | |
| ⇉ Address | |
| ⇉ Photo | |

# The 5 P's of Real Estate Social Marketing

| About You | |
|---|---|
| ▶▶ Short Bio | |
| ▶▶ Value Proposition | |
| ▶▶ Market/Niche | |
| ▶▶ Interests | |
| ▶▶ Hobbies | |
| ▶▶ Activities | |
| ▶▶ Favorite Movies | |
| ▶▶ Favorite Books | |
| ▶▶ Favorite Music | |
| ▶▶ Favorite TV shows | |
| **Work Experience** | |
| ▶▶ Positions | |
| ▶▶ Descriptions | |
| ▶▶ Summaries | |
| **Education** | |
| ▶▶ School/College | |
| ▶▶ Activities | |
| ▶▶ Affiliations | |
| **Other Info** | |
| ▶▶ Associations | |
| ▶▶ Honors/Awards | |
| ▶▶ Specialties | |

## The Fifth P is "Process"

This is where the rubber hits the road, meaning the integration, execution, and management of the previous four P's. There may be a host of initial issues to iron out depending on how complex your purpose, however, once the wrinkles are ironed out and you can get a handle on results, your comfort level will increase. You will also have a more accurate estimation of the time and resources it takes to meet your expectations.

Now that you have defined your purpose and connected all the parts, it is time to prioritize your schedule (or the schedule of your team) to prepare for the execution of your plan. Up until this point, you had *really* good intentions, but now it is time to block the time required to meet your purpose. At this point, you may realize your initial purpose is overwhelming and you may need to break up your original plan into smaller fragments so that your goals are attainable.

Each social marketing function takes time and unless you commit to a dedicated outsource solution or delegate to your team, then you may need to revise your purpose to fit into your priority schedule.

### Step 1: Initial set-up of selected places

▸▸ Create your account and build your profiles on the social places you have selected.

▸▸ Select the business photo and/or company logo you will use in all social places.

▸▸ Connect with others using the available tools within the network. Most networks have a feature to check your e-mail contact list to find other members using that specific network. You may be able to upload your contact list.

For example, Facebook has "Find people you know on Facebook."

### Step 2: Set up your monitoring and online reputation tools

| | |
|---|---|
| ❑ Google Alerts | |
| ❑ RSS Feeds | |
| ❑ Yahoo! Alerts | |
| ❑ Discussion Boards | |
| ❑ Twitter Search | |
| ❑ Blog Comments | |

### Step 3: Establish your schedule of social marketing activities

You will need to build your specific schedule based on the social places you select and your allocated time and resources.

The following is a recommended schedule based on a person who has selected these social places:

▸▸ Professional Blog
▸▸ Facebook
▸▸ Twitter
▸▸ LinkedIn
▸▸ YouTube
▸▸ ActiveRain
▸▸ RealTown
▸▸ Trulia Voices
▸▸ Zillow

# The 5 P's of Real Estate Social Marketing

## Daily
➼ Interact on Facebook – some ways to consider:
   -Post a link to a blog post.
   -Engage in conversation—select targets wisely.
   -Respond to friend requests/add friends.
   -Send a message to someone you know—watch for special events.
   -Encourage friends to become a fan (like) of your business page.
   -Post on someone's wall—don't promote, but thought lead.
➼ Post something of value on Twitter (your blog post, a resource, an article, tip, new listing, etc.).
➼ Review and answer any comments, e-mails.
➼ Review your RSS feeds.

## Weekly
➼ Write and post 2-3 blog articles that provide compelling, valuable content.
➼ Post a blog on ActiveRain, RealTown, at a minimum.
➼ Review your alerts and other monitoring tools; respond to any activity.
➼ Review and answer applicable questions on Zillow and Trulia Voices.
➼ Check your LinkedIn account and post a status update.
➼ Other LinkedIn Activities may include:
   -Reviewing posts and interacting with any groups you belong to
   -Responding to applicable questions in LinkedIn Answers
   -Connecting with other LinkedIn members

## Monthly
➼ Create 1- 2 videos based on your strategic plan.
➼ Upload and optimize your videos to YouTube and other video distribution channels.
➼ Post a blog on Trulia Voices and Zillow.
➼ Review and assess the metrics established to measure your social marketing ROI.

## Quarterly
➼ Review your real estate social marketing plan and make any necessary adjustments toward your desired outcomes.

## Real Estate Social Marketing Wrap-Up
Remember, with real estate social marketing, time is a virtue. This means, in order to see results, you must be patient. Do not expect a flood of business overnight. Do not give up on your journey if the results are slow. My recommendation is to monitor your overall plan every 90 days and make adjustments necessary to account for the reality of the situation. The key to any marketing program is consistency.

# Chapter 21

# Social Networking and Social Anxiety

I am not a psychologist and, thus, would not presume to offer any clinical insight or supporting data regarding my attempt to correlate the practice of online social networking with either the development or exacerbation of social anxiety.

Therefore, in this chapter, I will instead provide you with what will hopefully be an entertaining and thought-provoking quiz on the subject. The quiz was written by Dr. Virginia Taylor, a licensed clinical psychologist, and her colleague, Nicole Ferrari, Master's of Science candidate, in Research, Statistics, and Measurement.

Dr. Taylor contributed her work under the condition that I caution my readers that the quiz does not make any pretense whatsoever of being scientifically based or validated. Accordingly, if you do take the quiz, I suggest that you approach it in a light-hearted fashion and focus on how the questions may perhaps represent concepts that you would personally like to explore, but not with the anticipation that any conclusions represent any degree of certitude. Dr. Taylor recommends that if you are experiencing any significant issues related to the subject matter of social anxiety, or any anxiety in general, that you seek proper professional consultation.

Why then, you might ask, am I even devoting a chapter in *Leveraging Your Links* to the subject of the psychological consequences of social networking—which is a relatively new activity for most of us and, for many, has become a major consumer of their time, effort, and energy—if I am personally not an expert in such matters? The reasons are:

- ▸ To call attention to the issue of whether real estate professionals are either making money or, conversely, losing money, because of the time devoted to social networking; and
- ▸ To show that my concern for real estate professionals also extends to the relationship between the increased pressures and exposure generated from social networking, and their personal well-being.

The reason to examine the personal, and in some cases, psychological, impact of social networking is because while we have many social media measuring tools available for business ROI purposes—be they traffic ratings, inquiries, pay per click, pay per acquisition, CPM, pay per view, SEO, inquiries, leads, referrals, number of fans, friends, etc., and hopefully transactions—there does not seem to be as handy or accessible a tool to calculate or measure issues of stress and anxiety, which for some can be linked to social networking activities.

Part of my research on social networking/social media led me to the work of Robert Doede, Ph.D., an associate professor of psychology at Trinity Western University. Dr. Doede conducts social media anxiety-related research through experiments involving his college students. He challenges them to abstain from all social and traditional media throughout a three-month semester. Dr. Doede's research interestingly revealed that as his students abstained from media, they experienced a decrease in anxiety, lost weight, and their grades improved. Dr. Doede has concluded that "attention is something that diminishes as there are more demands on students' time in terms of information. This creates anxiety from within as we try to be as efficient and rapid-fire as possible in as many domains of our life as possible."

I am sure that real estate professionals can especially relate to his conclusion, considering the substantial demands on their time that pre-existed social networking and continue to occur over and above the social networking demands that the average citizen is confronted with.

Scores of social psychologists agree that many "friend-related decisions" could result in an anxiety disorder. Anxieties emerging from greater social media practices span a wide spectrum, from where individuals have been known to not terminate a romantic relationship because they did not wish to change their relationship status on Facebook ...to many more fretting over the implications of either rejecting friend requests or unfriending others.

Dr. Doede also asserts that if we are not extremely careful in how we allow these sites to enter our lives, we will find our capacities to attend to other humans, with the care and sensitivity they deserve, subtly yet profoundly diminished.

Miguel Cancino of MiguelCancino.com, a social media marketing and search engine optimization site, expressed how an element of stress or anxiety is experienced with the following question—a question that I am sure scores of real estate agents involved in social networking are routinely asking themselves: "Who the hell is this person and why is he requesting my friendship?"

For those of you experiencing what is being called "Facebook Fatigue" and/or, what I call, "Twitter Tiredness," or who are exhausted overall to the point of crying out, "So much information and not enough time!", you clearly need a strategy to ameliorate those feelings or challenges. You also need to be aware that your social networking activities and demands might be taking a great toll on the quality of your life and thus your business—or would it be your business and thus your life? Given the amazing dedication and amount of time that a stellar real estate career requires, many agents are actually focusing more on the demands of their careers instead of their lives in general.

For that reason, within this book, I have included numerous examples of social media time management and systematic solutions. Moreover, I also want to add some very personal observations regarding other possible and perhaps unintended consequences of adding thought leadership to your social networking activities.

It is very important to be prepared for negative online reactions to your thoughts. You need to approach your online communications with the same savvy that politicians exhibit, especially as you evolve as a professional who moves from the social networking level of youngsters—possibly your children, college students, and those social networkers who merely seek to connect, chat, post, and follow up on socially-related issues—to the more advanced level of posting robust content and thought-leadership manifestations, or linking articles you write or promote on your blog. Although you will now be inserting yourself in a way in which many will honor you for, there may be—or more accurately, will be—those who do not share your views. These people might, as a result, mount an online backlash campaign against you.

As an example, let's consider what happened to the former chief economist of the National Association of Realtors, Dr. David Lereah. Dr. Lereah, from this writer's perspective, was as charismatic, visible, and as great an advocate of real estate brokers and Realtors as our industry has ever seen. Dr. Lereah wrote extensively, and in a most enthusiastic way, regarding the benefits of buying real estate. Dr. Lereah was always, in my considered and very knowledgeable opinion, honest, ethical, factual, extremely well-written and well-spoken in everything he published. Nevertheless, a few years ago, David was excoriated by both the offline media and online in blogs, chat rooms, etc. for his thought leadership.

You may ask how this happened, especially given that virtually everyone else in the worlds of real estate and finance was encouraging homeownership... including U.S. presidents, the head of the U.S. Treasury, and chief economists throughout the world. Unfortunately, David wound up taking the hit for much of the industry due to the fact that he was not—in a Nostradamus-like way—prescient enough to predict a total, worldwide real estate collapse. Consequently, when homeowners and investors lost money, they needed to direct blame at someone, and who better than the real estate industry's leading symbol of the real estate market?

Therefore, I would be remiss in this book if I didn't suggest the need for everyone in real estate to be very careful regarding the degree to which you use social media as a way to stimulate real estate consumers beyond interest in the properties you're representing. For example, if you are constantly and categorically postulating and proclaiming that everyone should be buying now, or at any and all times, this could come back to haunt you…especially within your online communities, where participants can attribute their real estate difficulties to you. Also, please keep in mind that, oftentimes, online misrepresentations of what you truly said or did can create an insidious groundswell of negativity directed at you. Such backlash is typically not a result of harmless social networking musings and chit chat-oriented posts, but rather a consequence of your espousing content that is intended to significantly sway or influence consumers. At this point, you are becoming a real estate advocacy journalist.

I personally experienced an online backlash within our industry on several occasions. Several years ago, I was invited to debate Redfin at the legendary Inman Conference. I have always respected, and still respect, Brad Inman—as do RISMedia's John Featherston and Darryl MacPherson—for his immense journalistic and technological contributions to the real estate industry. At this particular Inman event, I was told by Brad that "60 Minutes" was going to film our debate/discussion, which was being held in Manhattan. In fact, I signed a release form from "60 Minutes."

Unfortunately, my observations during the debate created rancor in some online sectors. To me, what I said was not deserving of an online excoriation by anyone, let alone by so many. I'll let you decide. Please go to www.youtube.com and type in "Redfin Allan Dalton" in the search box to see the clip from the debate; you can be the judge as to my appropriateness and whether or not what I said should have induced so much online venom against me.

Specifically, my major point was that Glenn Kelman, the CEO of Redfin, was inappropriate in his claim asserting that home sellers would save money by using Redfin, instead of what he labeled "conventional" or "non-discount" companies, because, he claimed, Redfin generally returned two-thirds of its fee to the home seller. I responded that his assertion was a specious argument because to suggest a savings implies a set commission rate…which essentially would be price fixing and, thus, antitrust.

I, therefore, encouraged Glenn—a person I like and respect very much, as I do Redfin's aspirations on behalf of both the real estate industry and, for transparency purposes, consumers—to contextualize his remarks by acknowledging the following nuance: it was important for the "60 Minutes" audience to not conclude they would automatically save money because that would suggest that all companies and Realtors were able to create the same result and, thus, bottom line. Understandably, my comments ended up on the "60 Minutes" editing room floor, and only Glenn appeared on "60 Minutes," where he did an outstanding job promoting his agenda from his particular prism.

My point is that, because of my thoughts—even though I was applauded by the Realtors in attendance while Glenn was not—I was attacked online by many who are more geared toward cowardly online attacks. These are the folks who, lacking knowledge about the industry or the proper use of technology to help consumers, will always direct their online diatribes toward personalities instead of juxtaposing relative precepts.

The same thing happened when I was invited to debate Zillow. Zillow is a terrific, consumer-useful, and very innovative Internet-based service—one which can also be leveraged by sophisticated Realtors. Its founders and executives are top-shelf people as well as being very bright. When I debated Zillow and inserted my views as an industry thought leader, I became the subject of widespread attacks. You can check out a clip from the debate by going to http://www.youtube.com/watch?v=0DNtYtM_gX0.

There, you will see that my point was that Realtors are needed not only to refine a "Zestimate"—an opinion that Zillow has always offered—but that it is dangerous for our industry, and misleading for consumers, to conclude that price isn't also significantly influenced by the marketing skills, the negotiating skills, and the overall value of a Realtor.

Otherwise, if we believe a real estate agent's value is not part of what a home will sell for, we commodify our business—in the same way a company's shares are priced at $60, regardless of which stockbroker or discount broker you use to facilitate your transaction. It is important to realize that Realtors and the market process also determine the price of a home. For making these points, I was accused of throwing a chair and likened to Jerry Springer. The headline of the blog that accused me of throwing a chair at this debate was not only totally absurd and an outright lie written to attract blog hits, but it was also unfair to Jerry Springer because, even though I haven't watched his show, I know it's his guests who throw objects and not him. But why let facts get in the way of an online attack?

Now, admittedly, I was being unnecessarily facetious when I compared Zillow to a fortune teller and a carnival age/weight guesser. They deserved better treatment from me since they do provide a valuable service. Zillow has matured and is now a great consumer experience, and I encourage real estate companies and agents to integrate Zillow into their overall value proposition.

The reason I have shared with you a few of the scars I have accumulated for defending real estate industry value is that I want to impress upon you the reality that any time you take a stand on a controversial issue, you should expect a backlash. Therefore, are you ready to become an online rain maker or visible thought leader? To find out, I suggest that you first take this quiz.

## Social Networking and Social Anxiety

### Social Networking Quiz

*By Dr. Virginia Taylor, licensed clinical psychologist, and Nicole Ferrari, Master of Science candidate in Research, Statistics, and Measurement*

How ready are you to embrace the opportunities of social networking in growing your business? Are you a technophobe or a technophile? Take this quiz to discover your online networking I.Q.!

**Please rate your agreement with the following statements based on this scale:**
  **1 = Strongly disagree**
  **2 = Disagree**
  **3 = Neither agree nor disagree**
  **4 = Agree**
  **5 = Strongly agree**

1. I like to "spread the news" regarding my real estate accomplishments.
2. I feel I must maintain a professional appearance wherever I go because I never know who I may see.
3. For me, the opportunity to get to know people from my past in new ways is a valued benefit of social networking sites.
4. If I learned that an acquaintance had contacted me on a social networking site like Facebook, I would anticipate the professional opportunities that could follow.
5. With each additional 100 people who join my social networking site, I would be increasingly excited rather than increasingly anxious and vulnerable about what others might be saying about me.
6. If I had to choose, I'd prefer to have people inquiring more about me than about my properties.
7. I am very careful to only share pictures of myself that I consider to be flattering, both online and in person.
8. At social gatherings, I find striking up conversations with new acquaintances to be energizing.
9. To me, a significant number of friends, fans, and followers online signifies that I have a lot going on in my life.
10. The potential professional gains I experience from high online connectivity outweigh my concerns about privacy or personal criticism.
11. When I see someone's picture on a billboard or on the front of a shopping cart, I feel more favorably toward him or her.
12. If someone saw my picture on a billboard or on the front of a shopping cart, he or she would feel more favorably toward me.
13. When I need to lift my mood, I seek the company of others.

14. I am as comfortable first engaging potential clients through social networking sites as during open houses.
15. I am comfortable accepting all friend requests, even from people I don't know.
16. I am more comfortable with people commenting about me offline than online.
17. I give serious thought to what potential clients might think before I make online connections with certain people or organizations.
18. Even before I entered the real estate profession, I would look forward to bringing something over and introducing myself to every new neighbor.
19. I feel that I am able to judge a person fairly accurately through only online communication.
20. I tend to consider what I know about others before I decide how much and what to share about myself.

**To discover your social networking readiness score, add up your individual subscale scores as listed below, *and multiply your score on #10 by 5*; then find your grand total by adding together your individual subscale scores.**

Visibility subscale item #s: 1, 6, 11, 16
Impression management subscale item #s: 2, 7, 12, 17
Extroversion subscale item #s: 3, 8, 13, 18
Perceived value of social networking subscale item #s: 4, 9, 14, 19
Interpersonal sensitivity subscale item #s: 5, 10, 15, 20

**If your total score is between 90 and 120 points:** Congratulations! If you aren't already a major presence on several online networks, you will be soon! You are a natural and are ready to jump into social networking with both feet. You have the aptitude and attitude that will enable you to benefit greatly by maximizing your exposure online. Good luck!

**If your total score is between 60 and 89 points:** With a little preparation, you will be ready to build your business through social networking sites. But before you make your moves into the online business world, you may want to take some time out to learn what makes some Realtors more successful online than others, and consider how you can apply their secrets of success to your own Web profile. Start with examining the quiz subscales to see where your strengths and weaknesses lie, and where you can start making the changes necessary to achieve the level of success you are seeking.

**If your total score is between 40 and 59 points:** You can find some level of professional success through online social networking, but first you will need to do some serious research to prepare yourself for this new world of opportunity. Using social networking to build your business may require you to move out of your usual comfort zone, and make some significant changes in your online and offline communication style. You should continue focusing your energy on your personal connections in the community, and start by using social networking as a way to bolster those existing relationships.

**If your total score is below 40 points:** Social networking might not be the right direction to take for growing your business. Your energy may be better spent on more traditional ways of forging professional relationships. The good news is, five years ago social networking was not on anyone's radar, and five years from now the next new thing might be more suited to your style!

*This quiz was developed by Dr. Virginia Taylor expressly and exclusively for* Leveraging your Links.

# Chapter 22

## Meet Mr. Social Media–
## Dustin Luther

## Dustin Luther
Internet Marketing Strategy at 4realz
Speaking and Consulting

Founder at Rain City Real Estate Guide

**Allan Dalton:** Dustin, when did you first recognize the potential impact that social networking and social media would have on real estate careers?
**Dustin Luther:** I think it's safe to say that I recognized the potential impact of online social networking pretty early on. I created one of the first real estate blog communities, Rain City Guide, in March 2005 and my wife was closing transactions from the blog by June of that year; so it didn't take long for me to realize that the opportunity to benefit from online networking was huge.

**AD:** What in your background led to your becoming, in my opinion, one of the real estate industry's true pioneers in understanding the significance of social media?
**DL:** I'm sure that being an outsider definitely helped. After graduating from UC Berkeley, I spent years in transportation engineering and only got into real estate as a way to jump-start my wife's real estate career. One of the things that helped me early on was that I was both in and out of the real estate community. I was part of the community because I was there to earn real estate business for my family like most of the other players, but I was also an outsider who could comfortably question the status quo—and especially in 2005, with Zillow, Trulia, Redfin, Google Maps, etc. all coming on the scene. At that time, there was so much to question about the existing online real estate marketing options and strategies.

# Meet Mr. Social Media – Dustin Luther

**AD:** Dustin, I appreciate your terminology—"comfortably question the status quo." Now let me ask you, when a real estate agent retains you as their social media consultant, what does this process involve?

**DL:** First and foremost, it involves developing a strategy that will work for the agent and almost always starts with an analysis of what's worked for them in the past. An analytically minded agent who's found success in the past by going directly to consumers is going to require a very different strategy than an agent who's found success in the past by leveraging his or her referral network. However, either way, there are some standard themes to my consulting. We tend to develop an online hub (website/blog), as well as a promotional strategy where we'll coach agents on how to ask for business in online settings.

**AD:** When you were with us at Move, Inc. and REALTOR.com several years ago, you were among the first executives in the company to passionately talk about blogging and social networking. Why do you think others, like myself, didn't immediately seize upon the significance of these concepts?

**DL:** I don't think that you and others didn't try to seize it—there were always several projects being built and/or launched, including a social network for the REALTOR.com community and a blogging platform by the Top Producer team. So efforts were being made to tap into these markets.

However, the best online blogging and social networking tools (WordPress, Twitter, Facebook, etc.) have always been free (or at least nearly free), so getting a publicly traded company like Move to focus on "giving" things away will always be difficult, and it's really hard to blame anyone there for not getting more excited. If anything, I was a bit wrongheaded to focus on building social networking tools, when I could have focused on building the brand value of REALTOR.com within other real estate communities.

**AD:** Well, Dustin, retrospectively speaking, it is now clear that both concepts can be managed and integrated simultaneously. And speaking of integration, how do you recommend that Realtors who are active in social media reconcile the need to insert their real estate agenda while at the same time not violating the tacit understanding that certain online communities have regarding keeping solicitations out of the experience?

**DL:** I'm not sure they need to insert a real estate agenda. For the vast majority of successful real estate professionals, real estate is a networking game where they get their business from building and connecting within their sphere.

For example, if you add a real estate professional to a networking event with ten local people, the good ones will inevitably find out who has a real estate story to share (who's thinking of buying/selling or knows someone buying/selling) and find a way to get at least one client out of the event. They do this not by having a real estate agenda, but by knowing how to ask for business when the timing is right. Online networking is no different. If agents show up with a real estate agenda, they are likely to alienate the very referral network they need to successfully generate business out of social networks. Nonetheless, agents who don't have the skills to appropriately direct a conversation toward real estate and ask for business at an offline networking event aren't going to magically develop those skills when they go online.

**AD: I assert in this book that if Realtors conclude that social media and social networking are one in the same, or interchangeable premises, that this denies either full comprehension of each or integration of the two, because you cannot integrate sameness. Do you agree with this?**

**DL:** Although I don't know exactly how you're going to make the distinction in the book, I can definitely appreciate that there is a difference between social media and social networking. My take is that social "media" means that, thanks to Internet tools, any of us can broadcast our message, whereas social "networking" means that it's easier than ever to connect with a large group of people using online tools. Knowing when to use Internet tools to broadcast versus to connect is definitely an important skill set.

**AD: Dustin, I also assert in this book that if you do integrate social media with social networking for real estate business purposes, you can achieve a convergence leading to a real estate social marketing functionality. Another point I make in the book is that online communities and networks have different needs and organizational premises than real estate markets. In other words, FSBOs, expireds, short sale home sellers, etc. represent de facto markets versus communities or tribes. Do you agree?**

**DL:** I'm pretty sure I follow where you're going and I agree that if you're trying to reach consumers directly—as opposed to reaching and expanding your referral sphere—then it's definitely possible to organize a marketing plan and target those users directly...although, outside of some very specific examples—such as Zillow's and Trulia's message boards—I haven't seen real estate agents generate much business by targeting these types of users via social networks. A more common strategy to reach these types of users is to create targeted landing pages on a hub and then buy extremely targeted traffic, most often search traffic towards these pages.

**AD: Dustin, our Census revealed that only a small percentage of Realtors are making significantly more money via social networking and/or social media. Does this surprise you?**

**DL:** Not at all. Most agents approach online marketing as if it's foreign turf and don't put together a strategy that will work. However, if you asked the same agents from your Census where they generate the majority of their business,

you'd find the same results I found when I asked the question (http://4realz.net/2010/02/my-last-post-got-me-thinking-about-a-pol/). The majority of agents generate their business from their referral networks and online social networks are the most effective and efficient way to stay connected and enhance their sphere. I've noticed that when you teach agents how to use their online social networks to build their sphere, they start attributing much more of their referral leads to their online activity; even if it's to a connection to a client they originally met at an offline event. In other words, agents start to experience that their online sphere-building activities are the "cause" behind someone becoming a client and not just the initial contact.

**AD: What are some examples you've seen of great social media utilization by Realtors?**

**DL:** One of my favorite examples of reaching consumers directly comes from Dale Chumbley. He has created a Facebook page specific to his community, Vancouver, Washington (http://www.facebook.com/WhyVancouverWA) that has allowed him to network with thousands of local people within only a few weeks of launching it. His premise is that he publishes a new "thing to do" in his community each day. The locals not only appreciate his ideas, but they also send him new ideas, and even go so far as to thank him when they meet up with him at local events. After interviewing him, I was blown away by the number of clients he's picked up from this Facebook community (8,956 fans as of 4/13/2010).

**AD: What are the greatest misperceptions of social media that you have heard?**

**DL:** The greatest misperception is that agents can use social media to "reach" their next client. Every day, I see agents who think they can't "talk" to the larger real estate community because they need to talk with consumers directly. It's a recipe for failure as consumers are rarely looking to "connect" with Realtors in any meaningful way, so you end up with a lot of one-way conversations that show consumers a Realtor who doesn't know how to connect with other people. For the vast majority of agents, they're so much more skilled at using their social network to generate leads from friends, family, past clients, and the real estate community at large, that it's a shame they think they have to reach their next client with every blog post, tweet, and status update.

**AD: Do you think Realtors run the risk of appearing to be irrelevant if they use social networking primarily for contacts versus providing content?**
**DL:** Not really. Very few successful Realtors are known for creating content, and most of the content that's created is crap and super easy for consumers to ignore. In my mind, it's much better for agents to prove that they're fluent in real estate topics that matter. For example, I'd rather have a Realtor who follows and is fluent in housing tax law than the one who wrote the tax law. In my mind, creating original content is not only hard, but it's not a skill set common to most Realtors...or any other professionals for that matter. I actually think there's an over-emphasis in real estate on creating original content when there's a lot more value in micro-commentary and content curation (http://just-writeclick.com/2009/10/10/content-curation-a-manifesto/ ).

**AD: Dustin, your view is totally consistent with some of what I write in the book, where I illustrate how politicians, when employing social networking and social media platforms, only seize upon a few truly viral subjects. That said, Dustin, tell our readers if you would, the good, the bad, and the ugly regarding blogging for real estate professionals, as you are perhaps the industry's foremost expert on this concept.**
**DL:** I'm honestly not sure where to start with this question. The good is that more professionals are figuring out they don't need to spend a ton of money to develop an effective Web presence. I remember years ago when I told people that my wife's real estate blog (Rain City Guide) was also her website, people reacted like I was crazy. However, so much has changed and now it's quite common for real estate agents to create online hubs that integrate their blog into their website with beautiful designs that simply don't cost much at all. If I had to take things to the bad, it would be how many online hubs (websites/blogs) are missing a decent home search. If you're going to blog and have a decent website, then it really is critical to have a decent home search if you want to capture any consumer clients.

**Meet Mr. Social Media – Dustin Luther**

And now to the ugly: Prospecting. Even for the folks that have a decent home search on their website, they're often missing the tools to actively prospect their database of home searchers, which is just sad. Way, way too many agents wait for consumers to contact them (i.e., request a showing), which means they're inevitably leaving the majority of their potential clients to their competitors.

**AD: What are some sites that our industry is either overlooking or under-utilizing?**
**DL:** I'm not sure it's "underutilized," but my current favorite tool is Gist (http://gist.com). Because I've connected with thousands of people using tools like Twitter, LinkedIn, and Facebook, there's a lot of "noise" in my social networks and Gist lets me filter updates based on the priorities I set for each individual. Since I've been using the tool, I've been able to focus on connecting with the people that are most important to my business.

**AD: I agree, Dustin, Gist is a great repository for aggregating in one place all of one's contacts that otherwise remain disparately located and, thus, diluted from a consolidation, efficiency and time-management perspective. Dustin, since you have always been ahead of the curve, where do you predict we are heading?**
**DL:** I think you're going to see things happen on two fronts: direct-to-consumer and referral-building tools. For reaching consumers directly, I think you're going to see more real estate tools that focus on managing and prospecting data-bases—and in particular, databases that are connected to online home-search tools. In terms of building a referral network, I think you'll see tools similar to Gist, but more specific to the real estate network that encourages and enables agents to connect with the people who are important to their business.

**AD: As you know, Steve Hundley and I created an online real estate Social Media Census, which thousands of Realtors have participated in. Given that our market is the real estate industry, would this effort qualify for what you would classify as an adroit utilization of social media, and would you encourage Realtors to offer something similar online, directly to consumers in their local markets with a link to their websites or blogs?**
**DL:** Of course. It sounds like this has been a huge success regarding giving you the ability to start a conversation about the effective use of social media with your target audience. This sounds like a great use of social media tools.

**AD: Dustin, having you reinforce our work is appreciated and we certainly welcome and encourage Realtors to model how we are using social media within the industry in terms of our Census, the RISMedia Social Media Summit, and**

this book, and how they look to become more robust thought leaders within their online consumer communities. In fact, we plan on encouraging real estate agents to create their own real estate community census or become part of a national one we are considering creating online. I hope to see the day that the government census will be done online.

**DL:** Allan, thank you very much. Your questions covered a ton of ground about how a Realtor can develop a successful online marketing strategy. In terms of learning more about how I can help them, it should come as no surprise that I have my hands in a few different real estate projects. If people want to learn more about the websites my company develops—which integrate top-notch home search, mapping, and lead management tools into their blogs/websites—they should connect with the HomeQuest team at http://homequest-group.com/. They can learn more about my background, as well as find information on hiring me as a speaker, educator, or consultant at http://4realz.net/media/, although the best way to connect with me is to reach out to me directly on either Facebook (http://www.facebook.com/dustinluther) or on Twitter (http://twitter.com/tyr). Thanks again!

# Chapter 23

## DMAC on D.M.A.C.
Darryl MacPherson on Digital Media at the Company Level

## Darryl MacPherson
Executive Vice President
RISMedia

**Allan Dalton:** Darryl, you and John Featherston have been instrumental in overseeing, on behalf of RISMedia, the creation of a significant percentage of the real estate industry's digital media...digital media often referred to as B-to-C (Business-to-Consumer) content. Why did you make the decision to add a B-to-C emphasis after your many years of serving as the industry standard-bearer in B-to-B (Business-to-Business) content?

**Darryl MacPherson:** Allan, as you know, ever since RISMedia was founded by John Featherston over 30 years ago, its mission and privilege has always been to provide the real estate industry with necessary and valuable information, ranging from business development strategies and best practices all the way to surveys and broker rankings. Therefore, given our longtime role and responsibility of serving the industry's informational needs, it was only natural that we evolve to also provide consultative content assistance in order to meet the extensive and increasing external needs of the industry to now provide information to consumers.

**AD:** Darryl, what do you mean when you say, "external needs?"
**DMAC:** I am specifically referring to the needs of all real estate companies to respond to the online informational needs of consumers and clients in their respective markets—this need is now an acute one.

**AD:** The term "real estate industry" means different things to different people—who is the industry you serve?
**DMAC:** That is a very important question. Here is how RISMedia has both nuanced and integrated industry segments.

First, for 30 years, RISMedia was primarily focused on serving the needs of broker/owners and company management. Our major constituency was, and remains, real estate principals and their organizations, but our focus and service certainly does not end there.

**AD: Who else within the real estate industry, then, is a beneficiary of RISMedia's consultative service and "content chain," if you will?**
**DMAC:** RISMedia also provides social media content to industry service providers, the Top 5 in Real Estate Network®, and tens of thousands of leading Realtors who need content to educate consumers through their various social networking and social media platforms and efforts.

**AD: Darryl, please tell the readers of this book how RISMedia does this.**
**DMAC:** We have a seasoned in-house staff of writers and editors who are actively engaging real estate professionals every day in order to stay on top of the most pressing issues and trends, including those that affect consumers as well as agents and brokers. We also seek out and employ the best team of professional freelance writers and business experts in the field to help generate these ongoing streams of content. At RISMedia, we are immersed in the real estate business and are constantly monitoring various news sources in order to filter the most relevant information to our various constituents.

**AD: Darryl, you and John have recently introduced a program that relates to digital media at the company level called RREIN—RISMedia's Real Estate Information Network®. Would you explain what RREIN represents and why RISMedia has founded this network?**
**DMAC:** We created RREIN as a direct response to the needs and requests of many real estate companies. For several years now, numerous leading real estate brokers have approached RISMedia and asked us for a cost-effective, company-based solution that would enable these companies and their agents to insert themselves as information leaders in their local markets and, specifically, online.

Companies told us they were seeking actionable and relevant B-to-C real estate content that was customized and not costly.

**AD: I can appreciate that, Darryl, as real estate companies not only need a property IDX solution, but also what could be called a "content IDX" solution. Is this what you have found?**
**DMAC:** Absolutely, Allan. As you know, consumers are not only going online now for property listing information but also for relevant and contextually rich and robust real estate content as well. We have found that RREIN is the most sophisticated and efficient way for companies to accomplish this objective of providing consumers with the information they request.

**AD:** What makes RISMedia's content special to real estate companies?
**DMAC:** Our 30-year history of having a large team of real estate writers creating real estate content in a manner that:

- Encourages real estate transactions
- Respects real estate companies and brokers
- Is differentiated in our online and off-line vehicles
- Is significantly less expensive and more efficient than companies attempting to generate this information on their own

**AD:** What types of companies are RREIN members?
**DMAC:** Without exception, prestigious and respected marketplace leaders who recognize that ongoing market share is tied to online content share and who are dedicated to elevating their agents' relevance and increasing the consumer's knowledge and decision-making ability.

RREIN members are company leaders who appreciate that consumers are not only judging their companies and associates on transactional results, but also on their ability to deliver needed content and information. RREIN company leaders are also great communicators who are able to convey this industry paradigm throughout their organizations.

**AD:** What is the chief benefit to an agent who belongs to a RREIN-member firm?
**DMAC:** The principal benefit to agents is really the same benefit to consumers and the company. Everyone wins when useful information is accessible. RREIN, therefore, is totally in alignment with every real estate company's marketplace mandate.

**AD:** Meaning?
**DMAC:** That all companies are only successful if their agents are...and agents are only successful when their clients and customers succeed. Therefore, RISMedia's and RREIN's role is to provide content connectivity online to all parties involved and do it in the most efficient and effective manner possible in order to help facilitate success for all parties involved.

**AD:** Let's end with this. Tell me why, Darryl, if I were still the owner of my former real estate company, I would want my organization to become a member of RREIN?
**DMAC:** You would want to become part of RREIN because, number one, it would establish your firm as a leader in its marketplace—one that is committed to not only facilitating home sales, but to informing and educating consumers so that they can make the best possible real estate-related decisions.

## DMAC on D.M.A.C.

Second, being a member of RREIN positions your agents as consumer-centric and information-oriented real estate consultants...not just salespeople after a commission. Finally, as a member of RREIN, everything happens automatically and in a turnkey fashion, thanks to the systems and solutions put in place by RISMedia. It takes the onus off the brokers so that they can concentrate on the business of real estate.

# Chapter 24

# Mobile Is on the Move

## Seth Kaplan
President, Mobile Real Estate ID
## John Lim
Founder and CEO of Mobile Card Cast

Creators of The Mobile Real Estate ID system

**Allan Dalton: John and Seth, would you please speak to the mobile movement.**
**John Lim:** Right now, the mobile movement—being the fastest and largest-growing revolution in today's society—has allowed consumers, businesses, and everyone, to use their mobile device as more than just what it was invented for—simple phone communication. You can now access all of your social links and the Internet, you can buy products over your mobile device securely, or you can use it for news updates. It's even used now for an alert system to prevent tragedies, such as an earthquake or a shooting at a school. So, it's become the one device that guarantees that a person always leaves his or her house with the one point of contact that you're guaranteed to reach them on.
**Seth Kaplan:** Because of the advances in technology, the mobile movement has allowed for more than just the phone call or the text message. There's such a wide array of content that's available via the mobile phone now. It truly has become the equalizer across different socioeconomic conditions and countries. For example, there are more Google searches being made on mobile phones in the mobile-phone-emerging countries than there are on desktop or laptop computers.

**AD: How does the mobile device impact social media?**
**SK:** The evolution of the mobile device to include functions such as text mes-

saging, e-mail, and the mobile Internet has truly unleashed the power of real-time social media. Since contributions to social media can be made via the mobile device, people can add, update, post, follow, and friend, no matter where they are.

**AD: How do the advances in mobile technology affect today's real estate professional?**
**JL:** The mobile device of the present allows real estate professionals and firms to become more productive and efficient by cutting the cords created by traditional brick and mortar offices. They are no longer constrained to the confines of their desk for phone calls, e-mails, and information. Devices such as the BlackBerry, iPhone, and Android allow you to remain in constant communication and access all the information necessary to conduct your business in the field—such as, where the houses being sold are located. Furthermore, the size of that field—the geographic territories in which an agent can operate—is now expanded since agents don't need to be dependent on their physical office location.

**AD: In what other ways can mobile technology and your Mobile Real Estate ID system impact the real estate industry?**
**JL:** That's a great question, Allan. The advances in the technology of mobile devices are not only creating a new-found freedom for real estate professionals, but a new medium that real estate consumers are using to facilitate their search for information. These two factors have led to a number of innovations in mobile marketing programs that can be utilized to market real estate listings by connecting the agent and consumer through their mobile devices. The Mobile Real Estate ID system, which we have developed, is a perfect example of this. When implemented, a real estate agent or firm can leverage the 5 P's of our Mobile Real Estate ID system to create a mobile culture.
**SK:** In particular, as it pertains to social media, our Mobile ID truly allows someone to leverage his or her links. Your Mobile ID can be anything. Mine is my name. So if you text Seth to 88500, you will receive back a text message with my contact information and a link to my Mobile ID page. My Mobile ID page has information about me, my brand, and links to all of my social media outlets—Facebook, Twitter, my blog, LinkedIn, etc. It is the simplest and most efficient way to give people a way to follow me through the outlet of their choice. The Mobile ID is the gateway—the landing page to all of a person's links.

**AD: Can you elaborate about the 5 P's of Mobile Real Estate?**
**SK:** Well, first of all, Allan, John and I have *you* to thank for helping us to better package our real estate offering by suggesting that we introduce to the real

estate industry the concept of the 5 P's of Mobile Real Estate: Phoning; Property Promotion; Personal Branding; Prospecting; and an all-in-one Platform.

**AD:** You are most welcome, but all I did was give a name and concept to what you have already created and what is a phenomenal solution for real estate agents and companies. Please explain how your exciting mobile system works.

**SK:** We are happy to break down the 5 P's of Mobile Real Estate. Mobile Real Estate ID (MRE ID) is a comprehensive system for the incorporation of mobile marketing technology within the culture of the top real estate firms in the industry. The 5 P's of Mobile Real Estate outlined below detail the ways in which this system can shift and enhance the overall marketing efforts of agents, brokers, and brands by leveraging the mobile devices we all carry with us on a daily basis.

1. **Phoning:** With over 270 million mobile devices in the U.S. alone, the device itself provides us with the ability to make calls, send text messages, e-mail, and search the Internet. These capabilities provide real estate professionals with the ability to go across larger geographical territories with greater efficiency. The MRE ID platform connects calls, leads, and alerts directly to agents' mobile devices.

2. **Property Promotion:** Assigning a unique Mobile ID to each property listing allows buyers to access property information, pictures, and the listing agent's contact information directly on their cell phones via text message. They simply send a text message with the property's Mobile ID to a specific short code (i.e., text 123 to 88500). Mobile IDs can be used across all forms of property advertisements. For example, they can appear on the For Sale sign, in online advertisements, print advertisements, brochures, and direct mail pieces. When a real estate consumer clicks on the link for pictures within the text message, they are taken to a mobile Web page that not only allows them to see property photos but search for other listings through the mobile website.

3. **Personal Branding:** Agents will be branded in the text messages sent to consumers, in addition to having their own unique Mobile ID, which will allow them to brand themselves. The Mobile ID can be the agent's name or branding (i.e., text John to 88500). The agent's Mobile ID, similar to a property, will send back information via text message about that agent and include a link to the agent's mobile website. Mobile websites can range in functionality from a simple landing page with a picture and social media links (Facebook, Twitter, LinkedIn, etc.) to a complete site with a property search and a variety of additional features.

4. **Prospecting:** MRE ID allows firms and agents to reach potential clients in ways that have never before been possible. Each time a potential customer texts in to a Mobile ID for a property listing or agent, his or her cell phone number is captured and is simultaneously sent to the listing agent. This allows agents to follow up with that prospect

instantly. Furthermore, agents' Mobile IDs allow them to build a mobile database of prospects with whom they have spoken and networked. The Mobile ID also provides existing and former clients with a simple and efficient way to refer the agent—they can simply tell others to text their agent's Mobile ID to the specified short code.

**5. Platform:** The MRE ID platform allows brokers and agents to manage their entire mobile marketing solution in one easy-to-use portal. Brokers can track and manage all leads, generate reports, and send mass text and e-mail communications to all of their agents. Agents can track and manage all leads for their listings, generate reports, and customize messages. The platform will also provide detailed analytics with regards to mobile websites.

**AD:** Out of the scores of real estate agents who are now more successful because of your system, can you give me an agent or company that comes immediately to mind that we can use as an example?

**SK:** Ken Baris, of Jordan Baris, Inc. Realtors in Northern New Jersey, is a great example of a broker who has implemented the Mobile Real Estate ID system with great success. In his company's particular case, they wanted to make sure they provided their clientele—who they compare to upscale Nordstrom shoppers—with a second-to-none experience on the Mobile Web. They recognized that their clientele, who relied primarily on smartphones, was not able to access and navigate to their online website with the level of ease and ability they were used to, since the Jordan Baris website wasn't formatted for the mobile device. So, we took the look, feel, and content of their online site, and we streamlined and formatted it to fit any mobile phone with Internet access.

Once the Jordan Baris mobile site was created, we needed to make people aware of it and drive traffic to it. To do so, we leveraged the personal branding and property promotion features of the Mobile Real Estate ID system and created a unique Mobile ID for Jordan Baris. Now, anyone can text JB to 88500 and instantly get a text message back on their phone with a link to the mobile website. Furthermore, our phone detection software recognizes when a mobile browser is accessing the site and responds with the mobile website optimized for that particular handset as opposed to the traditional online site. In order to drive additional traffic, Ken implemented a unique Mobile ID for each property listing that the firm had and advertised the Mobile IDs on the For Sale signs. Each time a consumer texts in for a specific property, they are sent a link to a single property page within the Jordan Baris mobile site, where they can continue to search or learn more about the Jordan Baris brand.

Jordan Baris also uses the Mobile Real Estate ID platform in a variety of ways to connect with their agents on their mobile devices when they are out in the field. Not only do the leads from consumer text inquiries get routed directly to the listing agent's cell phone, but Ken uses the platform to send text message communications to the agents as well.

**AD:** How would you contrast the mobile technology assimilation process of most adults in North America versus real estate agents' adaptation for real estate purposes?

**SK:** Well, I think most adults in this country, certainly the 18-35 demographic, became extremely accustomed to mobile phones during the mid- to late-1990s, and as there were advances in technology. Younger adults don't look at it as their mobile phone; they look at it as their *phone*. And, households within that demographic are typically, and ever-increasingly, *only* mobile. They don't have a land line because they're home so little, or traveling, or whatever the case may be. So they don't see the need for traditional land lines. I think that, taking that to the next step, when you're getting into the demographic of 35- to 55-year-olds, the adoption of the mobile phone was obviously slower because this group didn't see the need for it; they were so accustomed to the land line. I think that's changing because of their need to communicate with their children and/or their grandchildren. There's a shift in overall communication methods across the country. People are now making fewer phone calls compared to the number of text messages they send on a monthly basis. So, just in terms of being able to communicate with those they know and love—their family members—they're forced to keep up and learn how to adapt to this technology. Not really because they *want* to, but because they *have* to.

**AD:** To what degree do you think the promulgation of hand-held devices has been responsible for Twitter's tremendous growth, because of the ease and convenience of responding to Twitter while on the move?

**JL:** Truth be told, without the mobile device, Twitter would never exist. Twitter was invented by two guys who were working for Google. As an innovation, Google let them release the product. Had there not been mobile devices, or the movement of mobile devices, Twitter would have been a product that *never happened*. Right now, Twitter sends the most text messages through the system from one single point, second only to 4INFO, which is a large, advertising text messaging ad server.

**SK:** And I would add that the mobile device and social networking overall go hand-in-hand because of the ease with which people can update Facebook statuses, tweet, and change their LinkedIn profiles. Whether you're updating your Facebook profile once a day or eight times a day, it wouldn't be nearly as easy to do if you couldn't do it from your mobile device. You're bringing what's actually going on in real time—while you're out there living your life—to the world of Facebook or the world of Twitter...and the mobile device is the conduit through which you can do that.

## Mobile Is on the Move

**AD:** What do you think is the single greatest benefit that mobile technology has brought to real estate careers?

**JL:** I believe that has yet to be defined. I'd say that, currently, the accessing of e-mail on the phone has made real estate agents more efficient in their day-to-day business. It has allowed them to do that from outside their office and not have to wait to get back to their office to respond to e-mails, and so forth. So, it allowed them to take that communication, while showing a house or doing a listing presentation, and respond back and close leads quicker.

**AD:** John and Seth, may I give you my perspective on the significance of mobile technology in terms of real estate careers?

**JL:** We would love to hear it. What are your thoughts?

**AD:** Well, for years, one of the reasons why so many real estate agents looked for business with limited success was because their manifest destiny was one that was very geographically limited. Many real estate agents' success was determined by the boundaries of their MLS. In my own company, people going from Saddle River to Woodcliff Lake, New Jersey—even though it was only a 30-second drive—thought they were crossing the Himalayas because of the MLS boundaries. And compounding that fact, many real estate careers were limited because if I were an agent who worked for Ridgewood Realty in the town of Ridgewood, New Jersey, the definitional confines of the town my company was named after automatically skewed my empowerment. If I went to another town and said, "Mr. and Mrs. Homeowner in Franklin Lakes, New Jersey, I'd like to represent you. I'm with Ridgewood Realty," I would be limited in what I could do for them. Back then, agents would even protect their farm areas, which also limited other agents. So, one of the reasons why so many agents never really exponentially gained in terms of income was because of the forces that defined their careers in such a way that it limited their geography…and the problem was exacerbated by their need to be constantly in one physical location.

So, in my opinion, mobile has been the emancipation of real estate careers because it's more in alignment with the agents' need to be on the move. So, even before considering all the applications or the greater utility of mobile technology, just the fact that agents are now not confined to the umbilical cord of the telephone or a PC on a desk, allows them to express their territory in new ways. Mobile is redefining their territory. All careers are defined by an addressable market and mobile technology is basically redefining addressable markets for Realtors because it's allowing them to be connected in real time to a vast marketplace. Because of that, it's as if Realtors have been launched from their offices and are now empowered, emancipated, and decentralized. This emancipation subconsciously even suggests to them to go out into the field. *It's not just what their mobile phone brings to them; it's also what it allows them to leave behind.* Because even if an agent's mobile phone is dead, even if it was working when she left the office but subsequently ran out of battery power, she is still more likely to be involved in the marketplace than to be tied down.

So mobile technology has ramifications for real estate professionals that doctors don't have, lawyers don't have, professors don't have, and students don't have. Therefore, it could be said that mobile technology is more valuable and indispensable to agents who want to exponentially increase their income than arguably any technology in existence heretofore. Is that making sense?

**JL:** Allan, you are making tremendous sense and are bringing out implications that are not always visible to the naked eye. Because, like you said, mobile, by definition, has changed the mentality of the real estate agent. For agents, their biggest weapon in battle is their mobile device because it's changed their thinking.

**SK:** Allan, your great observations lead me to my next thought, which is regarding your question about how mobile technology can revolutionize the real estate industry. Not only is it releasing the agents from the confines of their brick-and-mortar offices and their very tiny geographic territory, but as they transition their brand from the corner shop on Main Street to online and then bring their brand to the mobile phone, so that they can market to the consumer in an efficient manner on their phone, they have not only freed themselves, they've freed consumers to search for properties, making the entire transaction process more efficient for everyone involved.

**AD: How has mobile technology changed the dynamics of the relationship between consumers and Realtors?**

**SK:** I think it's changed the dynamic tremendously when you think about how things used to be done compared to the way things can be done today...if done right, and if implemented correctly. For example, I would guess that if you were working with a buyer many years ago, you would set up an appointment, they would come to the office, you'd show them which listings were available in the area, and then you'd physically take them to go see those listings. Then came the Internet, which was kind of the intermediary between the old days and where we are today. The Internet enabled you to bring your brand online and allowed you to give consumers your website URL so they could then search for homes online. Then you could go out and show those pre-selected properties to your potential buyers. Now, with mobile technology enabling agents' websites to be accessed via mobile devices, as well as making listing information available via text message, consumers are free to go out into a certain geographic area, or many geographic areas, with only their devices. But their agent's brand is still present with them and once consumers find the information they want, they can communicate with their agent to set up an appointment while they're out in front of a property or while they're two towns over.

**JL:** The short answer to that is that the mobile device has increased the potential efficiency level of agents.

**AD: I can't imagine there are many agents who are active in the business right now who are not using mobile technology to one degree or another. So, I would assume that your greater purpose is to help them discover the expanded functionality and utility they're not yet incorporating because they are not yet aware of it. Would you agree with that?**

**JL:** I totally agree, which is why we are confident that the way in which we are now positioning our value proposition as relating to the 5 P's of Mobile Real Estate will automatically offer real estate agents and companies a sort of "pilot's checklist" for how to employ mobile technology.

**SK:** Absolutely, especially—please forgive the pun—if they want to see their careers take off or get into a higher gear.

**AD: Most agents are using some version of mobile technology, but what aren't they using? What are some *not* using that they *should* be using?**

**SK:** I would venture to say that 99.9 percent of real estate agents are using some sort of mobile technology, even if it's just having a cell phone. I would say that what 90 percent of them aren't using are the mobile marketing solutions that allow them to promote their brand, their listings, and their content to their consumers via the mobile device. So they all have the hardware, but they've yet to find the application or the software or the solution that integrates them into their overall market. In other words, they are only using one of the 5 P's—Phoning—and none of the others.

**AD: Great answer, Seth. Now I'd like to know how real estate professionals can use their mobile devices to leverage their links.**

**SK:** When we think about our "links," this term has changed considerably over the past 24 months. Prior to that, if you mentioned your links, more often than not you would be talking about your website...possibly your blog, or even your e-mail address. Since then, we have witnessed a combination of things—the proliferation of social networking and social media combined with sophisticated mobile devices that allow you to feed information to all of these outlets no matter where you are.

Today, when talking about our "links," we are referring to not only our website, but to our Facebook, Twitter, blog site, LinkedIn, etc. The underlying success of these sites is owed to the mobile industry for creating device applications and networks that allow you to update your Facebook status, tweet, and blog constantly throughout the course of your day to detail your life and your work online. Conversely, since there are so many people now with so many links, how do you know where or how to follow them? What we have developed is the gateway to all of someone's social media links—their Mobile ID. Your Mobile ID can be your name, your business, anything you want it to be. When someone texts your Mobile ID to our short code (e.g., text John to 88500), they will receive back a message with one link. From this one universal gateway, followers can now choose the path they want to follow you on—Facebook, Twitter, YouTube, your blog, etc.

**AD: What is the technology that you represent?**

**JL:** Our Mobile Real Estate ID system is a system that we're introducing and making available to all agents. The Mobile ID system is the one gateway to all of your links. So, whether I'm talking at a networking function or at a speaking engagement, there's one point of entry on your phone. Right now, I have different "Follow Me's"—Follow Me on Facebook, Twitter, LinkedIn, my blog, and on YouTube. I can't put all of those on my business card, nor can I say that and get everyone in this room to follow me. However, I can bring you into my Mobile ID, which is a mobile-enabled Internet landing page—one that has all my links—and allow you, the consumer, or you, the networker, to pick which way you want to follow me. This way, I'm giving you one way into everything I do and that is the system we're bringing to the agents today.

**SK:** I would like to add to what John just mentioned with regard to the Mobile ID and the overall premise of what powers the different solutions we offer within the real estate industry—in particular, the Mobile Real Estate ID system. So, we have our Mobile Real Estate ID platform, which allows agents to assign a specific ID to an individual property. This allows potential buyers to simply send a text message and instantly receive back the information about that particular listing. Now, once the buyer gets that information back, where they go from there is all tailored to that agent. They may choose to go to the agent's mobile-enabled website or they may choose to learn more about that agent in particular, which is that agent's Mobile ID, where they can follow him or her on Facebook, Twitter, etc.

**JL:** They can also find other listings in the area.

**SK:** Yes, they can find other listings. Again, it goes back to the point about leveraging your links. By creating one little link for a single property listing, you've tied that link into your own personal Mobile ID link, your mobile website link, the links to other properties in the area—

**JL:** Your Facebook, your Twitter, etc.

## Mobile Is on the Move

**AD:** Can you give an example of how real estate agents are integrating their marketing needs with mobile-based technology?

**SK:** I can give you a great example of how an agent has incorporated mobile technology across all traditional forms of advertising. The gentleman, R. Ashley Brunner, of the Coldwell Banker agency, Brunner Burkhart Group in Lancaster, Pennsylvania, has marketing systems he uses for every listing he gets. It includes The Real Estate Book, print materials, a direct mail piece, TV advertisements, radio advertisements, and now, the mobile advertisement—the text messaging component on the For Sale sign of the listing. He has a unique code that he uses for the one property that tells him where each lead is coming from, anytime someone texts in, whether it be from the print ad to see additional pictures, or from the radio spot: "Great open house this weekend—text in to see the pictures first."

**AD:** What activities have survived from the pre-mobile days?

**JL:** Ten years ago, it was new for an agent to have a website that consumers could visit. What mobile has done, particularly the Mobile ID System, is bring things back to the beginning. We're using one URL—your personal URL, whether it be online or on mobile. You're still going to johnlim.com. What the system does is take everything else that should be on johnlim.com, like your Facebook icons, and enables that to the mobile device. So again, it goes back to the basics of promoting one website name, not many. On your business card, you're not going to put "Follow me at Twitter.com/john; Facebook.com/john." You're going to put, "Follow me at johnlim.com."

**AD:** John Featherston has always said that, if at all possible, every real estate-professional need regarding consumer contact and content distribution should be embedded into one's mobile solution. When do you see that happening?

**SK:** It's just a matter of time. For example, outside of this interview, Allan, you mentioned how you have religiously used a BlackBerry for the last seven years because you didn't want to be slowed down by a PC or laptop. *Mobile technology hasn't reinvented the wheel; it just made a more* efficient *wheel.* By the way, Allan, I have never seen anybody type as fast on a BlackBerry as you do, so I can appreciate how impatient you are regarding any product that might slow you down.

**AD:** Tell us about additional mobile efficiencies and usage.

**SK:** One of our core competencies is converting content for mobile devices. When we do so, we also create a mobile webpage, which is formatted to fit any mobile device with Internet access to host that content. Once we have created the page, we can then insert the link to that page into any outgoing text message or e-mail so those receiving the message on their mobile devices can view it properly.

**JL:** Now, if you took an article that was in an e-mail and wrapped it up into a link, Seth could come in and, with one push of a button, put that on his Facebook, and push it out to all of his distribution channels, all of his real estate networks. Now, when agents receive it, they won't get it as an e-mail; they'll just get it as a link, which they click on, and which then launches what looks like the e-mail. So it takes the e-mail function and makes it universal. You can even use it on Twitter. If you use Twitter, I couldn't copy that article because I'm limited to 140 characters. But agents could click on a link I send, which would automatically launch their Web browser, and then they could read the article as it came across their mobile device.

**SK:** I'd like to add to that point about a push campaign. One of the tremendous benefits of the Mobile ID system is that it creates the page with all of your different outlets—distribution channels like Facebook and Twitter—and one of the access points to that is the most universal access point in the world—the mobile phone. So I can become part of John's mobile ID network by texting the word John to 88500. Or he can send it to me via text message. Text messaging is the most common application in the world. More than three-quarters of cell phone users are using it on a daily basis. So, the real benefit is not only the fact that it's so common, but the fact that, if I'm in his network, he has my cell phone number. Because he has my cell number, besides putting content out across his Facebook and his Twitter, he can ensure that I get it by sending it out via text message. So, he can send a push campaign via text: "Hey guys, thought you might find this interesting: Here are 10 Ways to Appeal Your Property Taxes."

**AD:** Please explain to our readers why they should use text messaging that they pay for when e-mail is free?

**SK:** They would choose to text because the "open" ratio on e-mails sent is substantially lower than that of text messaging.

**AD:** Let me share with you what we are doing at Top 5 with mobile technology. We have taken our content and formatted it in such a way that each week our members can distribute, via their e-mail or social networking sites, a short, pithy real estate-related topic to their real estate social network that then encourages the consumer recipients to forward it to their friends. Now, while this process can also be facilitated through the use of a personal computer or laptop, we are finding that, just as Twitter is in a sense the synthesis of blogging and texting—which is why it is referred to as micro-blogging, and why Twitter is so popular on handheld devices—by keeping our Top 5 Real Estate Social Networking articles very brief, topical, and to the point, they have really been embraced by those who employ their mobile devices for content distribution.

**JL:** That's a great example of how content and consumers can be integrated into a mobile-promoted push campaign.

**AD:** There are communities being formed that are exclusively tied to mobile applications. For example, Friendster.com is a mobile social network specifically designed to be accessed exclusively through your mobile phone and text messaging. People have basically said, "We will form a community where we'll all just communicate in this mobile way." That said, do you think there will be an increasing number of social networks or communities that carry with them an explicit understanding or agreement that essentially all interactive communication will be via mobile?
**JL:** Yes, we completely agree.

**AD:** Let's move on to other topics. For one, how do you integrate voice with text for real estate purposes? At this point in time, are agents using their mobile device as a screen to make marketing presentations as they do on their laptops? How widespread do you project that practice to become?
**JL:** It is very feasible. It's starting to happen with the change from virtual tours to videos. You can now, via the target-marketing applications embedded in our Mobile ID system, target-market the video production of a property to the appropriate markets as opposed to being limited to the shotgun approach of You-Tube, which carries with it a totally different essence than a specifically targeted video-marketing campaign powered by mobile technology.

**AD:** Does your system interface with essentially all major mobile providers?
**SK:** Yes, our system has the capability to work on all devices. As long as the subscriber has activated text messaging, we can deliver content to his or her handset. If that subscriber has also activated the Mobile Internet on his or her device, then we can provide him or her with a much richer and more engaging experience.
**JL:** Our system is device-agnostic and carrier-agnostic. Nothing needs to be downloaded directly to the phone. Our mobile websites format to fit any phone with Internet access through unique handset recognition, which allows us to detect the device model, operating system, and browser when a link is clicked or accessed in order to send back the appropriate format for that device. Devices and carriers are changing all the time. We don't need to be updated on what phone you're currently using or what carrier you're with.

**AD:** What is your first step regarding integration?
**JL:** Well, to illustrate, we would create the Jane Smith Real Estate Mobile ID. We would pull the IDX listings from her MLS. We would then simply build her page by inserting her contact information, bio, picture, address, and whatever she desired. This mobile format would then generate an individually owned

and controlled real estate ID: JaneSmith.mccid.com.

**AD: Do consumers need to buy a dotmobile site to use Mobile Internet or can they use their existing dotcom site?**
**SK:** No, consumers do not need to purchase a dotmobile domain name. They can simply use their existing URL. Our phone recognition capabilities allow us to detect when someone is accessing the URL from a mobile browser and send the proper version of the mobile website for viewing on their device. While we know that there are two separate sites, the online and mobile versions, to the consumer it will act as one site formatted differently depending on their device.

**AD: How has mobile affected social networking platforms?**
**JL:** Without the mobile device, social networking platforms would not be as influential and powerful today.

**AD: What level do you believe most agents are at right now in terms of their mobile device usage? What are most using it for?**
**SK:** They're using it to communicate on the go—to make phone calls, send e-mails; correspond via text message.
**JL:** They're primarily using text messages to correspond with family members.

**AD: So the text message is more personal than professional?**
**JL:** Right now, yes.
**SK:** Although that is shifting. What I've heard from Realtors is that a lot more of their younger clients, the first-time home buyers, *only* communicate via text message. So agents have to communicate with them in this way.

**AD: What are the basic functions that most are using?**
**JL:** They're using the Mobile Internet primarily for search. The number-one use for Mobile Internet right now in the age group of 35–55 is for search—to find a location of either a restaurant or phone numbers.

**AD: What other things can real estate professionals do that they are not presently engaged in? And what can you do to help facilitate their mobile-based evolution?**
**SK:** What they *should* be using it for, and what we can help them with, is to promote their product. In the case of Realtors, their product is the listing that they're marketing. So they can use it to promote the individual listing; they can use it to promote their brand; and they can use it to coordinate and integrate the two. So, if someone comes to the listing first, they'll also get the brand; if someone comes to the brand first, they will also get the listing.

## Mobile Is on the Move

**AD:** There appears to be a mobile digital divide in the real estate industry between those real estate agents who always seem to gravitate to emerging technologies and others who cling to the traditional. Are you finding this to be the case in your extensive travels?

**SK:** Exactly. What we say all the time when we're out there talking to real estate agents is, "We know that there's a ton of stuff that you're hearing about mobile technology and that's going on around mobile. You all have phones, you're all hearing how important mobile technology is for you, and there are a lot of companies out there that offer a text messaging service, or an application, or a mobile web service, but none of them are showing you how to coordinate and integrate all of those things into a marketing platform."

**AD:** *It sounds as though your Mobile Real Estate ID system represents a simple solution for complicated careers.*

**JL:** That's very well put, Allan. I usually use a light switch to illustrate our thinking. For instance, I could sit here and talk to you about the complex technology that we use and how simple we have made it—the same way I could explain that when you turn your light switch on, the electricity goes through the wall, down to the building, down to the grid, down to the electric company—but nobody really cares. People just care that when you turn the switch on, the lights go on, and when you turn the switch off, the lights go off.

**AD:** I hope you are not saying that you "bring good things to life," because that marketing campaign has been taken. But seriously, how does mobile technology, when more fulsomely or robustly used, save agents and companies money?

**JL:** It increases the efficiency of individual real estate agents because, after all, time, as we always hear, is our most valuable possession. And it also leads at the company level, because company associates are a firm's single greatest asset to a more efficient deployment of their agent population. Therefore, the savings in terms of money and time are substantial.

**AD:** I'd like to end our interview by acknowledging that we have only really scratched the surface of the world and the wonders of mobile technology, specifically regarding how it relates to real estate brokerage application. This subject could be extended into a book by itself. Perhaps someday the two of you will write a book, but I know, for now, you are too busy enhancing the careers of real estate professionals and companies throughout North America. Thank you for contributing to *Leveraging Your Links*.

# Chapter 25

## The Power of Video

# Michael Krisa— "That Interview Guy"

**Allan Dalton:** Well, Michael, for starters I must acknowledge that I am somewhat struck by the irony of *me* interviewing *you*—a person widely accepted in the real estate industry as "That Interview Guy," but since I once watched Larry King being interviewed, it gives me comfort that I'm not in danger of incurring the wrath of the interview gods. Although, what I really want to have with you, as with all of our other mentors in this book, is a conversation.

So, let me begin by saying, Mike, that you've established yourself as a well-respected thought leader in real estate circles for many years now, and in many areas—for your knowledge and expertise, including the effective utilization of the medium of video online and, specifically, as it relates to the real estate industry. So why don't we begin by my asking you to trace your personal and professional journey for me, from when you first came into the real estate business up to this particular point in your career as it relates to and centers around the use of video online.

**Michael Krisa:** I like that, sounds good. I think if I were to sum it all up, Allan, curiosity is what's really driven me. The first modality was doing audio interviews and it started when I first got into the business as a practicing agent back in '88. I was fascinated by what it is that makes some agents successful while some aren't. It's that simple. My broker gave me a cross-directory with all of the street addresses and phone numbers and said, "Here's how you become successful: make phone calls," and I thought, "What an archaic way to do business." So I started going after the top producers in my marketplace, not so much my office because that was the "donut crowd," but I went after those individuals that were doing the 100, 200 transactions per year. I just asked them what they did and what I discovered was it was like mentoring, like Knights of the Round Table; they all studied *under* someone, a master, to hone their craft. And then people were asking me, well, how did I do this? So I took those and I recorded them and put them to the Web.

And then about six years ago, I was working with broker/agent Jim Hughes as his VP of Business Development and created this library of content, if you will. It was an ongoing audio series where I interviewed the Allan Daltons of the world—CEOs, coaches, trainers...the "Who's Who" of real estate. From there, we just expanded to the next natural modality, which was video. Four years ago, I noticed that video was exploding already within the Internet marketing field, but it hadn't yet graduated into real estate. I think I was one of the earlier adopters of video. I took my goofy style of doing interviews—but this time we did it with a camera—and went to NAR and other conferences and just interviewed the same people I had been interviewing, but added a whole different level of excitement with video. Now people could see us interacting and having fun.

**AD: I read some information, provided by the Pew Internet research people, which stated that more than 50 percent of online adults use the Web to promote online video and that more than 70 percent of broadband users are involved with online video, and that more than 50 percent share links to video with others and more than 70 percent receive video links. Given this incredible, compelling data, how would you rate the real estate industry's utilization, at this point in time, of video online?**
**MK:** We're still scratching the surface, Allan. I would equate it to a caveman inside of a cave with a brush versus people outside of a cave using laser printers. We're still so far behind in this industry to adopt it. And maybe it's the demographic. The average age of real estate agents is 55-plus. Maybe we're intimidated by the technology, but the agents that are doing it, Allan, are having phenomenal success.

**AD: That's great to hear. And that's why we're interviewing you, Michael, because you personally are a leader in this space and also you're so connected to the rainmakers—if you will, the video rainmakers—online throughout the industry. Michael, what would you say are the top uses of video that a real estate agent or a company can employ online?**
**MK:** From an agent perspective, and even from a broker's perspective, we know that people like to work with people who are like themselves...that "Principle of Like." So, I would say, Allan, that one of the first things you should be doing is testimonials. A broker uses testimonials for recruiting purposes; an agent uses testimonials for listings and getting more sales. Because when somebody comes to the website and sees heartfelt testimonials from clients, it's a slam dunk because it's unsolicited, and it has so much power because it's the human voice, which we're conditioned to relate to. The other thing is creating content— where we're actually educating potential sellers and buyers about the pitfalls of what they'll experience in real estate. Create a series that's going to educate the

consumer in terms of what they can expect through the real estate process. By doing that, you've got an educated consumer who's more likely to know, like, and trust you because they've had that experience with you online.

The other phenomenon that surrounds video is called the "Authority Principle." This goes way back to the '50s and '60s—when we saw people in white coats that played doctors on TV, we just automatically handed over that authority. Well, the same is true with online video. We cannot differentiate between a TV screen and a video screen. So that gives real estate practitioners an almost unfair advantage over their competition—by creating a series of content, they will be perceived as the authorities in their neighborhood.

Which brings up another point: let's say you don't have listings at the moment. Well, video is a natural extension of the neighborhood you're in. You could be out there doing reviews of pertinent points of interest, restaurants and tourist destinations so that when you've got clients that are coming from out of town or out of state, they already feel familiar with the place they're moving to. This is great for corporate relocations. To make a short answer long, Allan, I think the only restricting factor when it comes to video is your imagination.

**AD: Those are great applications. It's interesting you referenced the '50s and '60s because perhaps one of the greatest illustrations of the power of video when it's used properly happened during that time, specifically the Kennedy-Nixon presidential debate. Senator Kennedy won the debate on television but lost it on the radio. So it just shows you the magic of imagery. But that also calls into question how professional a video has to be in order to create that favorable response.**

**MK:** If you're talking to videographers that are doing this for a living, of course they're going to say it has to be spot-on professional. The example that I'd like to use is a horror movie that came out about 11 years ago. It was called *The Blair Witch Project*. And that was probably the shakiest video you'll ever see because it was shot with handheld cameras. It was gritty. It was almost guerrilla-style and the budget they used to produce that film was $250,000. To date, it has grossed over $250 million. So my point to anyone who's thinking about getting into video: guerrilla-style works. What people want is good audio and they want good content. Give them something in a story format they can relate to, and that they'll get entertainment and knowledge from, and they'll be engaged.

**AD: That's interesting that you reference *The Blair Witch Project*. I saw the movie, but the shaky video was almost purposeful and strategic because it gave the person a sense that someone was running and being chased in the woods and it was very destabilizing. I'm just wondering for those readers of the book that are really looking to get more engaged in video, how much of**

a difference, in your view, does quality make between them producing something of a personal nature, where it might be more generally accepted if it is of a lower quality, as opposed to when filming somebody's home and marketing a property? In that case, do you need to use a tripod to take away that whole shaky sense? Some of these video jobs that you see are very, very shaky.

**MK:** Some of the cameras that are available today, Allan, are so reasonably priced. They have stabilization software that's built into them, so you can get a really good quality shot. Cameras that used to be $50,000, $60,000, are now selling for under $1,000. So in terms of the equipment necessary to be able to shoot good video, it's out there. There are even entry-level cameras right now in the $200 range that will do an adequate job. I would say to you that the most important thing, aside from the shakiness, is knowing ahead of time what it is that you expect this video to do. So, the old adage is: what is your intended outcome before you even start producing this?

**AD:** Not only do we see video being distributed online but now with the whole magic of handheld devices and video on a cell phone—which I've read is up about 52 percent from last year—how does that further change the role of video in the career of a real estate agent?

**MK:** Well, let's look at the news industry where video and movies have been pertinent for as far back as we can remember. Videos, actually handheld video or amateur video, have revolutionized the way in which the news is being delivered now. Because anybody with a cell phone, in essence, is now a news reporter. And if they have a WordPress blog, they're actually now competing against news agencies that are no longer sending out news reporters because they have people living in those areas. If we jump back into a real estate perspective, you now have local practitioners who can be recognized as the authorities in their area because they're shooting videos, introducing their community's pertinent points—the shopping, the religious centers, the amenities, etc. By utilizing video, Realtors gain a tremendous advantage over their competition.

**AD:** In terms of the use of video in the marketing of property, what percentage of real estate professionals would you estimate are currently employing video to market properties online? I mean, really hosting a video and marketing it properly as opposed to a virtual tour?

**MK:** I would say single digits at best, Allan. Four percent, maybe, at the most.

**AD:** And why do you think that is?

**MK:** I think, if you look at the real estate landscape, per se—and you would know this better than I with REALTOR.com and your relationship there, once upon a time—the average Realtor has a website. So, in a business like this, it's incumbent upon you to have a professional image and to at least have a website. Since video is relatively new, I would have to say that only 4 or 5 percent of Realtors right now are using it.

**AD:** Given how much easier it is for some agents to post a video on their blog along with text, versus just text, you would think that more Realtors would be employing video on their blog. What is your sense of how prominent this has become?

**MK:** According to recent statistics I saw on YouTube, the average visitor who comes to a website that has video will stay there for six minutes. The average visitor who comes to a site that only has text will stay there for 57 seconds. That's a *dramatic* increase. And the other difference, too, is in terms of conversion—and I'm looking outside of real estate into direct-response marketing online. Sites that have video have a 12 percent higher conversion rate, meaning that somebody will actually buy something or be engaged enough to put in an e-mail address or supply some kind of information to the recipient of that website.

**AD:** Those are compelling statistics, Michael. I liked what you said earlier about employing video for the purposes of testimonials, either for the Realtor or the company. Testimonials obviously have been prominently used offline for centuries, but the difference with online video is it really promises to become a lot more viral. You know that people who appear in a video will send a link to their friends. So, I would think that's a great way to create a real support campaign within the community by involving and co-opting members of the community on the video. You have an extensive retinue of professional real estate agents who follow you. Are you seeing a lot of agents getting video testimonials and then having consumers pass it on to people they know?

**MK:** Oh, absolutely. And I would take it one step further. The real savvy agents who are using video are now engaging the seller. They record the walk-through of the home. Who could be more emotional, more passionate, more experienced at being able to tell a story about a house than somebody who's lived there for the past 10, 15, 20 years? And so now you've got this really heartfelt story that's being told firsthand by the seller and we know that, in all likelihood, the prospective buyer who's going to come to that house is going to be attracted to that same thing the seller was attracted to. So the Realtor, in essence, is taken out of this equation and it's no longer a selling proposition; it's almost like inviting someone in—here's an invitation to be a part of my home.

**AD:** Many years ago at my company, I created a program that I called the Co-operative Showing Suggestions. The program involved having the agent and the seller cooperate in the writing of a showing strategy, which was unlike highlight sheets and feature sheets. The showing strategy was a co-produced narrative for training purposes that we would then, back in those days, fax to potential showing agents who might not have inspected the property. So, Michael, are you seeing any real estate agents who are involving homeowners in the production of videos for the purpose of educating other agents before they bring their buyers?

**MK:** Oh, absolutely. And I see agents that are taking it one step further, Allan, where they're actually showing some of the *deficiencies* of the home. That way, when a prospective buyer or agent does tour that home, he or she is already aware of potential problems ahead of time. They don't have to start making excuses. Now, you have an educated, cooperating broker and you have an educated potential buyer who are both aware of any flaws ahead of time.

**AD:** Are you saying agents are also using videos for seller disclosure purposes to document problems within the home? Is that really taking place?

**MK:** Absolutely. One of the best things you can do for credibility, as opposed to saying "everything here is perfect," is if you can actually show some of the faults in your product. That just makes you come across as more sincere and more trustworthy. The same is true of a Realtor who's saying, "Here's a great house. It has some fantastic amenities, but look here, here's something: the roof may be a bit dodgy. The shingles are fifteen years old. We know the extended life is maybe seventeen, so the roof may have to be done soon." Or, "Here are some landscaping issues." By pointing these things out ahead of time, it gives that Realtor more credibility and the house more credibility as well.

**AD:** Again, something I did years ago was a program called "Neighbors Know Best," where we would go out and ask the neighbors of a particular property what they liked about the neighborhood most, and then we would do a brochure that had all of the neighbors' comments. Are you seeing agents who are interviewing people within a community and producing a video for that particular property's value within the community?

**MK:** Brian Copeland is a Realtor who gets it. His site is nashvilleandbeyond.com. He's out there with video and he's going to the local markets; he's filming the local streets. When you watch Brian's videos, you feel so engaged that, number one, you just love, trust, and want to work with Brian. That's a given after you've watched some of these videos. But you almost feel like you know Nashville as much as a resident does. I've never been to Nashville but I feel like I could walk up and down some of these streets, Allan, and actually take you out for a coffee and feel quite comfortable about where we're going. That's the power that video conveys. It makes us feel like we're a part of something even though we've never been there.

**AD:** That sounds wonderful, and what I'm specifically saying Michael is just imagine if an agent came to your home and said, "I'm marketing a property seven houses down and I'm interviewing everybody on the street. There's going to be a video that will be provided online and at the open house." I'm calling it "Neighbors Know Best." Wouldn't you think, Michael, that that would be one way to get the entire neighborhood involved because they have a vested interest in what the home sells for? It's almost like an IPO, an initial property offering, where you're taking not only the property—but the street—public and involving the entire street in that property where people will want to say, "Wow, I definitely want to say something good about living on this street because that's going to affect the value of my home."

**MK:** Oh, *think* of the viral nature of what you just said here, Allan. You can get a WordPress blog for free and give everybody in that neighborhood the URL so they can go there. You can bet that if they're on the video they're going to want to see it. And if they're there and they see themselves, they're going to send it to Aunt Betty and all of their relatives, friends, family, and coworkers. Suddenly that Realtor is at the center of this web and everything is going out virally—all he had to do was be nice.

**AD:** Regarding composing a video, how do you recommend that Realtors upload their video content to video-sharing sights in a way that drives traffic back to their websites and blogs?

**MK:** Basically, you would be uploading videos. I'd start off by having my own site. I personally use WordPress because it's so easy for me to navigate and I don't have to be dependent on a web developer, so I can automatically post my videos there. For somebody who just wants to get something up, quick and dirty, there's YouTube, Viddler and a whole host of social video sites that are free and automatically convert your video to make it Web-ready.

The downside of doing something like that, Allan, when you're depending on YouTube or another similar site, is that you're being held hostage by a third party. So, it's free today but they can decide to change the game tomorrow and say, "By the way, based on X number of clicks or number of videos, we're going to be charging a monthly fee." At that point, if all of your videos are hosted on YouTube and you're just putting the embed links on your site, you really can't say no. You're stuck.

**AD:** That's a great perspective. The name of this book is *Leveraging Your Links*. How do you suggest Realtors use video both to improve their page rankings on sites like Google, and also to entice their friends, fans, and followers to either pass on the link or to visit their website or blog?

**MK:** I think that with any marketing ploy, number one, you have to determine what your strategy is. For example, is this something I'm doing for search engine ranking, and if so, what am I being ranked for? Am I trying to be a specialist in a certain neighborhood and that's what I'm targeting? If that's the case, I would probably create a series of content for, let's arbitrarily say, Hanover, Ontario. My content might read: "Here are the 15 things that every savvy home buyer should know," and then I would write those out as 15 questions and then I would shoot a one-minute video to address each one of those questions. I would then upload it simultaneously to YouTube and to all the different sites that I could think of with long-tail key terms. That would be a slam dunk for creating localized traffic.

**AD:** Absolutely. Given the fact that Realtors do not wish to violate the boundaries of friendship on social networking sites with self-serving video streams, what are some of the best uses of general-interest videos for specific communities that you've seen Realtors employ?
**MK:** Allan, when you say "self-serving," I think you instead have to look at what you're doing, if you're living in that area, almost as a public service. I'm showing you who I am. Let's say, in my area here, I just happen to be kayaking up and down the Saugeen River. Well, for people who are thinking about moving here, it's a matter of lifestyle. So they see me engaged in what I'm doing in my natural element, which is Michael being Michael outside. In essence, they get to know me, but they're also getting to experience what I do recreationally and they know that I'm a Realtor because it's on my site. So it's almost like you get to convey the best of both worlds: here is who I am as a person; here is who I am as a professional…without my having to beat them over the head by standing on a coffee table and thumping my chest, saying, "I am Realtor!"

**AD:** I read a statistic that said that any video over 90 seconds loses 75 percent of those who clicked on that video. What are your thoughts in terms of length?
**MK:** The sweet spot for me, Allan, is usually three to five minutes, but let's go back a step. People will watch content if it's pertinent to what they're looking for and if they're engaged. So, I've watched videos online that are 30 minutes long. Why? Because they were about a subject matter that I'm interested in. When I was putting together my blog, I wanted to understand how to use WordPress. The videos that I was watching, a series of tutorials, had ten parts that were thirty minutes long. So did it serve my interest? Absolutely. Was I engaged? Absolutely. Now if it was somebody that had no interest in WordPress, he or she would watch the first five seconds and be disengaged. So, in answer to your question, if the content you're creating is pertinent to what that person is looking for, they will stay on and they will watch it.

**AD:** Absolutely. The only way we have access to people is through their concerns. Can you give me some examples of agents who are employing video for the short sale and the REO markets?

**MK:** For me it's always been about "leading with a giving hand." If I can educate a consumer ahead of time about what they're going to experience through the short sale process, I think, overall, that makes the process that much easier and creates that much more of a professional image for the Realtor. So, Tim Burrell comes to mind as someone who's doing this. He's a RE/MAX agent, short sale master, and that's exactly what he's doing on his website. He educates sellers as to what they'll experience through the short-sale process. By creating that series of video content, he's taken himself out of the equation so people can go there and just learn. In essence, they're qualifying themselves. And then it's up to them to raise their hand and say, "You know what? Here's somebody that I know, like, and trust. I think it's time to call him."

**AD:** Some lenders have stated that, for short sales, the homeowner and the agent have to show a world-class marketing effort because sometimes lenders are suspicious that the real estate community might just be looking to cash in on the property that has no equity for the homeowner and try to get the lender to accept what the market will bear, as opposed to trying to influence the value of the property. So, I'm wondering if there are many agents who are using video—as they're putting together short-sale packets or as they're trying to get REO business—not just to educate consumers about the short-sale process or about buying foreclosures, but to add a higher level of elegance to properties that have too often been tarnished definitionally by words like "foreclosure," "short sale," and "REO." I would think these lenders and financial institutions, who naturally want to protect their equities, would really appreciate somebody who highlighted the virtues of these properties by the use of a video that would enhance the property's celebrityhood.

**MK:** Am I aware of agents doing that? No. *But*, you can bet that once we get off this call, I'm going to be telling a number of them that this is something they should now add to their arsenal.

**AD:** Well, Michael, that's the purpose of this book: to bring as many valuable ideas to our readers as possible. And in this case, if I were a lender, when an agent said, "This is the most the property can command," I would immediately think, "Have you really put in an absolute world-class effort or have you just been capitulating to a down marketplace?" I would wonder if that agent was truly trying to do something remarkable for this property. And, I would think a lender would be impressed by an agent who said, "Everybody's in the newspapers, everybody's on the Internet, but I *enhanced* my marketing of this short sale. I did a feature-home ad and I did a video on the property." And, from the buyers' perspective, when they see a property in a really well-produced video, it gives that previously tarnished property a rebirth within the marketplace.

Mike, since video is such a powerful tool, why do you think we haven't seen it on the Web sooner?

**MK:** I think a lot of it has to do, Allan, with the fact that our computers weren't strong enough in terms of memory and hard drive. They just weren't there yet. And now computers are so cheap, memory is so cheap, that that hurdle has been tackled. Number two would be access to broadband or high-speed access. It's ubiquitous now across North America. Almost everybody has access to high-speed Internet. The third reason was the lack of software that would allow video to be streamed over the Net. And that was conquered with Adobe Flash. The other thing was the cost of production—the actual video equipment. Now you can get a great video camera for a couple hundred bucks. So, suddenly, with a laptop computer, video, and some editing software, in essence, Allan, you can do what TV studios would have to pay a million dollars for. On a simple laptop, you can now shoot, edit, and upload to the Web. I mean, that's amazing...and then add to that the fact that you can now tie it all together using a program like WordPress. We now have all the tools of production at our fingertips and the cost to do this is pennies. Pennies on the dollar.

**AD:** Michael, I'm of the opinion that video will also be very, very important regarding fee validation. With the evisceration of classified advertising offline because consumers are going online, one area has been taken away that was perceived by consumers as being an expense and a sacrifice. I can't imagine that Realtors are not going to want to exponentially increase their use of video for all homes, but especially expensive homes—where homeowners are paying tens of thousands of dollars in fees. What are your thoughts?

**MK:** Just look at what's going on around us. How can you possibly do justice to a property by taking one static picture and running it in a newspaper? Using the movie *The Untouchables* as an example, it's like bringing a knife to a gunfight. I look at the *New York Times* and the *LA Times*. They're actually contracting the size of their newspapers to save money. They're now running their newspapers in the late afternoon so that they can have the freshest news possible to save costs. The writing is on the cyber wall, Allan. Consumers are going online. When I look at numbers regarding YouTube—and granted these are 2008 numbers—72 million new unique visitors per month go to YouTube to watch video. That's 4.7 *billion* page views per month. Those numbers are staggering. What possible publication in print could ever match that? That aside, compared to that static picture, think about how much more you can do to paint a picture of the home by using video, by using audio, by touching all the modalities that are needed to spark human emotion and get consumers engaged.

**AD**: Exactly, and those are great qualitative aesthetic reasons, but what I'm also saying is that if you can't demonstrate or display that there's some significant and perceived cost and effort in what you're doing on behalf of the home seller, possibly something that they can't do on their own, I think it's going to be increasingly more difficult for fee validation, given the fact that the onerous need to be in the newspapers is going to be something of the past, and at least that was something that the home seller could fight for—to have more advertising. We want them now to really appreciate that video is over and above classified advertising. The other thing I'd like to ask you, Michael, is that given the fact that IDX has neutered, in a sense, the benefit or the differentiation of most Realtors because everybody's properties are everywhere and everybody else's properties are on your site as well, isn't video usage even more necessary?

**MK**: Absolutely. Even when you use something like IDX, you can only utilize static pictures versus using video, which has all the modalities covered.

I think the other part that we really haven't touched on is the ability to show a prospective seller what the reaction to their home is...what the numbers are. If you use something like Google Analytics, you can actually track the number of people that have watched that video, that have played it in its entirety, that have been even remotely interested in that property. This means we can now say to home sellers, "Look, we've had 3,000 visitors to our site. Here's how long, on average, they stay, and when they look at *your* home, Mr. and Mrs. Seller, they reject it after the first 30 seconds. Maybe there's something wrong with price or maybe it's a matter of the aesthetics. There's something we have to adjust because the numbers don't lie." What we've done here with video is we've armed the savvy Realtor with more tools, with more pertinent facts, that they can use in their defense to justify what they're doing online to help that seller.

**AD**: Absolutely. And, given the fact that there are video home-marketing companies that are enticing home sellers to use them instead of using their real estate professional, and given the fact that a non-Realtor, a non-real estate professional, can sell homeowners a professional video tour of their property and then distribute it online, doesn't that make it even *more* absurd for real estate professionals not to do that as well?

**MK**: I think, Allan, gone are the days of validating your worth by merely stating, "I'm worth it." Yet there are so many agents who still say, "I am worth six percent" and when you ask the question, "Why?" most didn't bother learning the answer. Video is another tool in your arsenal and if you don't use it...your competition will.

**AD**: Not just your *industry* competition, but people *outside* the industry.

**MK**: Yes, outside. We're such an inbred entity in real estate. We don't look over the fence to see what's happening outside. For instance, I can see ahead of time, if I need a knee surgery, exactly what the surgeon's going to do—in live time, they show the exact operations. So I'm educated and I know what to expect. Why is it that we haven't brought those core strengths into real estate to show consumers exactly what it is we do and how we do it and then justify what we do?

**AD: Would you recommend that every Realtor, when calling an expired listing home seller, say, "Folks, was there some reason why there wasn't a video story of your home online? If I were your agent that is the first thing I would do."**
**MK:** Oh, absolutely.

**AD: That's a very powerful, specific thing to point out when a home hasn't sold: "Was there some reason why your agent didn't do a video story on your property online, Mr. and Mrs. Homeowner?" And they'll say, "Oh my God! Sheesh! Wow! Why didn't they?"**
**MK:** I remember at one of your speaking engagements, one of the things you were addressing was: Is it a matter of price? If all that's involved is price to sell a house, and I remember you said this, you could have a basement full of dead bodies, but if it's priced right, the home will sell. Well, how ludicrous is that?

**AD: Because if all there were was price, there wouldn't be so many homeowners today saying they're going to wait until the market changes, because their home can sell right now but they don't like the price. So, obviously, it's more complicated than sometimes we put forth as an industry. Let me ask you this, Michael: Do you ever see the day—because the whole concept of rankings is so important in social media and social networking along with recommendations—that we'll give consumers the opportunity to rank properties that are being marketed online with video?**
**MK:** That's an interesting proposition because we're seeing that now. Customers are ranking the experience they've had at restaurants; they rank the experience they've had with a certain doctor. It's now starting to trickle into real estate where they're ranking the services they received from that particular Realtor. So, it's not much of a leap to say, "Will they be ranking properties?"

**AD: Let me ask you another question, Michael, from a housekeeping standpoint. What type of video camera would you recommend that somebody buy, or consider buying?**
**MK:** I think right now, entry level. But first, let's decide what it is you want to be doing with that camera. Will you be outside shooting testimonials or are you going to be sitting in front of your computer? You could use a simple webcam if you're planning to keep your butt stationary.

But realistically, if you're going to do testimonials, if you're going to do walking tours, that kind of thing, the easiest camera right now is the Flip Video Camera. It's about $150. The high-def version is about $200. It has a big red button that you press and now you're in business. It uploads automatically to YouTube. The downside is it doesn't have an external mike jack so the sound quality is dodgy. And one of the things that I was taught about video is that a good video is 70 percent *audio*. This brings us to the next camera, which I've been working with, which is called a Kodak Zi8. It's about $200. It's a great entry-level, it fits into your back pocket, you can plug in an auxiliary microphone, it has flash memory and all the bells and whistles—and it also shoots photos. So, it's a fantastic entry-level camera that does a phenomenal job.

**AD:** I know you can post high-resolution clips on YouTube. Can you do the same thing on most agent sites?
**MK:** Well, are you asking me about high-def versus standard def? Computer screens really don't do high-def; it's more related to TV screens. High-def is what they call 16 by 9, which is a more rectangular looking video player versus more of a square, which is the 640 by 280, I believe. So, I wouldn't really be worried about high-def. The cheater's way around it is just shooting wide-angle and you'll create that same appearance of high-def...the 16 by 9 look.

**AD:** That's great insight. In your opinion, who are some of the agents that are most effectively using video?
**MK:** I like what Ian Watt is doing. Ian Watt is a Canadian Realtor out of Vancouver, Canada (www.ianwatt.ca). This is a dedicated guy, Allan. Every single day, he's got his Flip video camera on the dashboard of his car and he shoots a two-minute video while he's driving to work, and he'll tell you what's happening in the market, he'll assess a certain property, he'll talk about condos for sale, he'll also talk about the state of the union in terms of what's happening in real estate, and he doesn't hold any punches. He'll come right out and say, "You know, some Realtors are lazy. They're not doing this, that, and the other thing." Other times he'll praise them. So, he's kind of a contrarian in that he wants to stir things up. That's an interesting site to take a look at.

**AD:** Michael, it's not surprising that your first example of a person who's that evolved would be from Canada. It's always been my experience that a high percentage of the most sophisticated real estate professionals in North America are from Canada. They're always willing to come to the U.S. to attend conferences and conventions but very few U.S. Realtors go to Canada for conferences. So Canadian agents have the best of both worlds and, because of that, many are the most sophisticated real estate agents in North America.
**MK:** Well, when you're under snow eight months of the year, Allan, it gives you

a reason to want to get out...and it gives you a lot of time to think.

**AD: Canadian real estate agents know everything about real estate in Canada as well as everything we know about real estate in the U.S. So, they know much more than most agents in the United States.**
**MK:** We're too humble to say it. Another guy who's pretty good is Tom Everitt, a Realtor who is the sales and marketing director of thinktom.com. He's another Canadian Realtor and he's got an interesting site. He proves that you don't have to spend a lot on a set. If you look at his, it's fairly professional. He put up a piece of drywall in his garage, painted it red, hung up some stuff on it, and now he shoots a daily broadcast in his garage. It has created such notoriety that the local TV station has actually come into his garage to film him doing an episode. This just shows the amazing power of video.

**AD: I would think, Michael, that one of the great benefits of video is that it's caused us to evolve as an industry from sending preordained direct mail letters to providing real estate content. What you're describing creates a sense of a real estate news show, one that's live, interactive, and daily.**
**MK:** What are some of the hottest shows on television right now? It's these reality-based TV shows. I think there's this voyeuristic nature that's in us that makes us want to look over somebody's shoulder to see what they're doing. And these types of programs satisfy that need, so if you're fairly articulate, you can get up in front of a video camera and put on a pretty good reality show.

**AD: I read once that when people do video online, the single biggest mistake they make is that they try to be funny...because everybody has a different sense of humor. Would you agree with that?**
**MK:** I have a tendency to be two sentences ahead of my brain at any given time, so for me, it's a toughie to bite my tongue at times. I would say, Allan, that the best thing you can be is yourself...because everyone else is taken. So, again, in real estate, some people have a tendency, once they put a suit on, to try to be more than they really are. They try to speak and use mannerisms that are really not them. And video captures that. My advice would be to practice. Get up in front of the camera until you feel comfortable and, if you're Allan Dalton, just be Allan Dalton. If you're Michael Krisa, be Michael Krisa. Your true self is going to come out on the video. If you happen to have a sense of humor, that will come out. I wouldn't try to force it. People will identify with you because of who you are. If you're not being sincere on video, when your viewers finally meet you face-to-face, they will sense that and they will disengage with you personally. So why do that? The video, the whole nature of video, Allan, is that it gives you such a distinct opportunity to create that trust, that friendship, *and*

it's being done online while you're working on something else. It's a wonderful thing if you look at it that way.

**AD:** What suggestions can you give to our readers regarding how they should dress, or appear, when making a video?

**MK:** I guess it goes back to what your personality type is and how you conduct your business with clients. For me, I'm fairly casual, so what you see on video is what you see when we get together, unless it's some kind of posh function, where I'll wear a suit. But again, I would suggest being yourself. If you're someone who's comfortable wearing a suit or a professional dress, that's the way you should be, because that is the audience you're trying to speak to. If you're like a Tupper Briggs, a real estate agent in Evergreen, Colorado, it's a lifestyle thing—they're outside in shorts and skiing...they're selling the lifestyle. So, going back to what we talked about earlier, Allan, first determine what you're trying to sell. What's the end game? Determine that and then work your way backwards.

**AD:** How can a real estate professional get hits on his or her site regarding a particular property?

**MK:** I'd be looking at long-tail key terms that will drive traffic to my site and position me as the authority in that particular area.

**AD:** And obviously, the more granular or specific or refined, the more powerful that becomes.

**MK:** Absolutely, and it's a tradeoff, too, because if I say, "Homes for Sale in L.A.," well, obviously I'll get millions of hits but is that quality? However, if I drill it right down to waterfront condos in Newport Beach, and even take it down to a ZIP code, I will get less in terms of numbers but I will get better results in terms of quality of lead.

**AD:** How do you feel about a Realtor hiring a professional to make a video?

**MK:** I guess if you can't do it yourself, if you don't want to invest the time to learn, if you don't want to hire a high school kid to come out—and think about it, kids today are already doing this anyway, Allan—if you want to hire a professional and spend thousands, if you've got that budget, then so be it. But again, what's the outcome? What is it that you expect? Just because you've spent $1,000 or $2,000 on a professional-looking video, now that you have it in your hands, how is that video any different from the professional postcards and slick advertisements that agents used to spend thousands of dollars on—that would sit on their desks and they would never use?

## The Power of Video

**AD:** In terms of the application that some refer to as the third or fourth screen—mobile devices—what are some of the nuances or various uses of video on the mobile medium that are different than online?

**MK:** You're talking about an application on a cell phone?

**AD:** Yes, as opposed to Web-based.

**MK:** I would keep it short, succinct, and one- to two-minutes tops. Make sure you're delivering exactly what it is they're looking for; if it's a basic tour of a home, then drive them to a website. For cell phone applications, I'd want to keep them impactful, short, and with a call-to-action at the end to drive them somewhere for more information. Employ some distinctive call-to-action that's going to get that viewer to do something.

**AD:** Is there anything else you'd like to share with the readers?

**MK:** I think the one thing that you and I talked about earlier, prior to this interview, was the distinction between social media and social marketing.

**AD:** Yes, how would you make the distinction and how does it apply to the world of video?

**MK:** When we talk about social marketing versus social networking, I believe that social networking is a digital extension of what we do in person when we walk into a room and we meet people. The difference is, because it's online, we now have the potential of touching hundreds of thousands of people. I think the breakdown is when agents mix up the two—social networking and social marketing or media. Media are the modalities that you're using to engage that prospective person to build a relationship. So is it audio, is it print, is it video? Of those, video seems to be the most impactful because it touches all the modalities and it gives the viewer the opportunity to know, like, and trust you that much quicker.

**AD:** Mike, that's a great distinction and a great summary.

**MK:** Thank you, Allan.

**AD:** Is there anything else that you'd like to share with the readers?

**MK:** Just that if they want to see video in action, in terms of what I'm doing, thatinterviewguy.com is how I'm helping Realtors by sharing interviews. The style isn't perfect—I call it guerrilla-style—but at least they can see how easy it is. And if I can do it, they can do it.

**AD:** Michael, I want to thank you very, very much. It's a privilege to have you in the book and I look forward to further conversations—maybe even interviews!

**MK:** My pleasure, Allan.

# Chapter 26

# Meet Real Estate's Internet Crusader—Saul Klein

## Saul Klein

CEO, Point2 Technologies

http://Point2.com

**Allan Dalton:** Saul, I'd like to hear your perspective on social networking and social media, in terms of the real estate industry.

**Saul Klein:** Social networking is a name given to online networking using what we generally refer to as Web 2.0–type tools. The Internet did not create social networking. "Social networking" has been around for as long as there have been people on Earth; we just called it "networking." Now, the medium has been augmented to include the Internet in general and the Web specifically. Real estate sales is a "people business" *and* a "networking business." The greatest tool to facilitate human interaction (networking) is the Internet. Realtors, therefore, must learn how to network in this new environment in order to make sales.

Making sales involves establishing rapport, building trust and confidence, and closing the deal, and getting referrals. Establishing rapport takes time and effort. You have built rapport with many people over your life with whom you have subsequently lost contact. Social media allows one to re-establish communication with people you "knew in another life" who may need to buy or sell a house—and if you have re-established contact, you have the potential to win that listing.

The Internet environment was not invented for the real estate industry. The industry must, therefore, learn how to integrate the capabilities of today's social networking functionality into the prospecting, home buying, and home selling process. When we first were introduced to e-mail, many were skeptical that it would ever be of any value beyond sending jokes to friends. We have since learned of the business power of e-mail. The same holds true for social networking; people will learn how to adopt (or is it adapt or both?) this technology to ensure the prosperity of their businesses. Social networking allows Realtors to remain at the "center of the conversation" about real estate.

## Meet Real Estate's Internet Crusader — Saul Klein

Realtors are being sold a bill of goods regarding social networking. It is not about social networking for real estate sales. It is about social networking because that is what people do; they network. The systems on how to maximize the time one spends online will come in time. But the problem exists right now and some people are asking, "When will I have time to engage in social networking?" It is a matter of priorities. Don't watch *CSI* or *Desperate Housewives* and you will have a few extra hours a week.

Have you ever known a Realtor who has been going to the same community lunch every month for 20 years and has never obtained a listing or a buyer from the group, yet he or she keeps going back? Much of one's prospecting efforts are fruitless. Eliminate the fruitless and experiment with "social media."

**AD: Could you provide us some background on the creation of NAR's e-PRO Technology Certification Program?**

**SK:** I designed and wrote the entire course. John Reilly was my editor. Mike Barnett worked with our developer to create the platform to my specifications. I proposed the idea to NAR when the REALTORS® Information Network (RIN) was launched. I knew that the initiatives proposed by NAR would fail without proper socialization and education. Not enough Realtors were going online. John, Mike, and I launched a crusade to educate Realtors as to the benefits of being online and to drive as many of them online as possible. We had also created RealTown and RealTalk, the first conceptual social networking communities in the real estate industry. We believed then, as now, that there is a power in connecting with others—i.e., "No one is as smart as everyone," the "Wisdom of the Crowds," etc.

**AD: How are social networking and social media impacting real estate careers, and how will they affect careers in the future? Why do you think so many agents are crying out that they are not getting results?**

**SK:** *I think that expectations regarding what social networking can and will do are out of alignment with reality. It will not turn a lousy Realtor into a good one. It will not manufacture leads overnight with little effort. Agents are being told to expect the moon, so they do. When they don't get it, they're disappointed.*

**AD: What, if any, are some of the misuses of social networking and social media that you have identified?**

**SK:** Some of the misuses include having too many followers, and a mixing of "family," "social friends," and "business friends" that may not be appropriate; posting anything if one doesn't know what to post; asking for references on LinkedIn from semi-strangers; confusing which information really needs to be posted in "real time" versus what can wait.

**AD: How do you think agents can best balance their personal and professional posts and tweets?**

**SK:** Determine who you want to communicate with and what is appropriate to communicate. Write about something about which you are passionate. Your writing will get better and you will find others who share your passion. That is what you are looking for—connections.

**AD: How much of what an agent has always done offline regarding networking can and should be replicated online?**

**SK:** This goes back to my point on passion. If one can write, the world opens up. There is a buyer for everything somewhere (the long tail). Theoretically, almost all business-related networking (prospecting) can be done in an online environment. The question is whether that's the way your audience wants it. Much of this is truly generational.

**AD: Where are you seeing the highest usage of social networking and social media?**

**SK:** The demographic groups consisting of Gen Xers and Gen Yers see this as the norm.

**AD: You do a lot of work in Canada. Is there any difference between how agents in Canada and agents in the U.S. approach social networking and social media?**

**SK:** Actually no. I think the biggest differentiators are the generation gaps.

**AD: Saul, you created an online real estate community before anyone else. Can you tell me why and how it works?**

**SK:** When I began to play on AOL and CompuServe in the early 1990s, I believed that what I was seeing was a miracle...nothing less. At the push of a button, at the speed of light, all of the information in the world was available to everybody in the world—and today, in near real time. I read a few books about online communities and the new economy, and it made sense to me that the world was converging into a tool or a machine that would greatly enhance collaboration and produce incredible results. Human beings like to share.

My early experiences online allowed me to share my expertise with others, and I loved being able to help people. I believe that most people like to help others. The next step was for us to set out on a crusade to connect the world— and by the way, the world is now connected. It would have happened without us, but it is fun to think that, at least in our chosen industry, we have contributed. This was our mission statement, back in the late-1990s, when we formed the InternetCrusade:

## Meet Real Estate's Internet Crusader—Saul Klein

"InternetCrusade™ envisions a global cultural shift to online communication, commerce and information exchange over the next few years. To facilitate and enable this shift, REEPco has created the InternetCrusade. Its mission is to:

1. Drive online as many people as possible through the year 2000.

2. Provide a support mechanism to enable people to comfortably and efficiently utilize the power of the Internet—by shortening the learning curve and reducing the frustrations of technology. We make sense of the Internet.

3. Encourage and promote community activities online.

4. Give people a stake in their Internet future by assisting them in the acquisition of their own domains and the creation of their Internet Marketing Presence.

5. Enable human beings to optimize the power of the personal computer and the Internet in their life—helping them become Web-efficient in the shortest period of time.

6. Find Partners whose interests are enhanced by the work of the InternetCrusade™ and create and develop an ongoing relationship with them.

While I was in the Navy, I took my first programming language course in 1968. I played on computers during every class while at the Academy, and my second ship was the first computerized class of ships in the Navy. What the technology can do today is amazing. They don't even teach Celestial Navigation at the Academy anymore (I would have never believed it).

**AD:** Thank you, Saul. I would expect nothing less from a graduate of the Naval Academy in Annapolis and, by the way, thank you for your service in the Navy. Do you have any additional suggestions for Realtors regarding social networking and social media?
**SK:** Yes, Realtors need to:

1. Accept the reality of change.

2. Use their strength to maximize their positioning in the future.

3. Do more of the things they should be doing and less of the things they should not be doing.

4. Focus on high-value targets.

5. Know when to say NO.

**AD:** Thank you, Saul, for your tremendous contributions to this subject.

# Chapter 27

# You Only Have One Chance to Make a First Impression...Online, Too

The vast opportunities provided to enterprising real estate professionals through social networking/social media platforms have understandably led to an enormous degree of emphasis being placed on how one can best connect online. Equal attention, however, seems to be lacking in terms of how one can best communicate with, and to, these ever-growing online connections and contacts.

While an uncountable number of courses, training classes, books, tapes, and coaching efforts have been devoted to the subject of how a real estate professional can best communicate with consumers and clients either face-to-face or via the phone, our industry and, better yet, our society is in its mere infancy regarding how one can most effectively communicate online—especially for business purposes.

In fact, the argument could be made that online communication requires a much more intense level of forensic-like attention than the offline communication of real estate professionals. That's because face-to-face communication—and even telephone communication to a lesser degree—is comprised of not only the message but also body language, physical appearance, and tonality, whereas online communication, even when video is employed, is more straightforward and less nuanced. Even though there are opportunities to employ pictures and streaming video online accompanied by voice, in the overwhelming percentage of cases, the first impression online will be text. It will absolutely require the right text or taglines to cause consumers to delve deeper into your online communications repertoire. Therefore, as I set the stage for just how important your communication is online, and especially when you are making your first impression, I need to ask you to contemplate this question:

*"What percentage of your real estate income would you attribute to how you communicate with consumers and clients?"*

This is a question I have asked of myself and have posed to literally hundreds of thousands of real estate professionals throughout the world over the past 30 years.

On virtually all occasions, the preponderance of answers was, "100 percent." Granted, during most of the years—or as I reluctantly admit, decades—I asked this question, we were not in an age of online communication. However, once we entered this new era, I revised my question. Beginning with my tenure at REALTOR.com, I started posing the question in this fashion:

*"What percentage of your real estate income do you believe is based upon not only how you're communicating offline to and with consumers but also, now, online?"*

Unsurprisingly, the answer was still "100 percent."

Indeed, not only are you making lasting first impressions online, you're now making them to more people—more friends, fans, followers, networks, and communities—than you were offline. While most real estate professionals have experienced the trauma of an ineffective picture or video of a marketed property, oftentimes we overlook the serious consequences of the inappropriate use of our text or words. Inappropriate verbal speech can be casual and forgotten, but online text is documented and subject to being reproduced or even forwarded to an unintended audience. There exists a major need, therefore, to further focus on the subject of how real estate agents communicate and differentiate themselves online. Remember, thoughts lead to words, actions, behavior, character, and destiny. Consumers will now be judging and comparing those in the real estate profession based on how they communicate—both online and offline.

Although most real estate agents will, I'm sure, agree that the need to differentiate themselves is paramount, many lack a sophisticated online differentiation strategy. Perhaps this is because they lack a real estate business plan. If this is the case with you, chances are you might not have invested enough time—or better yet, dedicated sufficient time to rigorous introspection—while creating an online plan for differentiation.

Regarding differentiation and the need to develop new capabilities, I am reminded of a thesis proffered by the dean of the Stanford University Business Department. At a symposium he conducted for a small group of executives in Palo Alto, California, which I attended, the dean asserted that all businesses and many professionals must compete in two major ways: first for a positional advantage and then for a capabilities advantage. He explained, using McDonald's as an example, how this fast-food icon had built a positional advantage, represented by their brand, locations, and relationship to the consumer. Yet, if they failed to also differentiate themselves through a series of capabilities advantages—for example, drive-through windows, Big Macs, their breakfast menu, etc.—then their positional advantage would either recede or possibly disappear. Consequently, I inferred from this unassailable, at least to me, logic that if real estate companies and agents—who spend fortunes on locations, offices, and brand building in order to create a positional advantage—do not develop a corresponding capabilities advantage—be it technology, information, social networking/social media, short sales, etc.—then they, too, run the risk of losing their hard-earned positional advantage.

# You Only Have One Chance to Make a First Impression...Online, Too

Enterprise Rent-A-Car is a stellar example of how a new entrant into a marketplace—one that did not have prime airport locations and thus no positional advantage—rapidly ascended through the development of a capabilities advantage: they picked up rental car customers at their homes or businesses, while Hertz, Avis, etc., did not.

While differentiation and capabilities advantages are paramount in all professional arenas, the concept takes on a different meaning within real estate, because, as I've mentioned before, no real estate company attains differentiation due to its product. Therefore, until we reach the day when consumers tell their friends to buy only homes with Coldwell Banker family rooms, or RE/MAX kitchens, everybody within the real estate industry will need to discover and create alternative means of achieving necessary differentiation. Moreover, now that essentially all company listings in many markets can be displayed online by their competitors, the most obvious differentiating opportunities have been blunted. Let's examine the concept of digital differentiation in your career.

## Digital Differentiation

Can you have significant differentiation through IDX?

Yes____          No__X__

Can you get great differentiation from MLS?

Yes____          No __X__

Can you achieve differentiation from the product (i.e., homes), as in RE/MAX kitchens, Coldwell Banker living rooms, Century 21 patios, Keller Williams contemporaries, etc.?

Yes____          No __X__

Can you enjoy great differentiation by preventing your friends, fans, and followers from "friending" other real estate professionals?

Yes____          *No __X__

*No, because others can have many of the same friends, fans, and followers. Many consumers have friends in the real estate industry, both offline and online. So, that alone is not going to allow you to achieve significant differentiation.

How, then, does one digitally differentiate oneself through words, text, video, and overall content? You can have a great SEO strategy and keyword placement but, at the end of the day, if consumers do not recognize your value or want to do business with you, then you have not really differentiated yourself in terms of real value; you have just appeared in front of more people. You're connected to more people, but you're not influencing more people because in order to influence more people, you need differentiation. In order to differentiate yourself online, you need compelling content. If consumers' online experiences with you are unsatisfying, then all of your efforts could be subverted. In fact, you might have been better off not exposing your shallowness to that deep an audience. As the old saying goes, "One is better off allowing others to assume he or she is ignorant, rather than speaking and removing all doubt."

Indeed, the need for a digitally linked differentiation strategy is unsurprising, considering that ours is an industry that has shown a preference for imitation over innovation regarding its communication patterns. As an example, wouldn't you like to have a dollar for every time you've heard an agent say, "I want to help you get the best price in the shortest period of time with the least inconvenience?" Even worse is this following example of imitation used by thousands of agents during what they have been told to call a "listing presentation":

**Agent:** *Folks, how will you be selecting an agent? Will it be based upon someone who will tell you anything—meaning lie—to get the listing, or someone like me, who will tell you the truth?*

Well, it's one thing to communicate this desperate, anything-but-Sophie's Choice question to consumers on a one-to-one basis, and it's quite another thing when this approach is exposed to the whole world online. Just imagine the consequences of the entire online community experiencing such dreadful real estate-imbedded communication—especially when you are the messenger.

That particular question, where an agent asks home sellers whether they're going to select an agent who lies versus an agent who tells the truth, presumably like him or her—surprise, surprise—actually conveys the following unspoken statement:

**Agent:** *Mr. and Mrs. Homeseller, before I can even begin to concentrate or discuss your needs this evening, we first must try to resolve my needs or competitive worries. I might not get this listing! I could lose this listing, folks, so therefore, before we can talk or delve into the marketing needs of your property, I first have to put you through the torture of telling me, face-to-face, upfront, almost like you're being held hostage, how you're going to go about selecting an agent.*

This self-serving and obvious ploy only encourages home sellers to become repelled by you. This, in turn, leads to them having to interview multiple real estate agents. My point here is to suggest that our industry must carefully re-examine its long history of beloved anti-consumer clichés. Otherwise, some of these thoughts will find their way into our online lexicon and will forever memorialize our industry as one that is either not able to focus first on consumer needs, or not intelligent enough to disguise its motives. Online communication has to be considered very carefully because it differs greatly from one-to-one communication. This type of common communication disaster that our industry is noted for has prevented many home sellers from taking immediate action offline for years. Again, how would you like it if a stranger came to your home and asked whether you wanted to hire him for a job because he'll tell you the truth, as opposed to his professional colleagues, who will lie to you?

If we bring this pattern of communication online—and I know most of my readers won't—it will spell disaster. Not retooling our offline rhetoric for targeted online purposes, when using Twitter, Facebook, blogs, etc., is a terrifying proposition, and not just for consumers. Please allow me to expand upon this premise.

**Readers:** *Allan, can you give us examples of some of the trite, tiresome, and hackneyed clichés used offline by real estate agents, and to which consumers have developed antibodies, so that we don't bring this type of communication into our social networking platforms, communities, and communications?*

**Allan:** *Happily. People constantly ask real estate agents offline, "How's the real estate market?" I don't think there's another answer to a question that consumers want to find online or offline that's greater than this one. Please remember that consumers are also going online to get a sense of the real estate market. Therefore, let's optimistically hope that we can end the ridiculously ineffective and insulting way in which many in our industry have responded offline to this genuine consumer inquiry over the past several decades. Here's an example of what's taking place offline, in this case at a high school soccer game:*

**Consumer asks:** *How's the real estate market?*

**Agent offline will say:** *Either, "Great, I've never been busier," or, "All I need are a few more listings," or, "Do you want to buy or sell a home?" or—the granddaddy of all regrettable rhetoric and an all-time conversation killer—"It's unbelievable!"*

**Consumer thinks (but does not say):** *Oh my God! This person is a moron. I cannot imagine a less nuanced, less sophisticated, or less analytical mind at work than this real estate agent is displaying in my very presence. Therefore, I'd better change the subject because obviously the subject of real estate is clearly one that he is not prepared for or even truly interested in discussing even though he is in the real estate business. Why else would he destroy the potential of this whole subject matter by saying something either so disingenuous or as superficial as, "It's unbelievable?" Obviously the word "unbelievable" literally means "not to be believed." I can't believe this agent is responding to me in this way. In fact, I don't think the market is unbelievable. This agent is unbelievable.*

**Consumer remains polite and says:** *Oh, it's unbelievable? That's great. By the way, which player out there is your daughter?*

Again, the agent responses listed earlier cause consumers to switch away from the topic of real estate because they've learned instantaneously by our communications that we're really not ready to have a meaningful discussion about the overall marketplace. They are. We're not.

Now here's a recommended alternative, which you also need to bring online:

**Consumer:** *How's the market?*

**Agent:** *Thank you for asking.*

The reason you thank the consumer for asking is not just because it's polite but also to give yourself subliminal permission to ask the consumer a follow-up question. Since he or she first asked you a question, you'll be able to ask a question in return because it's nice and symmetrical.

**Agent continues:** *We are in a very opportunistic marketplace. There are great opportunities for buyers, sellers, and investors. Now, let me ask you a question: When do you think you might be making your next real estate move?*

If you just say, "Do you want to buy or sell?" it might create uncomfortable pressure, and that question does not create enough of an opportunity for you to do follow-up business; the consumer might not be able to either buy or sell right now, but he or she might be ready in a year or so. For example, if somebody is planning to sell four months from now and you ask, "Do you want to buy or sell?" he might think you mean this week, and you'll be told, "No." But if you ask that same person when he might be planning his next real estate move, the consumer might be more willing to volunteer, "In about nine months," or, "A year from now, when my youngest son goes away to college." Then you can say, "Well, it might be too soon to start the marketing of your home, but why don't we get together over the next few weeks or so? We can start creating a pre-marketing strategy." Regarding online communication, if you only tweet, "Do you want to buy or sell?" and offer a link to your website or blog, or only mention tax credits for buyers, etc., you limit a larger market. For the larger market, ask, "When do you think you might be making your next real estate move?"

Hundreds of millions of dollars have been lost because real estate agents did not seize this unique-to-the-real-estate-industry selling opportunity by communicating in a more effective way. Instead, they copied many of the communication patterns from 30 or 40 years ago—communication patterns to which consumers have developed antibodies. Many real estate agents are playing online checkers instead of online chess, by not realizing that when they tweet or blog about how "it's a great time to buy," or that "it's a buyer's market," this causes most of the people in the marketplace and communities they serve to further hibernate.

You should only blog forcefully about how "it's a great buyer's market" if you are in a destination market like Florida—where most people do not have to buy and sell their homes in the same market at the same time—or if you are trying to stimulate first-time buyers online throughout your social networking platform. Otherwise, be very, very careful not to polarize the online community by asserting that it's either "a buyer's market" or "a seller's market." Remember: it's always "an opportunistic market." Realize, however, that by characterizing a market as "opportunistic," you are now challenged to create specific and customized solutions for each niche or opportunity.

Another important thing to consider while you develop your online communication strategies is that you need to truly understand your social networking demographics. I suggest that you be especially strategic regarding matching message with marketplace because the vast majority of your consumers— meaning online friends, fans, communities, and even tribes—are typically local people. Therefore, in most markets, 80 to 90 percent of these local connections—these human connections that you are working assiduously to nurture and expand upon—typically have to sell before they buy. This perspective is further reinforced when one considers that the average age of many successful real estate agents is higher than the average age of most renters or first-time buyers who may not be as inclined to friend or follow particular real estate agents online. Therefore, by labeling or posting text referring to the market as a "buyer's market," you are probably unwittingly disenfranchising your natural online following and depriving yourself of an enormous career opportunity online, even more so than offline, because of the tweets, chats, blogs, online communities, and networks with which you are involved.

In the high percentage of cases where people have to sell before they buy and where you want to engage them, you should tweet, for example: "If your home value has dropped, that could be great news for you if you take this opportunity to move up. Please e-mail me for information." Now you're using Twitter to effectively relate to the needs of the marketplace.

The only way—as I've always said—that you have access to people is through their concerns. And most people who own homes are initially more concerned about the circumstances surrounding what they own than they are about the opportunity to buy another property. Therefore, you need to address both aspects of their real estate world simultaneously online, as part of your real estate social marketing system. For example, I might tweet to Top 5 Members: "In 1989, I created the industry's only move-up system. If you want the updated version by Maria Patterson of RISMedia, please visit my blog."

When you tell people that it's a great time to buy, you might think that's positive, but that's actually negative to a lot of people. Today's consumers are very astute and they know, intuitively, that if there's never been a greater time to buy, then there's never been a worse time to sell, in many cases. And they also know that when they see that there's never been a greater time to buy, that statement is oftentimes accompanied by information about short sales, REOs, and foreclosures. As a result, you might become the personal epicenter for negativity. However, when you say that this is an opportunistic marketplace, you're now differentiating yourself from all the "doom and gloomers."

You also don't want online visitors to think you are taking on a predatory posture by trolling online communities looking for other predators you can satisfy because of the misfortune that some are experiencing. So, you've got to be very, very careful, politically, in the way you communicate online. That's why I'm suggesting that you assert, both online and offline, that it is an opportunistic market.

To be deliberately redundant, you've got to become expert in crafting solutions. For example, for some consumers, it's an opportunistic market because they can sell their homes before they lose more equity; for others, it's an opportunistic market for those with built-up equity; for some, it's an opportunity for first-time buyers; or it's an opportunistic market because there's more inventory and selection. I don't have to go much deeper, because I know I'm singing to the choir. You all know it's an opportunistic market. Stockbrokers understand that it's never a stock market; it's a market of stocks. We have to understand in our online communication that there's no such thing as a real estate market, per se; there's a market of real estate that spells different opportunities for different niches.

Here are some other examples of how you can have a greater impact regarding your online communication and how you can leverage social networking and social media opportunities among your friends, fans, communities, followers, and tribes. I call these examples, "Dalton's Digital Don'ts and Do's."

### Dalton's Digital Don'ts and Do's

**Don't:** Tweet that you just got a new listing. For many home sellers, that indicates to them that their homes just went down in value in certain markets, and it's more personally celebratory for you than it is for the consumer. It's announcing something that many people think is unnecessary, redundant, or unremarkable, and it appears as though you're bragging; any consumer with half a brain realizes that, on a minute's notice, he or she can go to any number of search engines and not only see your new listing but also see a hundred others. So, instead of tweeting that you just got a new listing, as though it's another notch on your gun handle...

**Do:** Tweet that you are bringing a magnificent new property to the marketplace. Now, I ask you, what would impress you more—to hear that an agent just got a new listing or that he or she is bringing a magnificent new property to the marketplace?

**Don't:** Tweet that you have a listing presentation. Again, listing presentations are what you want. Consumers want marketing proposals. Listing presentations are about you. Marketing proposals are about what you are going to do for the client. So, instead...
**Do:** Tweet or post that you have a new marketing proposal that you'll be making that night.

**Don't:** Tweet or post about how you offer a complimentary market analysis, or that you are presenting a CMA. Don't tweet, blog, chat, retweet, or post anything that talks about a CMA. Instead...
**Do:** Post that you can help people with an MMA, a master market analysis. A CMA is just a complimentary or competitive market analysis, which really doesn't even describe the phenomenon because if you really wanted to be technical, it would be a CPA—a competitive property analysis, since we're not analyzing markets. It's not competitive markets or a market analysis; you're really comparing properties. I, therefore, would recommend that you talk about your MMA instead of your CMA. What's the difference? A CMA gives home sellers an estimate of value. An MMA not only provides an estimate of value, but it includes ways in which they might be able to enhance their value through merchandising and staging ideas. What do you think would differentiate you more online: telling people that you'll do a market analysis or a master market analysis?

**Don't:** Tweet, post, or blog to anybody or to any community that you will be "sitting an open house this weekend." The only thing that would be worse would be for you to say that you'll be "sleeping" an open house. Because "sitting" is the next thing to saying you'll be "sleeping" at it. Instead...
**Do:** Tweet, post, or blog that you will be marketing 10 open houses this weekend. This statement sounds as though you've got something going for yourself; the other sounds like you are sitting at someone's house waiting for people to visit.

**Don't:** Refer to properties as either "beautiful," "lovely," "charming," "elegant," "spacious," "cream puff," "Shangri-la," etc. These terms are overused and non-remarkable; you need more distinctive dialogue.

**Don't:** Refer to virtually every property you represent that has remarkable landscaping as either having been "professionally landscaped" or being located in a "park-like setting." It's as if the entire industry knows of only two ways to describe all of the properties in the world. Again, you're denying yourself digital differentiation.

**Don't:** Blog or talk about how you are different from other real estate agents. Instead...
**Do:** Focus on how you can help clients' properties achieve differentiation. Why? Because you cooperate with other agents, but homes do not cooperate with the other homes on the market. Therefore, the way you are different is in how you market homes differently. Find a way to convey this message throughout your online communication as it relates to real estate.

**Don't:** Tweet, post, or blog about how you qualify buyers. That's a massive turnoff. Instead...
**Do:** Tweet, post, or blog about how you can help establish purchasing power for prospective buyers. There's a major difference. When you communicate online that you "qualify" people, it intimidates people; it's a negative. When you speak in terms of helping to establish consumer "purchasing power," that verbiage is appropriately seductive online.

**Don't:** Tweet, blog, or post about how you can help first-time buyers. Instead...
**Do:** Tweet, blog, or post about your "rent-to-buy" program, since the majority of first-time buyers are essentially renters and, therefore, do not see themselves as first-time buyers. Again, by talking in terms of how you have a rent-to-buy assistance program, you're demonstrating a major digital difference and you are giving yourself the opportunity to encourage retweeting and leveraging your links.

**Don't:** Tweet that you speak several languages. Instead...
**Do:** Create multilingual links to your publications on your website.

**Don't:** Tweet, blog, or post about how you sell more homes. Instead...
**Do:** Tweet, blog, or post about how you are dedicated to selling homes for more. Again, consumers offline have developed antibodies to people boasting about the number of homes they sell. Which would appeal to you more online: reading that an agent sells more homes, or reading that an agent loves to sell homes for more?

**Don't:** Tweet, post, or blog about homes not selling because they're overpriced. Instead...
**Do:** Tweet, post, or blog about how homes do not sell because they're not

properly marketed. Remember, price is just a part of marketing. If all you are communicating online is that home prices have to be reduced, or that they don't sell because they're overpriced, you're subconsciously asserting that all you are is an overpaid appraiser and that your whole value proposition is tied into one thing that you can do, which is reduce prices, as opposed to having greater skills that are tied to marketing, which also includes pricing.

**Don't:** Tweet, post, or blog—ever—about how you provide great service. Instead...
**Do:** Tweet, post, or blog about the value of your great skills—unless you're in a marketplace where your competitors are going online and proclaiming they give horrible service. If your competitors are all saying they give horrible service, then it would impress somebody if you say you give great service. But, since they're probably not saying this and are probably all saying they give great service, there's no differentiation value; there's very little perceived value in service when compared to the value of skills. To demonstrate my point: when you get on an airplane, there are two groups of employees—the service sector (flight attendants) and the skill sector (pilot and co-pilot). Which sector do you want the pilot to be in: the skill sector or the service sector? Real estate agents provide service and possess skills, but you will only be able to have one great differentiator. Do you want that to be based on your skills or your service? Service, to the consumer, is presumably the frosting on the cake, and is referred to as "value-added." To many real estate agents offline, the hackneyed expression of "service" represented the cake, and those agents run the risk of bringing that same communication behavior online, which will be as equally unimpressive and equally non-remarkable. Start to always talk in terms of your skills on LinkedIn, Facebook, etc., or when you're blogging about what consumers need from a real estate professional.

**Don't:** Post, tweet, chat, or blog about your real estate "assistant." Instead...
**Do:** Post, tweet, chat, or blog about your exceptionally skilled "associates," "partners," "colleagues," or "team members." To illustrate how much of a negative the word "assistant" is, in both the offline and online marketplace, think back to a time when you went to a store seeking help and you asked for the manager, and you were told that the manager wasn't available, however, the assistant manager could talk to you. Did that please you or was that a letdown? Don't let consumers down online, and don't let your partners down online, by demeaning them as being your "assistants." Instead, refer to them as your "colleagues," "cohorts," "collaborators," "coworkers," "employees," and "team members," like the rest of the professional world does online.

## You Only Have One Chance to Make a First Impression...Online, Too

**Don't:** Announce on your LinkedIn or Facebook profile, or as part of your blog, that you are a "waterfront," "condo," or "two-family" specialist, to give a few examples. Instead...
**Do:** Position or post that you have developed a waterfront marketing system, a condo marketing system, a two-family home marketing system, etc.—especially if you are targeting people with those specific real estate-related needs or interests.

**Don't:** When chatting with other real estate agents, use the word "commission," or say you "mine leads," or you "scrub leads," or that you "incubate leads."
**Do:** Talk about your "fees" and how you "serve the needs of online consumers."

**Don't:** Claim or boast that you have 5,000 people in your database.
**Do:** Let us, at RISMedia and Top 5, show you how to convert your 5,000 names into your personally branded real estate social network. You want people to be members of your network, not numbers or names in your database; it's too impersonal and antiseptic, you can't leverage it, and you'll never sell a database as easily as you will be able to sell a network that's been organized.

**Don't:** Highlight online that you will be serving food at your open house. Consumers might think you're trying to bribe other real estate professionals, by enticing them with food, to come see your listings—as if we are an industry of "gastronomic incinerators" who need to satisfy their food addiction in order to assume the professional responsibility of learning about the properties within their marketplace so they can more effectively educate buyers and sellers. Imagine if doctors went online and chatted with each other, or posted to fellow physicians: "Please come and examine my patients. If you do, I'll feed you; there will be a buffet." Instead...
**Do:** Post or tweet: You need to learn about my great property for your interested buyers and to educate yourself.

Real estate companies must also ensure that certain words in their offline lexicon are purged. Here are two great examples—which I realize don't describe most real estate companies or circumstances—that are significantly illustrative.

Years ago, when I was president of my company, during a visit to one of our 32 offices, I walked in with a young couple who were house hunting at the time. As we entered the office, I heard one of our agents yell from the back of our conference room to our floor-time, or opportunity-time, agent, "Hey Becky, you've got a couple of walk-ins." Almost before this consumer-commodifying comment was complete, this young couple abruptly left our office.

Also, many years ago, while consulting with a major broker in Hawaii, he said to me, "Allan, if you could improve the results for my ICs, I will pay you anything you ask for." I thought, "I'm going to lose any credibility I have right now because I don't know what he's talking about." Then I asked him, "What do you mean by your 'ICs'?" To which he responded, "Oh, I'm sorry, Allan. I was referring to our company's independent contractors." I feel guilty that I actually commanded a higher consulting fee by including among my suggestions for increasing his office's productivity the notion of redefining his "ICs" within his communication models and policy procedure manuals as his "Realtor associates," and honoring them for what they truly were: the company's greatest asset.

Now, again, that is obvious and not a breakthrough, and hopefully doesn't represent my seminal consultative value, but it has always underscored for me that most companies and agents, at times, given the demands of their careers and lives, overlook the way in which they communicate and, therefore, are not aware of the negative consequences. And this oversight, I'm beginning to see, is happening in a massive way for real estate agents and companies in their online communications as well. For instance, perhaps someday our industry will come up with a better way of referring to homes that didn't sell than what we do now, which is to call home sellers and their properties "expired listings." In fact, I have personally tweeted and asked online for suggestions regarding alternate ways of describing this market. Perhaps you'd like to pass on a suggestion as well.

In summary, we must always be cognizant that language is the clothing of our ideas. One of the multitudes of factors that has caused our industry not to be fully appreciated for the greater good we do for society is the communication patterns we use to represent our value. Simply expressed, your great efforts and value are at times not congruent with how you convey your professional essence to and among consumers and clients. This offline syndrome of short-cut and thoughtless or lazy cliché language must not proliferate online. Online verbiage is very visible and will be scrutinized and memorialized to a degree not ever contemplated with offline conversation. Therefore, as an industry, we must retool our rhetoric for online use as we become more visible, transparent, and engaged as members of an ever-evolving and sophisticated community.

Clearly, there is a major difference between the abbreviated syntax, pithy taglines, and straightforward comments that you use in your posts and tweets, and the rich scholastic levels of literacy that you exhibit in the articles you write for your blogs. Regardless of whether you are writing more extensively on your blog or using concise or even abbreviated language elsewhere online, always remember words matter because your words reflect your thoughts.

# Chapter 28

## Spelling and Grammar Matter...
## Even More So Online

*By Maria Patterson*
Executive Editor, RISMedia

As Allan explained in the previous chapter, your online communications—even a quick 140-character tweet—carry more weight than your spoken words. Why? Because they're forever etched in cyberspace. While you might be at the top of your game when it comes to real estate sales, your stellar status and professionalism can quickly be tarnished by an innocent grammar, style, or spelling blunder in the online world.

Rest assured, you're not alone. Many a savvy businessperson grapples with the nuances of spelling and grammar that are, otherwise, second nature for journalists and authors. In the past, this Achilles' heel rarely caused a problem; however, today, thanks to the wild popularity of social media sites, we're all suddenly in the business of written communication...professional writer or not.

While there is a certain level of acceptance and forgiveness when it comes to online writing errors, in my opinion, if you are putting your professional persona out there for the world to see, you must advance your grammar and writing skills. Think of it this way: would you be okay with a grammatical or spelling error on the home page of your website? Probably not. So start taking a similar level of care with your social media sites.

For many a discerning reader and client, a foolish misspelling or grammar mistake on a post, tweet, or text can bring you down a few notches in their eyes. If there is a slip of the fingers and you do make an error, you can quickly redeem yourself by catching it and making amends, so be sure to immediately reread anything you post or send. The problem is, there is no way to completely undo the error in the online world, in other words, once the text has been sent, the post posted, the tweet tweeted. You can delete a tweet, but not before it has gone out to every follower who is set up to automatically receive your tweets via text message. However, while you can't erase the error, you can correct it... and the sooner, the better.

As an editor and writer, I realize that it can be very tempting to ignore a typo in the hopes that no one will notice, but trust me, it's never the right move.

## Spelling and Grammar Matter...Even More So Online

Sometimes I try to rationalize that posting a correction will only make things worse because it simply draws more attention to the fact that I made a mistake in the first place. But the truth is, someone is noticing that mistake whether I correct it or not...so better to "stand corrected."

The following is an unofficial, but apparently widely accepted, technique for correcting typos online and in texts among the younger crowd. I picked this up from my in-house social media expert, my 14-year-old son, and his own social network. When you make a mistake, simply correct it by re-entering the word or words correctly in a subsequent post/tweet/text followed by an asterisk.

**Example:**
This is an actual comment from my son on a recent Facebook post of mine:

*Thanks, everone, for the birthday wishes.*
Immediately followed by his next post (after suffering a brief tirade from his editor mother):

*everyone\*...sorry, Mom.*

I've used this same technique on the RISMedia Facebook page instead of deleting and re-entering a particular post. Since fans were already commenting on the post, deleting and reposting wouldn't have been the right option.

Correcting oneself in this manner—or whatever manner you're comfortable with—is also a must in text messaging where it's literally impossible to delete what's already been sent.

**Example:**
Text 1: *You're closing is scheduled for next Friday.*

While many would argue that it's acceptable to make grammar and spelling errors via text and social networking sites due to the casual and quick-fingered nature of this form of communication, I advocate that it's not...especially when used for any type of business correspondence. So, correct yourself as soon as you've noticed the error with a simple follow-up text:

Text 2: *your\**

Not only does this prove that you really do know how to spell, but that you're also the type of professional who prides himself or herself on attention to detail—always a good thought to have about one's real estate agent, no?

### My Top 10 Grammar Offenses
While it's impossible to catch every typo and make sure every verb agrees with every subject, becoming fluent in at least the most common grammar and spelling rules will go a long way. Most experts agree that certain errors are just

plain verboten...or should be. While the lists vary a bit, you will usually find the offenses listed here among the most common—and the most glaring. So commit to learning at least the following to keep the grammar police and discerning consumers on your side.

**1. It's and Its ... and *never* Its'**
Whenever you see an apostrophe in a contraction such as *it's*, remember that the apostrophe is replacing a letter, in this case the *i* in *is*. Therefore, *it's* is short for *it is*. In this particular word, the apostrophe does not connote possession. In this case, in fact, the word *its* is actually the possessive word, even though there's no apostrophe in sight:

> *It's going on the market next week.*
> *It's priced perfectly to sell.*
> *Its best feature is the wrap-around porch.*
> *Its owners are going to refer me again and again.*

As for *its'*...it's not even a word. So don't use it!

**2. They're, Their, and There**
If you remember the apostrophe rule—that when you see one in a contraction, it's taking the place of a letter—then you'll always remember that *they're* is a contraction for *they are*: *they're* going to the movies; *they're* making an offer; *they're* being unrealistic.

*Their/theirs* is the possessive term. For me, remembering grammar and spelling rules comes down to little idiosyncratic memory triggers. Since there is an *i* in *their* and I am a person, *their* spelled with an i refers to people: *their* neighbors; *their* community; *their* good taste in furniture; the prize is *theirs* for the taking.

How do I remember that *there* refers to a place or timeframe? Because it's the only one left: the key is over *there*; *there* is going to be an offer soon; I can head over *there* now.

**3. Effect and Affect**
I have personally struggled with this one for years until I recently, finally, came across an explanation that made complete and logical sense to me. *Effect* is a noun; *affect* is a verb. How could I have missed this for so many years?

> The *effects* of the struggling economy are felt far and wide.
> How will the struggling economy *affect* consumers?

His weight loss is the *effect* of consistent exercise.
Consistent exercise *affects* your metabolism.

One caveat, however: the word *affect* is also used as a psychological term meaning one's observable expression or emotion: His *affect* was flat upon losing the home to a higher bidder.

### 4. Your and You're

This is perhaps the number-one nemesis of many a writer and is one of the most frequent and gut-wrenching errors I see. Again, let the apostrophe be your guide; it replaces the letter *a* in *you are*: *you're* the highest bidder; *you're* in control; *you're* a great golfer.

That leaves *your* as the pronoun signifying possession: *your* house; *your* family; *your* life.

Deep down, I believe that most people know the difference between *your* and *you're*, but simply forget to pause and double check. This still happens to me and I still cringe every time because this error can always be directly attributed to haste. So avoid this common, but painful, mistake by taking a second to confirm that *you're* using *your* words correctly.

### 5. Then and Than

No special tricks for remembering this one, although *than* is often used in conjunction with the word *rather* so that's a great clue. *Then* connotes time and *than* connotes comparison.

I'll do the dishes and *then* walk the dog.
I'll walk the dog and *then* watch a movie.

I'd rather walk the dog *than* do the dishes.
I'd rather watch a movie *than* walk the dog.

### 6. Possessive Apostrophes

Willy-nilly apostrophes are a sure sign of an amateur writer, so take the time to understand when and how to use them.

For singular nouns, use *'s*: the *dog's* collar; the *home's* front porch; *Ted's* listing.

For plural nouns, use *s'*: the *cats'* toys; the *neighbors'* property lines; the *owners'* home.

For most proper nouns that end in *s*, just use the apostrophe: *Dr. Seuss'* books; *Jesus'* disciples.

Also remember that all it takes in most cases to make a word plural is an *s* or *es*—no apostrophe is necessary: new *homes* for sale; more *listings* available; the best *schools* in town.

### 7. The Non-Words
I'm not talking about the occasional acceptable slang word used here and there. I'm talking about words that simply don't exist and never did, so please don't use them!

> *Orientate*—While this may technically be a word, it has become common practice to use it to mean *orient*, which is the correct word. The most common misuse I hear is *disorientated*. The correct word is *disoriented*. A good agent *orients* his clients to the sales process; he doesn't *orientate* them.

> *Irregardless*—Unfortunately, there is no such thing. The correct word is *regardless*.

### 8. Starting a Sentence with "And"
I won't lie. I've done this. And will continue to do so from time to time (see?). But it's best to live by the "Never start a sentence with *And*" rule, reserving the right to do so once in a while for creative or dramatic effect, or, as seen often in this book, when transcribing a conversation or interview.

Using *and* to begin a sentence can be quite effective when it comes to promotional and marketing copy. For example, imagine in big block letters on the front of your next postcard:

TIMES ARE TOUGH.
AND THERE HAS NEVER BEEN A BETTER TIME TO BUY.

Catchy, right? The point is, when used for dramatic effect in such a way, *and* as the starter becomes quite a powerful word. Reserve it for those special few occasions, however, to keep the grammar patrol at bay.

### 9. I and Me
I think we all had it drilled into us as little kids—*Charlie and I*, not *Charlie and me*—almost as much as we were pestered about saying please and thank you. But the truth is, it's not always *Charlie and I*. In fact, depending on where the phrase falls in the sentence, it can be downright wrong and will stand out like a sore thumb to any halfway-decent grammarian.

In English teacher-speak, the general rule is this: Use *Charlie and I* when you and Charlie are the subject of the sentence—meaning that you and Charlie are responsible for the action (the verb)—and *Charlie and me* when you and Charlie are on the receiving end of the action (objects, or objects of a preposition):

> *Charlie and I are cooking an amazing dinner for Emeril.*
>
> *Charlie and I are heading to Emeril's restaurant instead.*
>
> *Emeril is cooking an amazing dinner for Charlie and me.*
>
> *Emeril is taking Charlie and me to his restaurant instead.*

### 10. Reserve the Exclamation Point!

I know real estate is exciting. But the poor exclamation point has been tossed around, misused, and overused ad nauseam throughout social media sites. There seems to be a natural tendency to believe that every tweet is exciting, every post thrilling, and let's face it, promoting ourselves and our business just begs for that exclamation point.

The problem is, as with anything that's overused, the exclamation point is losing its oomph in the online universe and is, therefore, turning many people off. Most experts advise not using the exclamation point in formal business writing at all. While social media is anything but formal, overusing the exclamation point is much like the boy who cried wolf. The reader winds up thinking, "*Sure*, he has something exciting to say…for the 20th time this week." Unfortunately, this particular punctuation mark has become so commonplace that it's lost all meaning and can often make the writer appear self-absorbed with his or her own importance.

So, please—lay off the exclamation points and save them for the truly important and/or exciting news:

> *At 7:02 a.m., I welcomed my first grandchild into the world!*
>
> *I just sold a house to Tom Cruise!*
>
> *A-Rod just hit his 600th home run!*
>
> *The Yankees win the pennant!*
>
> *The Fed just dropped the interest rate to 1.5 percent!*

Now, that's exciting!

**Resources**

With a world of grammar and spelling aids at our fingertips, thanks to the Internet, there's no excuse for making consistent mistakes. Here are just a few of my favorite resources:

**Grammar Girl: Quick and Dirty Tips for Better Writing**—Quick, useful, easy to understand and entertaining. What more could you want?
http://grammar.quickanddirtytips.com

**AP Stylebook Online**—For serious journalists and a smart investment (yes, you need to pay for a subscription) for budding citizen journalists.
www.apstylebook.com

**Dictionary.com**—I highly recommend their mobile application for all of you PDA-enabled real estate professionals. Just pull out your smartphone and find the correct spelling, along with a handy thesaurus, wherever you are.
www.dictionary.com

**DailyWritingTips**—A comprehensive blog site on all things related to writing, including usage and grammar, but there's also a special section just for business writing...and plenty of fodder for your creative side.
www.dailywritingtips.com

**Google**—For the ultra-fast answer, simply type the word "define" followed by the word in question in the Google search window, and a definition will appear directly under your search term. Perfect for quickly checking the meaning or spelling of a word.

# Chapter 29

# Social Networking and Social Media: Understanding the Legalities

I am very fortunate that within my professional and personal network, there exists a very rare individual as he relates to a subject I wanted to include in this book. Specifically, I was in search of a person who could combine three backgrounds: law; real estate brokerage; and social networking expertise. Such a person was found in my friend Scott Forcino who, when asked to contribute some important content regarding the legal implications of social media, graciously agreed to provide some very limited, yet important, basic information on the subject. Scott, who recognizes the complexity surrounding social media and the law, suggests that anyone with personal questions or concerns should consult with an attorney who has expertise in an applicable field.

## The Legal Implications of Social Media
*By Scott Forcino*
*Co-founder, Counsel, Real Estate Advocates*
*Principal Broker, Westchester Real Estate Advocates*

Did you hear the news? For the week ending March 13, 2010, Facebook got more traffic than Google, according to Internet tracker Experian Hitwise. Social networkers tweet to their followers through Twitter and post updates to their fans and friends on Facebook. You're the publisher and instantly connect to your sphere of contacts.

That is interesting because it proves that Web 2.0 has surpassed the "static Web." User-generated content and search are now the main purposes of the Internet.

Social networking can be a lot of fun as a way to share daily events and it is also very productive for businesses to get their message out to their fans, followers, and friends. Although initially a college yearbook, Facebook is now the social platform for all ages, and the demographic group aged 35-54 is the fastest-growing segment. Users' photos and updates are shared all day. Twitter is the "broadcast channel" for users' social lives and business interests. LinkedIn is a professional site, where users can network for business purposes.

# Social Networking and Social Media: Understanding the Legalities

All three social networking giants are free to use and have seeped into our everyday lives. There is a race to monetize these efforts unlike anything seen since the '49 Gold Rush. However, there is a real danger of civil liability or even criminal culpability for careless users of these platforms. The following information topically addresses these areas of concern.

There are three areas wherein liability could result from careless engagement in social networking/social media. These are the pitfalls to engagement.

**Potential liability lies in the laws surrounding:**
1. Privacy
2. Intellectual Property
3. Tort (civil claims)

Regarding the issue of privacy, normally, the custodian of another's "personally identifiable information"—such as one's Social Security Number, or even one's date of birth or birthplace of origin—must not transmit, or even allow to be conveyed, this sensitive data. This is accurate with regard to a school, employer, or lender.

However, in the realm of social networking, this information, in addition to one's interests and "likes" and where one lives, is accessible to those who are intent on mining that data, or to those who buy that information from the social networking site. As such, there is no reasonable expectation of privacy on the part of a user. An important element in Facebook's "Terms" or "Statement of Rights and Responsibilities" section, that no one reads, is:

> For content that is covered by intellectual property rights, like photos and videos ("IP content"), you specifically give us the following permission, subject to your privacy and application settings: you grant us a non-exclusive, transferable, sub-licensable, royalty-free, worldwide license to use any IP content that you post on or in connection with Facebook ("IP License"). This IP License ends when you delete your IP content or your account unless your content has been shared with others, and they have not deleted it.

Each time a user posts an update, that user adds data as though answering a survey, all without that user's knowledge. One's occupation, gender, and personal interests all are packaged into trends and patterns and sold commercially. This discussion should also involve the danger inherent in alerting anyone with a criminal intent that you are "going away for the weekend" or "can't wait to go on vacation" or that you are "working late again tonight, uuggghhhhh." For the foregoing reasons, social networking sites are target-rich.

Regarding the issue of Intellectual Property, this addresses the unlawful use of another's copyrighted or trademarked work. Both categories are protected and the owner has rights to exclude the use of all others. If a user of a social

# Social Networking and Social Media: Understanding the Legalities

networking site uses third-party content such as articles, pictures, videos, or graphics, with no permission from the owner, this conduct can result in civil liability, including treble damages and attorney fees under the U.S. Copyright Act, 17 U.S.C. Section 101. There are enforcement measures implemented in the context of a Copyright Infringement action. Furthermore, within the realm of employer-employee relations, there is strict liability for the unauthorized acquisition of "trade secrets" or the "special sauce" used by a company and known by its employees.

However, the sophisticated online social networker can reduce content-related risks by establishing a policy for the publication of other's content. This policy should include attribution disclaimers, a screening of other's content for copyright permission demands, and obtaining the appropriate releases from the owners.

With these safeguards in place, liability should be avoided. Please be aware that it has been held that postings on social networking sites do not meet the minimum creativity standard to be copyright protected. That standard is evolving, however, and posts could be considered Intellectual Property in the near future.

Lastly, regarding the issue of "tortious" behavior, a user of a social networking site may become liable for damages for defaming another or engaging in libelous activity. This occurs when a user expresses as factual a false or derogatory statement. Some instances of this type of expression do not even require the claimant to demonstrate any damages or that they were actually harmed! Other civil actions include the "intentional infliction of emotional distress" or "interference with advantageous economic relations." It is necessary to note that all of the requirements of a Realtor still exist in an online setting such as a social networking site.

The Fair Housing Rules/Anti-Discrimination statutes, RESPA, and the Realtor's Code of Ethics all apply unabated. Specifically, a Realtor may not "knowingly or recklessly make false or misleading statements about others in the business" and also must be "truthful and honest in real estate communications." The Internet is not The Wild Wild West, or a lawless environ.

Additionally, it is all too common for agents to post updates and send tweets without any reference to their broker or the office in which they work. All of the foregoing actions will grant the user a first-hand look at the interesting field of tort law and will necessitate the user to remain in close contact with his or her favorite attorney and to take time off from work to appear in court. Not fun stuff. Not to mention the attorney's fees and the potential money damages stemming from a settlement or a verdict. It is important to remember that everyone has an opinion and that truth is the absolute defense to an allegation of any of the torts mentioned above. Do you want to assert those rights?

## Social Networking and Social Media: Understanding the Legalities

A famous incident concerning the foregoing involved a Miami agent/blogger who stated that a developer was "gonna go down and had been 'bankrupt' prior." In fact, the developer had never filed for bankruptcy protection and sued the blogger for defamation and sought damages of $25 million. The blogger retained counsel and within one year the suit was dismissed. This, however, was no victory for the blogger, who was terminated from his firm.

Based on the explosive growth of social networking sites and all the statistics that show the amount of time users commit to these sites, it is clear that these sites are here to stay. There is a very useful business purpose and much to gain through their use. However, some discretion should be used while enjoying the real benefits. Be careful out there.

Most sites will post a statement of Rights and Responsibilities. Here is Facebook's:

You own all of the content and information you post on Facebook, and you can control how it is shared through your privacy and application settings. In addition:

1. For content that is covered by intellectual property rights, like photos and videos ("IP content"), you specifically give us the following permission, subject to your privacy and application settings: you grant us a non-exclusive, transferable, sub-licensable, royalty-free, worldwide license to use any IP content that you post on or in connection with Facebook ("IP License"). This IP License ends when you delete your IP content or your account unless your content has been shared with others, and they have not deleted it.

2. When you delete IP content, it is deleted in a manner similar to emptying the recycle bin on a computer. However, you understand that removed content may persist in backup copies for a reasonable period of time (but will not be available to others).

3. When you add an application and use Platform, your content and information is shared with the application. We require applications to respect your privacy settings, but your agreement with that application will control how the application can use the content and information you share. (To learn more about Platform, read our About Platform page.)

4. When you publish content or information using the "everyone" setting, it means that everyone, including people off of Facebook, will have access to that information and we may not have control over what they do with it.

5. We always appreciate your feedback or other suggestions about Facebook, but you understand that we may use them without any obligation to compensate you for them (just as you have no obligation to offer them).

I strongly recommend that should you have any personal questions regarding legal issues related to any communication off- or online, consult an attorney who specializes in that area.

# Chapter 30

## Ask Not What Social Media Can Do For You...But What Social Media Can Do For Consumers
(with apologies to President John F. Kennedy)

The need for politicians to connect with their constituencies, so as to influence their voting preferences to gain political support for themselves, is closely aligned with the business goals of a Realtor who also seeks to gain the personal commitments and trust of his or her respective and varied consumer base.

In my year of research for this book, *Leveraging Your Links*, it became impossible to escape links and references to how today's politicians use—and, in some cases, have mastered—social networking and social media for both campaigning and governance purposes.

Comparing and contrasting how politicians leverage social networking/social media with how most real estate agents employ this opportunity was, for me, quite relevant, interesting, and admittedly, exciting.

How could I not be intrigued with the apparent similarities between politicians and real estate professionals regarding how they both need to be memorable and meaningful in the marketplace—especially considering that I grew up in Boston's inner city? Every young Bostonian, as I once was, soon learns that politics is in your blood—just as much as Boston baked beans, the Red Sox, Celtics, Bruins, Patriots, chowda, and pahking the cah in Hahvahd Yahd.

I now wonder if the years I personally devoted to working on numerous political campaigns—from mayoral, to congressional, to Boston school committee elections (hello, Paul McDevitt, former Boston school committee member)—were major influences and motivations, not only in my real estate career, but also for my writing this book. With all due respect to anything and everything I have done or witnessed within the real estate industry, I must say that it all pales in comparison to what I experienced in the political world. I observed politicians master an offline skillset for reaching and influencing members not only of one community, but many diverse communities. Today's politicians are

## Ask Not What Social Media Can Do For You...
## But What Social Media Can Do For Consumers

now beginning to master this ability online. My background in politics, perhaps, also explains why—after many years of my knocking on doors, telephone
canvassing, writing campaign letters, stuffing envelopes, and inserting political
messages into all sections of the city of Boston, and reaching people of all eth-
nicities, religions, and nationalities—Joe Murphy, my real estate partner, and I
decided many years later, in 1990, to be the first and only real estate company
in North America to publish home guides in six different languages. Alphabetically, the languages we published, in addition to English, were: Chinese, Japa-
nese, Korean, Russian, and Spanish.

I am also confident that the newspaper column I wrote covering the community of Hyde Park, for which I won a journalism award as a high school student,
was also a direct result of my work in the community on behalf of politicians.
Indeed, growing up and becoming immersed in all aspects of these political
campaigns—short of running for office myself—I soon learned that it is important to craft one's message differently for each community, network, or "tribe,"
if you will. How could I escape this political truism, when, after all, one of our
more prominent local politicians, former Speaker of the House Thomas "Tip"
O'Neill coined the expression, "All politics is local."?

As mentioned, years later, when in real estate brokerage, I began to also understand that keeping it "local" should include publishing in locally used languages. I must say that, more than 20 years after our company began to market
multiculturally, I still have not seen another real estate company or agent in
North America replicate the practice of publishing content in glossy, four-color
buyers' guides in six distinct language versions. Rather, all I see is the typical
real estate website approach, "We speak 38 languages at our company." While

it's a lot easier to merely promote that different languages are spoken than it is to publish content in different languages, the payoff is substantially less, as well.

What I also learned from my political campaigning years was that even though all consumers, and thus individuals, belong to multiple groups, networks, activities, and even gangs, in order to reach and influence them, you need to discover the one area that represents their dominant need. I've always said that the only way we ever have access to people is through their concerns. If you agree with my assertion, then the question becomes: How does this awareness translate into online marketing effectiveness? The answer is then: It begins with truly identifying which issues carry the most weight with certain individuals and/or groups.

Using politics again for illustrative purposes, a particular voter may be a registered Republican and a Protestant, live in a distinct neighborhood, and belong to a fishing club, the V.F.W., and the Young Republicans. Yet each of these affiliations might be transcended by a specific personal concern. For instance, let's say he is also intensely opposed to a nuclear power plant being built in the very harbor that his home overlooks. This then becomes his predominant concern—the one for which you can use your influence, if as a local real estate agent you decide to either join or mount an online campaign against the power plant to engage him or attract him to your blog. This issue is the one that you will need to adopt in order to appeal to not only him, but also his neighbors and the many others in the community affected by this issue—provided, of course, that opposition to the nuclear power plant is congruent with your beliefs as well.

Essentially, even though people who live within the town may belong to myriad online networks, each created around similar interests held by similar participants (such as hiking), there are transcendental issues that may be employed to create links *throughout* these numerous communities. Proper expression of these issues can create greater results than merely socializing on the issues that caused the network to be formed. Simply said, talking to fellow hikers on a hiking social network site about mountain climbing may not produce the same real estate results as mentioning, "One thing I like about hiking is that it's away from the nuclear power plants. Maybe we should all hike in opposition to it."

By inserting yourself as a leader of an issue—one that is not directly related to your business, but an issue that enjoys a tangential relationship to real estate—you condition online community participants to begin to view you as a thought leader within real estate; you are seen as one who is not taking time away from real estate functions and responsibilities in order to chit-chat online, but rather to galvanize people around causes that lead to action and directly benefit the online participants.

## Ask Not What Social Media Can Do For You...
## But What Social Media Can Do For Consumers

This would be the role that politicians would intuitively choose for themselves as they seek to create viral campaigns within various communities. Politicians assume this strategy because they realize it is virtually impossible to coalesce sufficient numbers of voters, either offline or online, via the hundreds of other common interests that lead to the formation of various networks and communities.

This is precisely why I respectfully recommend that strategically oriented Realtors emulate the aforementioned methods of politicians, rather than merely settling for the conventional online social networking and social media-like participation within a plethora of communities, networks, and tribes, or only seeking to aggregate thousands of friends, fans, and followers. *I strongly suggest that you identify online the five or six major issues that the community is focused upon, and then essentially subsume these community concerns as a major part of your social media communication strategy.* By doing so, you will emerge as the most credible and respected real estate thought leader or organizer within your online community.

A great example of what you can do *online* requires me to illustrate how I effectively employed such strategy *offline* years ago. I determined that members within a community should be reached strategically with specific content relating to how to move up, so I created the industry's first home move-up system. For expired-listing home sellers, I created an earlier version of my PDF and offline pamphlet, *There's Only One Reason Your Home Didn't Sell...and It Isn't Price*, which, at the time, I entitled, *The Realist Marketing Upgrade Program*. For homeowners who wanted to sell their homes by themselves, I created *The For Sale by Owner Marketing Partnership Program*, which was both a booklet and a system. For two-family homeowners in the community, I created *The Two-Family Home Marketing System*. For consumers who owned homes on corner lots, I created *The Corner Lot Home Marketing System*. Finally, for community members who were more comfortable speaking a foreign language, I had my guides translated into their languages, because their predominant issue was language. I also created *The Real Estate Financial Planning System* for those consumers who regretted not owning enough real estate at some time in their lives, but who also conceded that their real estate agent never encouraged them or showed them how they could develop a real estate financial plan for life. Their real estate agent had only asked them if he or she could be their agent for life.

Notwithstanding all of these systems and campaigns I created—some of which went on to become national marketing systems that I sold to various brands—I still recognized that there was an even larger community need and issue I wanted our company to lead: to connect with the interests of *every homeowner in our state*. This led me to ask myself, "What was the major concern of every single buyer and seller in New Jersey?"—where we had over 30 offices at that time—and how our company, and I, personally, could galvanize all homeowners in our state around a real estate issue that our company could uniquely champion.

My decision did not require rigorous introspection. Here is why it didn't: anyone who's driven down the New Jersey Turnpike should know which issue is the most prominent among all New Jersey homeowners. Within New Jersey, one of America's most beautiful states, in my opinion, there paradoxically exists a small section that is arguably one of the country's major—if not, greatest—eyesores.

Unfortunately, this small section is the only glimpse of an otherwise magnificent and exquisitely beautiful state that the overwhelming percentage of visitors never get to view and experience. Consequently, people who drive through the state think this unique landscape of oil refineries, gases, and foul odors defines the entire state of New Jersey, which it most definitely does not. I have personally owned homes in the leafy Boston suburbs of Needham and Medfield; in downtown Boston; in Westlake Village, California—which is exquisitely beautiful, as is virtually the whole, majestic state; and I currently own a home overlooking the Long Island Sound in the magnificent city of Norwalk, Connecticut, which is in the heart of highly coveted Fairfield County. I have also traveled many times over to all 50 states, every province of Canada, and throughout virtually all of Europe, and I can say without any hesitation, that New Jersey in its entirety, rates at the very top of my favorite places due to its physical beauty, luxuriant countryside, magnificent farms, the college town of Princeton, the dynamic and beautiful coastal communities, the easy access to and stunning views of Philadelphia and Manhattan, as well as the daily ferry service that takes mere minutes to travel from New Jersey to Manhattan. Wow, what a thrilling and fantastic state to live in!

Unfortunately, *my* perception is one that much of the world does not share, but my view is one that every homeowner and citizen of New Jersey wants to have communicated...especially homeowners.

Homeowners understand that the *perception* prospective buyers, corporations, relocating corporations, executives, and citizens of the world have regarding the state and community in which the homeowner's commodity (their property) resides, is inextricably "linked" with the market value of their real estate asset.

Consequently, I concluded that my media and marketing strategy should be one where our real estate company would take on the cause that all New Jersey residents would rally behind. I concluded that they would appreciate relief from the decades of New Jersey jokes and denigrating comments, and they not only would respect our message on behalf of the state as a real estate company, but would conclude the following: "This real estate company is very marketing- and media-savvy. They realize that the more they promote the state, the more they'll attract buyers as well as home sellers who want them to represent their interests. Therefore, they must also be great at marketing homes."

This is the type of messaging and content that I not only suggest, but I implore all real estate agents to embrace as an integral part of your social media strategy in order to rally online communities to your website or blog. Clearly, people in the state in which you practice real estate are more interested in learning how you champion the property value of all homeowners in your state, than in learning where and with whom you had dinner last night.

This is why I have included, for illustrative purposes, my New Jersey media campaign from years ago as a way to encourage readers of this book to not only tweet and post about yourself, but also about the town or state you represent. Better yet, try to come up with a slogan for your state, as I did. Spread the word online and you'll find that people will follow you with exponentially greater loyalty.

I encourage all of you to make sure that you have information on your blogs—almost like you're the tourism bureau—about the state, or the county, or the city you represent. Then you can tweet and post, "If there's anyone you know who wants to know why this is a great place to live, come to my blog. I have 10 reasons why you want to live in [Chicago] (or 15 reasons why you want to live in [Delaware County])." It's very, very important that you do this online.

Gregg Neuman, whom Steve Hundley and I proudly feature in this book, is a great example of being part of and connecting with the community. He has essentially taken on the entire gamut of cultural concerns for all downtown San Diego high-rise-living homeowners. For example, if the city of San Diego were to try to exact an extra high-rise property tax, as some type of new California Proposition 995, for instance, Gregg would, I am positive, try to lead the opposition even more strongly than developers or homeowner associations would. This is because Gregg has become, and has inserted himself as, a San Diego real estate, downtown-living community organizer. He has organized his social media and social networking in a way that assures people are following him because he's first and foremost following *their* issues, *their* needs, and *their* concerns, as opposed to having them follow *his* issues. I believe it's not a question of if, but when, hundreds of thousands of real estate professionals will become illuminated by these following facts or opinions:

1. Few, if any, of us have achieved an Ashton Kutcher-, Madonna-, President Obama-, or Sarah Palin-like charisma, or are seen as interesting enough by consumers to create or sustain a significant degree of satisfied followers and fans for the long run. I am always reminded of the adage, "If we knew how little other people were thinking about us, we would worry less about what they thought."

2. Many consumers either are, or will become, turned off if we ask them to follow us, ostensibly for the purpose of providing them with guidance, only to denigrate their expectations. One consumer told me that a real estate agent asked her to follow him on Twitter and all that the consumer ended up experiencing was an endless parade of gender-based, insulting jokes. When this type of betrayal by a real estate agent happens—when an agent asks people to follow him or her or to tweet about him or her, only to disrespect them by getting too personal, instead of providing valuable real estate content—the agent runs the risk of being perceived as a false prophet who means, but does not say, "Follow me for real estate but what you're really going to get is a voyeuristic look into my life." Therefore, be careful that consumers do not view your motive in using social networking as a means of satisfying your narcissism.

3. We have to be aware that we could be reaching the point where *everyone* is connected. When this happens, we essentially arrive at the point where *no one* is connected. When everyone is connected, in a sense, no one becomes connected, because when everyone is buried under an avalanche of commingled and shared contacts, which no one can maintain, the result is that it really won't matter if you don't keep up with your contacts, because everyone else is also feeling guilty for falling behind, or too tired to notice that you're not keeping in regular contact.

4. Social media should be utilized more in line with how politicians convey potentially viral thoughts, as opposed to providing incessant, self-centered daily reports about their everyday activities or routine.

5. Regarding politics, you need to be very careful when inserting yourself online because politics can be very divisive and polarizing. To illustrate my point: When I was 16, I was campaigning outside a voting location in Brighton, Massachusetts on Election Day. Nearby, was a man in his mid-20s who was campaigning for my candidate's opponent. He approached me, grabbed my candidate's political sign from me and threw it into a trash can. This led to a fistfight between the two of us, resulting in mutual bloody noses and my ending up with a dislocated shoulder. So, instead of joining everyone else at my candidate's victory celebration, I was across the street from the polling location in St. Elizabeth's Hospital. This was all a consequence of politics' divisive nature. Thankfully, due to technology, people can now use more sophisticated and strategic ways of disseminating their advocacy online, even when it's an opposing view.

Therefore, I would suggest that you support, for business reasons, *all* politicians, in the way that many corporations do, even if you don't support their ideologies. However, that's a very personal decision and one that you will have to make for yourself. I know that some people, and I respect them for this, will not connect with anybody whose political ideology is abhorrent to them. Otherwise, it's a good strategy online to be as apolitical and as neutral as possible. As an example, I appeared on a paid advertisement on the front cover of a real estate publication that featured both a former Democratic and Republican president. I offer this illustration as a symbol to remind you that you need to stay impartial online when you're talking about real estate.

We're an industry that wants *everyone* to buy or sell a home. We want *everyone* to get the tax benefits of homeownership. Thus, we should get along with *everyone*. Therefore, watch your online behavior and be aware of who you're linked to. Otherwise, you could wind up friending somebody who is very divisive in the community politically and you might automatically become associated with that person's polarized thinking.

6. When social networking becomes either too light or too self-centered—which can be fine for social purposes—it can destroy your professional essence or value. Valerie Fitzgerald said it best in my interview with her earlier in this book. She said that she absolutely never, under any circumstances, shares personal or self-congratulatory comments online. It's always all about helping people through her real estate knowl-

edge and she never diverts or strays from what she feels has to be her total premise—conveyed through her website, her blog, and in all of her different communities—that she is totally enraptured with and engaged in all things real estate. Valerie's strategy is fine with me as, quite candidly, I don't need to know that a top real estate attorney in my town also likes to cook.

When a real estate professional has the proper social media content and properly inserts the same through his or her appropriate social networks, this integration leads to effective real estate social marketing. Otherwise, the historically less-than-effective offline real estate behavior of many also contaminates their online reputations, images, and essences. A great example of this offline behavior is exemplified by how many real estate agents meet a potential client and quickly ask, "Do you want to buy or sell a home?" or proclaim, "The market's unbelievable!" as I covered elsewhere in this book. This pretty much sabotages any hope that the real estate agent would receive referrals.

For instance, what would you think if you asked a real estate agent that you ran into at a barbecue how she was doing and she answered, "I'm doing great. Are you interested in buying or selling a home?" Would her response inspire you to refer this unsophisticated, desperate-sounding agent to your friends? Not likely.

Now, of course, if someone in real estate asked every single person she met under any circumstances, "Do you want to buy or sell a home?" trust me, she will make a lot more money than another real estate agent who is not engaging anybody in any way, shape, or form. The key is that you want to meet and connect with as many people as possible, but you also want to have the greatest impact, and that requires a little bit more sophistication than saying, "Do you want to buy or sell a home?"

My experience in the political arena led to my creating the Real Estate Social Networking System concept, which is: instead of just expecting people to come to your sites, visit your blog, or participate with you in communities, you can now, through the use of e-mail combined with content, actually target specific real estate content to a target area, bypass spamming, and then encourage other people to forward those e-mails and, in so doing, create what becomes your *personalized* Real Estate Social Network. You can also then invite the same consumers to visit your website/blog and become members of your *real estate social network* and then sustain your relationship with ongoing relevant content, such as how to appeal your property taxes, etc.

I am sure that this concept was influenced by my realization that people want to be called either Democratic, Republican, Independent, Catholic, Jewish, Protestant, Muslim, etc., or to belong to *named* groups and companies. Why not give your friends, fans, followers, and all those you are participating with in a wide range of communities, a similar opportunity to join your specific and real estate only-based social network by actually naming it after yourself? For

## Ask Not What Social Media Can Do For You...
## But What Social Media Can Do For Consumers

example, if it were my network, I would call it the "Allan Dalton Real Estate So-cial Network." You need to create your own real estate social network—one in which *you* become a destination or niche market for consumers as opposed to your just targeting or participating in niche markets or belonging to hundreds of other communities.

This is exactly what politicians do; they create networks where everybody follows *them*, and their networks have their names attached to them. I would like to see this happen for all the readers of this book. Let's take a look at some specific examples of how politicians are using social networking and social media, and how they're combining the two into their own privately labeled political social networks.

Of course, as I offer these political examples, I'm trusting that you, the readers of this book, will put aside, as I did, your personal political opinions; otherwise, your ability to extract relevant and leverageable examples of how politicians use social networking and social media could be impeded. Being sensitive to the varying ideologies of my readers, I made sure to include examples of politi-cians from different political parties.

### President Barack Obama

President Obama has been widely regarded as the first "social media" presi-dent, due to his wildly effective use of social media and social networking prior to, and during, his run for the U.S. presidency in 2008. While then-Vermont Governor, Howard Dean, and his campaign manager, Joe Trippi, were the first to use the Internet to raise substantial sums during Dean's 2004 presidential campaign, President Obama and his team were able to raise the bar due to the use of technology that was not available to Dean in 2004. President Obama had the resources of Web 2.0—websites, blogs, social networking sites, as well as photo and video sites— which enabled him to reach millions of supporters and potential supporters, who then, in turn, spread the word about him and his powerful online presence.

In *The E-Campaign: Rallying Volunteers and Voters*, writer David Talbot points out that "the political campaign of Barack Obama made extensive use of the Web, creating simple interfaces for supporters to organize themselves, donate money, raise awareness on specific issues such as health care reform, and contact voters. This was done at a scale that not only far exceeded what had been done in previous elections, but also surpassed the Web operations of Obama's opponents—Senator John McCain in the general election, and, ear-lier, Senator Hillary Rodham Clinton in the Democratic Party primary elections." (*The E-Campaign: Rallying Volunteers and Voters* by David Talbot; http://www.america.gov/st/democracy-english/2009/March/20090309105245ebyessedo0.9717371.html)

In the article, *How Obama's Internet Campaign Changed Politics*, Arianna

## Ask Not What Social Media Can Do For You...
## But What Social Media Can Do For Consumers

Huffington, the editor-in-chief of The Huffington Post, maintains that President Obama owes his presidency to the Internet. "Were it not for the Internet, Barack Obama would not be president. Were it not for the Internet, Barack Obama would not have been the nominee," she said, while on a panel at the Web 2.0 Summit in San Francisco in November 2008, along with political consultant and Dean's former campaign manager, Joe Trippi, and San Francisco mayor, Gavin Newsom.

Trippi credited the president's use of the Internet for enabling him to successfully amass an enormous group of supporters and organizers, and in a fraction of the time and for a fraction of the cost it would have taken in pre-Internet days, which would have "required an army of volunteers and paid organizers on the ground." Trippi went on to say that President Obama's campaign also received 14.5 million hours of free advertising by creating official videos for YouTube that went viral. "To buy 14.5 million hours on broadcast TV is $47 million," he said. (*How Obama's Internet Campaign Changed Politics* by Claire Cain Miller; http://bits.blogs.nytimes.com/2008/11/07/how-obamas-internet-campaign-changed-politics/?pagemode=print)

In the article, *How Obama Tapped Into Social Networks' Power*, writer David Carr makes the point that President Obama's "relationships are not just the traditional ties of Democrats—teachers' unions, party faithful and Hollywood moneybags—but a network of supporters who used a distributed model of phone banking to organize and get out the vote, helped raise a record-breaking $600 million, and created all manner of media clips that were viewed millions of times. It was an online movement that begot offline behavior, including producing youth voter turnout that may have supplied the margin of victory." In the same article, Ranjit Mathoda, a lawyer and money manager was quoted as saying, "Senator Barack Obama understood that you could use the Web to lower the cost of building a political brand, create a sense of connection and engagement, and dispense with the command and control method of governing to allow people to self-organize to do the work." Mathoda added that, "Mr. Obama had very little in terms of brand to begin with, and he was up against Senator Clinton, who had all the traditional sources of power, and then Senator McCain. But he had the right people and the right idea to take them on."

Now, Carr points out, "All of the Obama supporters who traded their personal information for a ticket to a rally or an e-mail alert about the vice presidential choice, or opted in on Facebook or MyBarackObama can now be mass e-mailed at a cost of close to zero. And instead of the constant polling that has been a motor of presidential governance, an Obama White House can use the Web to measure voter attitudes." (*How Obama Tapped Into Social Networks' Power* by David Carr; http://www.nytimes.com/2008/11/10/business/media/10carr.html?_r=1)

After he was elected, President Obama continued to maintain his connectivity with his supporters, as well as with the whole nation, through his transitional

## Ask Not What Social Media Can Do For You...
## But What Social Media Can Do For Consumers

website, www.change.gov, and upon his inauguration, that website was shut down and replaced with www.whitehouse.gov.

### Howard Dean

On January 14, 2004, BBC News Online reporter Kevin Anderson wrote, "With the help of his net-savvy campaign manager Joe Trippi, Howard Dean is revolutionizing American politics." (*Internet Insurgent Howard Dean* by Kevin Anderson; http://news.bbc.co.uk/2/hi/americas/3394897.stm) While former Vermont Governor Dean (D) wasn't the first politician to utilize the Internet to garner support and raise money—John McCain raised $2 million after he beat George W. Bush in the 2000 New Hampshire Republican primary—Dean was the first candidate who went from being a relative unknown to a viable candidate, due to his use of the Internet and Meetup.com. Anderson explained what happened: "At the beginning of 2003, William Finkel of Meetup.com decided to set up groups for the campaigns of Howard Dean, John Edwards and John Kerry because their campaigns were generating buzz in political blogs. Riding a wave of anti-war sentiment, Howard Dean's blog-driven buzz turned into a roar, and Meetup gave his campaign a way to turn his virtual support into a real political force. On 2 March 2003, an overflow crowd mobbed Mr. Dean at a Meetup in New York City. 'It was a watershed moment,' Mr. Finkel said." (*Internet Insurgent Howard Dean* by Kevin Anderson; http://news.bbc.co.uk/2/hi/americas/3394897.stm)

Meetup.com was an online venue that enabled Dean's supporters to connect and plan where to meet offline to discuss their agenda. Meetups could occur anywhere there were people who wanted to get together. Another advantage of Meetup.com is that when supporters visited their candidate's group, they were able to leave their e-mail addresses, which were then used by candidates for fundraising purposes. According to Anderson, Meetup was paid for a weekly "data dump" of the e-mail addresses by Dean's campaign, as well as by other campaigns, including those of John Kerry and John Edwards. (*Internet insurgent Howard Dean* by Kevin Anderson; http://news.bbc.co.uk/2/hi/americas/3394897.stm)

By targeting these donors, via their e-mail addresses, Dean was able to raise millions of dollars. This was a new concept: collecting small donations from thousands of supporters, which added up to a huge amount of money.

Besides being an effective fundraising tool, the Internet's influence in the political process was just being discovered during the early years of this century's first decade. In the article, *Howard Dean's Internet Love-in* by Joel Roberts, Trippi credited the Internet and Meetup.com with enabling Dean supporters to organize their friends into a 1,200 member group that attended a rally in Washington state. Trippi said that those people were organized strictly by Meetup members, and without any assistance from Dean's campaign staff. (*Howard Dean's Internet Love-in* by Joel Roberts; http://www.cbsnews.com/stories/2003/06/04/politics/main557004.shtml)

## Ask Not What Social Media Can Do For You...
## But What Social Media Can Do For Consumers

### Ron Paul
Congressman Ron Paul (R) of Texas is another beneficiary of the Internet's political power. In the article, *The Web Takes Ron Paul for a Ride*, Katharine Q. Seelye and Leslie Wayne claim that, without the Internet, Paul's 2008 presidential campaign "might have gone the way of his 1988 Libertarian campaign for president, as a footnote to history." *(The Web Takes Ron Paul for a Ride* by Katharine Q. Seelye and Leslie Wayne; http://www.nytimes.com/2007/11/11/us/politics/11paul.html?%20_r=1). However, because Paul's supporters were able to connect with each other online, they were able to create an offline strategy involving old-school methods: having yard signs printed, stuffing campaign literature into envelopes, and coordinating pro-Paul campaign rallies. The authors illustrated how online support of Paul's cause—started by James Sugra of Huntington Beach, California and Trevor Lyman of Miami Beach—ramped up the campaign's momentum: "How much the Paul campaign had snowballed on the Internet became evident last week when supporters independent of the campaign raised $4 million online and an additional $200,000 over the phone in a single day, a record among this year's Republican candidates." Paul said that the media coverage of this extraordinary event supplied his campaign with an additional "$10 million worth of free publicity."

### Sarah Palin
In pre-social media days, Sarah Palin, former Alaska governor and 2008 Republican vice presidential nominee, would have been the natural successor to Senator Dan Quayle in regards to his treatment by the media. The mainstream press and late-night comedians would have reduced her to a cartoon and a joke, and she would have been dismissed as a know-nothing in the country's collective consciousness. However, the Internet and its tools did exist during the 2008 U.S. presidential campaign, and Palin wasted no time in figuring out how to use them—instead of traditional media outlets—to get her message directly to the people.

Palin had no other choice than to explore social networking and social media. After all, she had been ridiculed interminably for her television interview with Katie Couric, and Tina Fey's impression of her on *Saturday Night Live* portrayed Palin as a clueless caricature.

While Obama was blazing a social networking/social media trail for the Democratic Party, the Republicans lagged far behind. Palin, by necessity, jumped with both feet into the social networking/social media pool and yanked the Republican Party in with her. As of this writing, she has more than 2 million Facebook fans, over 200,000 Twitter followers, and in excess of 500 LinkedIn connections. She has chosen to mainly bypass the usual media outlets and speak directly to her friends, followers, and connections.

## Ask Not What Social Media Can Do For You...
## But What Social Media Can Do For Consumers

In *Palin Emerges as Facebook Phenom*, Andy Barr writes that, "For several days in August [2009], the national health care debate turned to focus on so-called 'death panels,' in large part because of two widely-publicized Palin Facebook posts accusing Democratic authors of the House proposal of creating bureaucratic entities to decide end-of-life care. The [posts were] immediately rebuked by Democrats, and even by some Republicans, as untrue and irresponsible." Palin ignored the mainstream media's request for a response and waited out the firestorm. Then, five days later, right before midnight, she posted her response on Facebook. By late morning of the next day, the home pages of numerous national and local newspapers were featuring articles about her post. As of the date of his article, Barr wrote that Palin was second only to President Obama as the most popular politician on Facebook and Twitter. (*Palin emerges as Facebook phenom* by Andy Barr; http://www.politico.com/news/stories/0909/27344.html)

Former White House press secretary and media strategist Ari Fleisher was quoted in the same article as saying, "Facebook is perfectly suited for someone as polarizing as Sarah Palin. It's the ideal way for her to keep in touch, to rev up her base and go around mainstream media."

Palin's strategy to cut out the mainstream media, i.e., the middleman or filter, is now affecting how the middleman reports on her. In *Sarah Palin Shuns Press: Talks to Twitter, Facebook Instead*, Pete Cashmore writes, "Palin is talking to no one...except Twitter and Facebook. ... The press appears somewhat frustrated by the decision, with the AP producing a full-length article today discussing the governor's most recent Tweets, including: 'Lots of celebration of Independence & Alaska's 50th Anniversary of Statehood.' It was only thanks to Twitter that the media know where Palin was today, the Associated Press adds—she was at the Juneau Fourth of July parade." (*Sarah Palin Shuns Press: Talks to Twitter, Facebook Instead* by Pete Cashmore; http://mashable.com/2009/07/04/sarah-palin-facebook/)

### Other Politicians
Politicians of all stripes—those regularly reported on, those who don't receive regular coverage, and those who get unfavorable coverage—have recognized the necessity of embracing social media and social networking in order to connect with their constituents and supporters, as well as to spread their message, and this goes for local politicians as well as national ones.

Mayor Scott Smith (R) of Mesa, Arizona told Steven Davy of pbs.org, "As money becomes tighter as traditional media outlets become either non-existent or more and more restrictive [as] to how much they cover and the scope of their coverage, I think social media is going to play an increasingly important role in local campaigns because they are all we have." (*Local Politicians Use Social Media to Connect with Voters* by Steven Davy; http://www.pbs.org/mediashift/2009/09/local-politicians-use-social-media-to-connect-with-voters272.html)

Indeed, politicians of all levels are flocking to social media to access people they wouldn't reach by way of traditional media. In the article, *Republican Politicians Make A Social Media Push*, Republican strategist Mindy Finn said that it's hard for a member of the House to get national media coverage, but "now if they build up a network of blogger support, if they have a presence on Facebook or on Twitter, and they put out ... information, it can go virally across the Internet." (*Republican Politicians Make A Social Media Push*, December 27, 2009; http://www.npr.org/templates/story/story.php?storyId=121891988)

Mayor Gavin Newsom (D) of San Francisco recalled an incident during his reelection campaign that served as his wake-up call. He said he attended one of his rallies and didn't see the usual people there. His aides explained that his audience was composed of his Facebook friends. At the time, he had no idea what Facebook was. Now, he says, he's "obsessed with Facebook." (*How Obama's Internet Campaign Changed Politics* by Claire Cain Miller; http://bits.blogs.nytimes.com/2008/11/07/how-obamas-internet-campaign-changed-politics/?pagemode=print). Newsom has since discovered the wonders of social media and how it can connect him to his constituents. As a result, his administration has been able to respond to his city's needs by creating programs, like DataSF, which address their needs and concerns. (*How Local Politicians Are Using Social Media* by Josh Sternberg; http://mashable.com/2009/10/19/social-media-local%20politics/)

Politicians are not only posting written content; they are also posting videos on YouTube. Olivia Ma, the video site's news and politics manager, said that, as of December 2009, about 80 percent of Congress had started using YouTube, including House Minority Whip Eric Cantor (R-VA), who created a popular mashup video of Republican doctors talking about why they were opposed to President Obama's health care plan. (*Republican Politicians Make A Social Media Push*, December 27, 2009; http://www.npr.org/templates/story/story.php?storyId=121891988)

Governor Deval Patrick (D-MA) and his Director of New Media and Online Strategy, Brad Blake, utilize all of the facets of social media. "What I try to do, both internally and when working with others on using social media, is to talk about the need or communication gap first, then figure out which tools best fill that need or gap. ... Twitter is great for getting quick reactions to information coming out of the office and to understand what people need help with. YouTube has been great to both disseminate important information...and to respond to constituent questions in a way that others can benefit from," said Blake. (*How Local Politicians Are Using Social Media* by Josh Sternberg; http://mashable.com/2009/10/19/social-media-local%20politics/)

The key to using social media for politicians—and for real estate agents—is to merge all of the possibilities into one effective tool. As Micah Kellner (D), Assemblyman for New York's 65th Assembly District, said, "All of these tools work best when they're integrated—when we use each of them in a way that's [complementary] to the others. Rather than focus on them primarily as separate pieces, I prefer to think of them as parts of our overall communications strategy." (*How Local Politicians Are Using Social Media* by Josh Sternberg; http://mashable.com/2009/10/19/social-media-local%20politics/)

The reason I have included a series of examples from the political realm regarding the ever-increasing utilization of social networking and social media platforms among forward-thinking and social media-savvy politicians and their respective campaigns is that, as I said earlier, I do believe we can learn much from the way in which they use these tools.

Moving on, I'd like to ask you a politically oriented question: *Who's campaigning for you?* Why is it that politicians are able to inspire volunteers to knock on doors, stuff envelopes, stand in the cold with a placard on Election Day, and donate money—oftentimes without any hope or promise of a personal reward other than the joy of supporting someone who stands for their beliefs?

Are consumers willing to make phone calls for you, stuff envelopes, stand in the cold, or even get into a fight—as I did—on your behalf? Probably not. That, in and of itself, should inform us that politicians must have a better sense of how to access the political concerns of people than real estate professionals do regarding accessing the real estate concerns of consumers. This difference is also reflected in the way in which politicians campaign. Most social media-savvy political pundits have opined that in the most recent presidential election, President Obama was able to create more connectivity online than either Senator Hillary Rodham Clinton or Senator John McCain because his message was one that responded to an existing need of potential voters—more than his competitors. Specifically, consumers were ready for change and President Obama's entire social media premise was either "Change," or "Change You Can Believe In," while Hillary Clinton's message was described as "Hillary for President," and John McCain's online strategy was "My Life Story."

Perhaps some real estate agents are not enjoying greater success through social networking and social media because their messages and their essences are incongruent with consumer needs. Hillary Clinton's message of "Hillary for President" appears to have been adopted by some agents and repurposed into "Vote for Me for Real Estate Office," and John McCain's into "My Story as a Real Estate Professional." Apparently, these messages, which have more to do with the messenger than with the consumer, don't appear to become especially viral online. So again, if you'll kindly put aside your opinions of the politicians I referenced and instead focus on the tactical and strategic approaches they employed to manage online connectivity with content and communities, it might shed greater light on how you need to view the way in which you manage your social media campaign.

It is my hope that all of us might take a page out of the playbook of prominent politicians. If we do, it will be for a good reason. Congress people get re-elected over 95 percent of the time. Real estate professionals cannot point to anywhere near that level of consumer loyalty. And yet, the approval ratings of politicians, in general, are atrocious. Why then this disparity between overall consumer sentiment and specific loyalty to local individual politicians? Unquestionably, it is due to how local politicians targeted the marketplace historically offline, and now online as well, in a heterogeneous manner where they artfully matched message to market, by customizing approaches to various and distinct consumer groups, e.g., their work on Medicare, which they directed to senior citizens, and their support of college loans, targeted to younger voters and their parents.

Most real estate professionals, however, have heretofore not displayed similar demographic acuity. But now, through the power of online social networks, they can and they should, and—most importantly—in a cost-effective and time-efficient manner.

For this technologically driven transformation to occur, relevant content is required. Relevant content emerges out of a relevant spirit of intent; therefore, you need to examine your spirit of intent. If you think about the messages conveyed by the candidates in the last presidential campaign, you can decide if you want your message to reflect your desire to affect change like President Obama's; your run for office like then-Senator Clinton's; or your life story as Senator McCain's did.

Again, if you are able to leave your politics, as they say, "at the door" and consider what some say about how these three great American politicians employed social media in order to determine how you can become the most viral online, then that exercise may lead you to ask yourself the following question: "Am I going to use social media to affect change in the marketplace, to run for real estate office, or to tell the ongoing story of my life?" My recommendation is that you learn a lesson from each of these three outstanding leaders. Part of your strategy should be about change, in terms of changing the lives of real estate consumers for the better, like first-time buyers, down-sizers, those who need short-sale relief, tax credits, etc. You've also got to run for real estate office by letting people know about your credentials, your background, and how much you love real estate and want to serve the real estate needs of others. And you also need to tell your life story, both personally and professionally, but do it in a relevant way as Senator McCain did.

In fact, I have written this book, using that very formula. *First*, I—along with John Featherston, Darryl MacPherson, Steve Hundley, our respective compa-

## Ask Not What Social Media Can Do For You...
## But What Social Media Can Do For Consumers

nies, RISMedia and 1parkplace, and all of the true real estate luminaries featured in this book—want to use this book and social media and social networking platforms to initiate necessary change. *Second*, I have always been running for real estate office by seeking your support (votes) for my real estate thought-leadership. *Third*, throughout this book, I have committed to sharing some of my life story, which is nowhere near as remarkable as Senator McCain's, through the use of personal and professional experiences and photos. When we utilize or manage social media in a way that advances the interests of others, it not only can create a viral online/offline campaign but can actually cause both politicians and others to jump onboard either by how they offer links to your blog-hosted content, retweet your information about your cause, or actually ask to participate in your movement. A classic example of how media, community, real estate, and politics can all merge can be found in the picture below of when New Jersey State Senator Lautenberg asked to join Joe Murphy and me in support of the slogan I created to promote the state of New Jersey. One must remember that politicians want homeowners to choose them...but then again, we want homeowners to choose us, too.

*My mentor, Joe Murphy, Senator Lautenberg, and a much younger me.*

*Author's note: My thanks to Patricia Bahner Porco who researched and then wrote the portion of this chapter on how politicians utilize social media.*

# Chapter 31

## Conclusion: Embarking on "Social Media 2.0"– Upgrading Friends, Fans, and Followers to "Members" of a Real Estate Social Network

The value of the principles I debut in this book will be directly proportional to the degree that you, the reader, personally and successfully apply them to your real estate business, be it at the company or individual level.

From the outset, I understood and accepted that my major motivation in writing this book was to shape and direct first your thoughts, and then of course, your actions, all in order to help you gain greater social media and social networking effectiveness and results-oriented proficiency.

Otherwise, there would be no point in writing this book. In fact, I believe that the foundation upon which the concept of "social media" is built is one that challenges all of us to not only seek to connect and create within online communities but, more significantly, to employ this digital medium to more powerfully influence, and presumably enhance, not just our careers but the lives of others.

Very few words or precepts have been as elevated in prominence in recent years as the concept of *transparency*. Accordingly, I seek to be fully forthright regarding what I hope this book will accomplish. Specifically, my objective now is to invite all of the real estate professionals who have read this book, and who have dedicated their valuable time to examining and evaluating its contents, to join me in determining if the objectives of the book have been reached. In a sense I ask that you write the book's conclusion with me...or at least part of it. What I am particularly interested in learning from you are your responses to the following questions:

A. Did this book expand your understanding of social media as it relates to your business?

B. Did this book inspire you to provide consumers with more valuable content?

C. Did this book provide you with valuable examples and illustrations from your industry contemporaries of direct applications of the book's principles?

## Conclusion: Embarking on "Social Media 2.0"– Upgrading Friends, Fans, and Followers to "Members" of a Real Estate Social Network

D. Did this book motivate you to become even more successful through the development and execution of a personal and effective social media/real estate social marketing strategy?

In order to determine whether these objectives have been realized, or will be in the near future, requires that you, the reader, expend the effort to reach conclusions of your own. To facilitate these conclusions, I ask you to consider the following objectives.

To complete these questions online, send comments and receive a free copy of survey results, visit http://www.surveymonkey.com/s/leveragingyourlinks-conclusionsurvey.

### *Leveraging Your Links* Objectives

1. To provide numerous case studies from industry-based social media mentors in order to share concrete, specific examples and illustrations so that the readers can contemplate changes to their personal real estate social media strategies.

Favorable Conclusion _____        Unfavorable Conclusion _____
Comments:

2. To cause readers to rigorously assess and resolve their own distinctions between social networking, social media, and real estate social marketing.

Favorable Conclusion _____        Unfavorable Conclusion _____
Comments:

3. To offer the opinion, by way of personal example (e.g., my writing this book as a non-professional journalist), that all of us have the right, which should be encouraged, to publicly express our views on real estate social media, etc., because citizen journalism is one of the hallmarks of social media.

Favorable Conclusion _____        Unfavorable Conclusion _____
Comments:

4. To provide valuable research from the industry to the industry by means of the *RIS-Media 2010 Dalton/Hundley Real Estate Social Media Census*.

Favorable Conclusion _____        Unfavorable Conclusion _____

# Conclusion: Embarking on "Social Media 2.0"– Upgrading Friends, Fans, and Followers to "Members" of a Real Estate Social Network

Comments:

5. To provide Steve Hundley's case study of Gregg Neuman, enabling readers to emulate a highly successful real estate social media strategy.

Favorable Conclusion _____          Unfavorable Conclusion _____
Comments:

6. To present research demonstrating how politicians apply community and networking strategies through the effective employment of social networking/social media resources as a basis of comparison.

Favorable Conclusion _____          Unfavorable Conclusion _____
Comments:

7. To provide readers with information and guidance regarding the critical importance of effective grammatical online communication. *Reminder*: The first impression someone has of you online could very well influence your future opportunities with that person.

Favorable Conclusion _____          Unfavorable Conclusion _____
Comments:

8. To provide the reader with a legal perspective regarding social media/social networking.

Favorable Conclusion _____          Unfavorable Conclusion _____
Comments:

9. To provide the reader with information and a quiz regarding the theoretical correlation between social networking and social anxiety.

Favorable Conclusion _____          Unfavorable Conclusion _____
Comments:

## Conclusion: Embarking on "Social Media 2.0"– Upgrading Friends, Fans, and Followers to "Members" of a Real Estate Social Network

10. To provide readers with information on how to develop their personal real estate social marketing plan.

Favorable Conclusion \_\_\_\_\_     Unfavorable Conclusion \_\_\_\_\_
Comments:


11. To provide information regarding the relationship between mobile technology and social media.

Favorable Conclusion \_\_\_\_\_     Unfavorable Conclusion \_\_\_\_\_
Comments:


12. To introduce the concept of real estate social marketing as representing the convergence of social networking and social media for strategic real estate business usage.

Favorable Conclusion \_\_\_\_\_     Unfavorable Conclusion \_\_\_\_\_
Comments:


13. To cause readers to expend considerable thought in order to either embrace or repudiate their individual implementations of the principles of the book.

Favorable Conclusion \_\_\_\_\_     Unfavorable Conclusion \_\_\_\_\_
Comments:

14. To demonstrate the distinction between a real estate professional who merely participates in online communities versus one who creates his or her own personally branded and led real estate social network that offers consumers *membership* and constantly seeks to provide appropriate content to consumer members who visit their website or blog. *Please do not answer this part yet, but defer your response until the end of my summary/conclusion/solution.*

Favorable Conclusion \_\_\_\_\_     Unfavorable Conclusion \_\_\_\_\_
Comments:

## Conclusion: Embarking on "Social Media 2.0"– Upgrading Friends, Fans, and Followers to "Members" of a Real Estate Social Network

Once again, you may complete these questions online and register to receive a free copy of the results by visiting http://www.surveymonkey.com/s/leveragingyourlinksconclusionsurvey.

The reason I have asked you to defer your response to question 14 is because I have not yet dedicated the proper time or focus within this book to what I believe is *the single most valuable use of social media* now available to real estate professionals—one which has not yet been adopted by even the most forward-thinking real estate professionals in North America, including the esteemed social media mentors whom I feature in this book.

After interviewing and carefully reviewing the social media business plans and business practices of those we selected and featured in this book, and also considering what I learned from additional research and travels throughout the industry both offline and online, I am convinced that there exists a momentous social media-related void that needs to be effectively addressed. I'm referring to the way in which real estate professionals can best and fully leverage the powers of social media—a way that, as I write this book, remains unexplored and unexploited.

I need to reference philosopher Hegel's treatise regarding change one last time. His assertion that all great change reveals three stages, with the final stage, or synthesis, representing a correction period, leads me to assert that our industry needs to experience a correction period for real estate usage of social media—or what I'm going to call Social Media 2.0 in deference to Web 2.0. In the world of Social Media 2.0, real estate professionals should not be satisfied by merely statistically measuring how many fans, followers, or friends they aggregate or how many communities, networks, organizations, or even tribes they participate in. Instead, this Social Media 2.0 correction period can represent for them the ability to create and manage their personally branded online and offline real estate social network, one which functions as a *membership* relationship similar to numerous other consumer/business relationship models. This personalized and branded *real estate social network* I speak of would, for the first time, afford consumers the luxury and appeal of not only connecting with a real estate agent through generic social networking sites, i.e., Twitter, Facebook, and LinkedIn, but would also provide consumers with the option of becoming a declared and accepted member of their real estate agent's personally led, proprietary *real estate social network*.

For illustrative purposes, the consumer would be approached in the following noteworthy fashion: "I'd like you to become a member of my John Doe *Real Estate Social Network*," or "Click here and learn the value of becoming a member of the Jane Doe Real Estate Social Network," or how about, "Membership has its privileges. Become a member of the Any Agent Real Estate Social Network. It's free, it's fun, its interactive...and informative. Please visit my web-

## Conclusion: Embarking on "Social Media 2.0"– Upgrading Friends, Fans, and Followers to "Members" of a Real Estate Social Network

site/blog to learn about the benefits of becoming a member of my *real estate social network*."

Ostensibly, most real estate professionals are apparently not interested in creating a deeper and more sustainable relationship with consumers as evidenced by their greater devotion to the concept of "customers for life" as opposed to "members for life." Now, of course, if you are a consumer, a real estate agent will always be willing to invite you to become a fan, friend, follower, or visitor to his or her website, blog, or online hub. But please, as a consumer, don't ever expect to be invited into a more meaningful and symbolically connected relationship, one that carries a greater commitment than the elusive and centuries-old "customer for life" failed strategy. Now of course, you, the consumer, can continue to feel and experience a higher level of bonding through the membership relationship you enjoy with your church, religion, political party, and civic and community organizations, and, of course, you can continue to gain a sense of inclusion from Facebook, Twitter, and numerous other thriving online organizations and networks. However, please do not expect that level of invitation or commitment to sustainable engagement from real estate agents. Instead, continue to expect only a consumer "catch-and-release" program to remain intact. Little wonder why the consumer's practice of Russian real estate roulette is so enduring.

Real estate agents seem to perceive themselves as only possessing the ability or value to belong to, but not *lead* communities. For example, over the years, tens of thousands of real estate agents have appropriately and enthusiastically asserted that they are "Ferryites," "Buffini-ites," "Sweathogs," "Proctorites," or that they are members of the venerated STAR POWER, ABR®, CDPE, CRS, e-PRO, GRI, the Top 5 in Real Estate Network®, etc. And this level of mutual loyalty and engagement is for good reason. Each of these magnificent networks, course designations, or certifications—along with their charismatic leaders—has provided either membership or networking opportunities, or has personally led networks that have helped to monumentally transform the careers of literally thousands upon thousands of real estate agents. Especially helped have been the careers of those agents who are the most vigilant regarding their professional development. And, of course, where would real estate agents be if they did not possess a sense of belonging, not only as Realtors, but also as members of branded real estate companies?

Now that I have reviewed how the real estate industry ensures that each of its own can enjoy multiple opportunities for inclusion or membership, either at the industry level (Realtor), the educational level (CRS, GRI, etc.), the business development level (STAR POWER, Top 5 in Real Estate, etc.), or the company brand level (franchise or independent), let's examine how uninviting we are in the way we treat consumers. The reason why it might be instructive to as-

## Conclusion: Embarking on "Social Media 2.0"– Upgrading Friends, Fans, and Followers to "Members" of a Real Estate Social Network

sess the issue of what we offer consumers in the way of inclusiveness is that it might help to explain why so many real estate professionals actually bemoan the fact that consumers do not display loyalty to them. Could this be explained by the principle of reciprocity?

No doubt some of my readers are thinking, "Oh Allan, come on! Did you forget how we already group or include consumers? You know, we group them as FSBOs, expireds, first-time buyers, looky-loos and, of course, that is after first honoring them by scrubbing them, incubating them, and announcing that they have qualified to become members of our database?" No wonder so many real estate professionals are perplexed regarding a history of consumer indifference considering the inelegant way in which we engage them!

Those who think that consumers should remain in the "buyers are liars" network, or that they will obtain referrals from consumers by merely asking for them on the back of their business cards, will see no need to offer a higher or more meaningful level of consumer engagement, and certainly not membership in anything to do with real estate. If this remains your thinking, you can rest assured that no other industry or profession will threaten to infringe on your intellectual property or business model.

*American Express, for one, will definitely not be seeking to emulate the real estate industry's business strategy for engendering consumer loyalty.* I first discovered how they think differently in 1976, when I qualified for an American Express card. American Express actually perceived much greater potential in me than I saw in myself. I thought I would be fortunate to just receive their credit card. However, they must have had a private conversation with my blessed mother, Rose, about my relative merits, because they told me that not only was I going to receive their credit card but that they were also going to confer upon me membership in American Express. Wow, did I feel important!

Unlike real estate agents, who for 50 years have been asking consumers if they could be their real estate agent for life, or attending conferences with banners reading "Customers for Life," American Express and their business model, to the contrary, concluded that they could effectively skip these trite and blatantly self-serving relationship-building steps by simply informing anybody doing business with them that they were now *members* of their exclusive "club." Perhaps our industry's inability to command consumer loyalty is related to the fact that we have always merely *requested* loyalty from consumers in business transactions and we have shied away from displaying reciprocal acts of loyalty to consumers beyond the transaction. This is something we can now do by offering them membership into our personally led and branded real estate social network. The reason why I suggest that we have an unprecedented opportunity to build online real estate memberships described as one's own real estate social network is because human online aggregators like Facebook, Twit-

## Conclusion: Embarking on "Social Media 2.0" – Upgrading Friends, Fans, and Followers to "Members" of a Real Estate Social Network

ter, Plaxo, LinkedIn, MySpace, etc. have already performed the heavy lifting for you. These sites and social networking concepts have conditioned consumers to enjoy the benefits of online participatory community sharing.

Amazingly, while there are very few major real estate social networks, there seems to be an almost infinite number of social networks based upon almost every other conceivable interest. To the consumer, it must appear that real estate professionals are not interested in leading a real estate social network, but instead have been seduced by the concept of consumers following them on Twitter or friending them on Facebook where possibly from time to time the subject of real estate might make that day's digital docket. I believe consumers would love for top producing real estate agents to post or tweet linking invitations to their websites or blogs so they could join others in declaring themselves a member of a successful agent's particular real estate social network. The technology is in place and consumers accept online aggregation around ideas, so all that is necessary at this point is to invite consumers to become members—and stay members—of your real estate social network, instead of just inviting them to visit your blog or website.

This distinction should not be seen as one of merely semantics, or as a ploy to achieve greater personal gain without true benefit to the consumer. Membership implies a higher degree of customer value and service, without additional fees. This relationship development provides continuous informational value that we initiate, rather than our only responding to consumers when they need our services to conduct a real estate transaction or because on a particular day a real estate agent had an interesting article on their blog or retweeted a topical issue that week. *Rather, it is the true real estate professional who can view the long-term potential of the valued member relationship, as opposed to always chasing down the immediate short-term—and immediately compensated—transaction-based relationship.* Perhaps for some, it may be helpful to consider "the worst-case scenario," which would be our providing to some members of our community valuable real estate information, which may never result in direct compensation from that person. We are then contributors, through social media, of positive community service which, at the very least, will likely be compensated with good will and referrals.

Please consider the difference between the following examples. Which one is more effective, in your opinion?

**Twitter Post #1:**
Hey folks, I invite everyone to become a member of my Jane Doe Real Estate Social Network. It's free, so check out what members receive.

*Versus*

**Twitter Post #2:**

## Conclusion: Embarking on "Social Media 2.0"– Upgrading Friends, Fans, and Followers to "Members" of a Real Estate Social Network

I'd like to be your real estate agent for life.

Now, here's a post that will work for you on Facebook:

**Facebook Post:**
I invite all of my friends and your friends to become members of my John Doe Real Estate Social Network. To learn what members receive...for free...please visit my website (or blog).

To illustrate my next point, I'm going to once again employ my Boston-based political metaphors that I use throughout the chapter, "Ask Not What Social Media Can Do for You...But What Social Media Can Do for Consumers." Starting several centuries ago, when new arrivals, who were mostly Europeans, landed in Boston after being "aggregated" by the shipping industry, they were immediately greeted by and offered membership into political parties. These membership affiliations were passed down to the immigrants' descendants and have endured, for most, to this day. Today, we at RISMedia, Top 5, and 1parkplace, have the technology and content to make this type of approach work for you. You can now upgrade your friends, fans, and followers from steerage or coach class to your first-class real estate social network. All that's required is a tab or link on your website, blog, or hub linking to a description of all the services you provide to your real estate members. To see how easy this is to accomplish, simply e-mail me at Allan.Dalton@top5inrealestate.com.

Perhaps one of the reasons many real estate professionals do not receive the respect they truly deserve is because they have not found a way to attach value to the free advice, information, and considerable counsel they provide to consumers. It's for that reason that I'm advocating that you, at the very least, enhance the perceived value of the informational and consultative services you provide by making such elements more special for your *members*. Hey, if Costco can do it, why not you?

I'll leave it to you to decide for yourself, but I believe that most consumers would prefer to be treated as "members" for life, as opposed to "customers" for life. I am purposely not saying "clients" for life because our industry has limited its definition of client along agency practices. But if the word "client" will continue to be defined by agency, then at the very least, let's use social media resources to encourage the evolution of our consumer relationships from where we now only ritualistically imitate the rest of the population by seeking friends, fans, and followers, to where our emphasis is on inviting consumers to become members of our personally branded real estate social networks. I suggest that most real estate agents will be better off having 1,000 intensely committed members in their personally branded real estate social networks than by having 10,000 casual friends, fans, followers, and visitors to their websites—all

## Conclusion: Embarking on "Social Media 2.0"– Upgrading Friends, Fans, and Followers to "Members" of a Real Estate Social Network

of whom they must share with hundreds of other Realtors.

*Therefore, I encourage you, the real estate professional, to obtain loyalty to you...through Facebook, Twitter, LinkedIn, etc., and not just organize loyalty through you...to Facebook, Twitter, LinkedIn, etc.* This distinction is especially significant because, as I have often said, many consumers will create connections online with multiple real estate agents just as they have done offline for decades. Unless real estate professionals learn how to use content and actively cause consumers to not only link to their websites, blogs, etc., but actually *enroll* as members in their personally branded real estate social network once they get there, then I fear that an unprecedented amount of time and effort will be directed toward promulgating one of the greatest zero-sum-gain outcomes in history. Simply said, you must look to employ social media to organize a community based on real estate interest *under your direct leadership*, and not just seek to insert yourself into myriad online communities in which you merely participate. In fact, you need to do both.

Although the information I'm about to share is certainly not original, it nevertheless is indispensable if one hopes to form a successful social media strategy: We must always look at our use of social media from the prism of the public. Continuing with my overuse of alliteration and penchant for the use of "P's" as in the 5 P's of Marketing, the 5 P's of Mobile etc.—which all began when my eighth-grade teacher ordered me to write 1,000 times as punishment for misbehavior in class, "Petulant pupils who perpetually perturb a patient pedagogue shall be punished." I must call attention to three other words that also begin with the letter "P" that should enjoy prominence with any professional perusing this publication: *Prospecting, Prowling, and Partnering.*

Taking these terms one at a time, from the public's perspective, "prospecting" is an activity that real estate agents are more passionate about than the public. In fact, I recall visiting one of the largest real estate organizations in the world recently and, as I entered, I was stunned to see appearing prominently on their front glass door, "No Solicitation or Salespeople Welcome," which ironically represented the very activity or behavior that was responsible for this company's entire existence. This vivid and most negative proclamation regarding the appeal of being prospected to suggests that most consumers do not possess a strong desire to be at the other end of prospecting activities.

Let's move to the next "P" — "prowling." While this word immediately offends many professionals whose professional methods would never be described in this fashion, many consumers believe that real estate professionals ask to friend them or invite them to join their numerous social networks in order to garner their real estate business. This online zealousness, therefore, runs the risk of being categorized as a light version of prowling.

## Conclusion: Embarking on "Social Media 2.0"– Upgrading Friends, Fans, and Followers to "Members" of a Real Estate Social Network

The last "P" is "partnering." Partnering is demonstrated by those real estate professionals who use social media with the spirit of intent to partner with neighborhood interests, community interests, the public's interest, and their overall clients' interest. Partnering or creating members means that everything relating to their use of social media is powered from the consumer perspective.

Social media, in my view, should be employed in such a way that real estate professionals who are hoping to win the confidence of prospective home sellers are now able to say (as I wrote in Chapter 5), *"Folks, my goal in using social networking and social media platforms is not to create friends, fans, and followers for me... but, instead, to create friends, fans, and followers for the properties, like yours, that I am privileged to represent."*

The notion that consumers are more likely to favorably respond when they believe that something benefits them, and are not enthralled by the self-serving or self-praising boasts of others, is certainly no remarkable revelation. What is remarkable, however, is how often the real estate industry seemingly overlooks the opportunity to provide information and solutions that respond to the clearly expressed needs of real estate consumers.

Ironically, in time, we may conclude that the Internet—the very thing so many in our industry (including me) originally viewed as a potential threat to the consumer perception of industry value—might actually be the catalyst for enhancing, if not transforming, our value to consumers.

Since few, if any, real estate brokerages or real estate agents were inclined to, or could afford to, make a deep commitment to research and development (R & D), as most corporations who serve consumers do, it led to years of stunning examples of industry approaches that seemed more dedicated to celebrating our needs instead of serving consumer needs—for example, approaches like hanging banners across real estate offices that exclaim, "Listings Needed" or "Agents Needed." I have respectfully suggested that few, if any, other business or service providers would imitate this attempt to publicly memorialize one's own needs.

The reason why the Internet and social media can now emancipate us from self-focused marketing is that the principles that govern Internet effectiveness—algorithms, SEO, key words—are all predicated upon consumer interest and preference. Had our industry enjoyed an SEO or algorithmic mindset offline in earlier decades, perhaps the pumpkins, calendars, and park benches that celebrate "Spouses Selling Houses" would not have led to our unofficial "page ranking" offline by consumers.

Moreover, since social media represents citizen journalism, and social networking, at a minimum, means interaction, ratings, rankings, and online feedback and forums, we now have much of the R & D we need, and it's being

**Conclusion: Embarking on "Social Media 2.0"– Upgrading Friends, Fans, and Followers to "Members" of a Real Estate Social Network**

provided at no expense.

The challenge now is to truly listen. Maybe we'll even discover that, all along, we've wanted to contact consumers more than they have wanted to be contacted and that consumers have always wanted real estate information more than we have been willing to provide same. I'll leave that research to you, as it will influence how you strategize your business career, but I assure you that not getting the answer right does carry with it what I have coined as "contentsequences."

In closing, please allow me to acknowledge that this book—although replete with research and factual examples and illustrations—also reflects great subjectivity. *Leveraging Your Links* was written by me in a very flexible and opinionated fashion and not as a legal brief or imperial dogma. Consequently, I harbor no illusions that my specific content will command universal assent. Moreover, to those who may think that something as simple as social networking does not require the degree of attention that I devoted to it in this book, then I also need to remind them of the unending number of courses, coaches, mentors, gurus, and books that the subject has attracted and will continue to attract. Regarding this book, my deepest desire is to have each reader not only become edified by its contents but, more importantly, continue on a personal social media and, perhaps, real estate social marketing journey. To that end, you have my very best wishes.

P.S. I now invite you to answer statement 14. Are you interested in creating your own personally branded and led real estate social network—which generates *members for life* instead of continuing to attempt to generate *customers for life*? If so, please let us know.

*"If I am not for myself, who will be for me? If I am not for others, what am I? And if not now, when?"*

—Rabbi Hillel

# Glossary of Terms

**1parkplace**

1parkplace is high-level marketing technology for agents, real estate teams, and brokerage firms.

**ActiveRain**

ActiveRain operates the largest and most active social network in the real estate space with a goal to "empower the real estate professional" and as an extension, empower the consumer. This network helps agents to create business relationships both within the industry and with the consumer.

**AOL**

America Online is arguably the first active social network. Starting in the early 1990s, AOL became a dominating service that connected millions of consumers to the Internet. Free start-up floppy disks were used to market the service and were given to prospective users, such as airline travelers or magazine subscribers. Although many new networks have developed over the years, AOL still has millions of users and offers a robust closed network of content.

**Backlink**

Backlinks are incoming links to a website or webpage. Inbound links were originally important (prior to the emergence of search engines) as a primary means of Web navigation; today, their significance lies in search engine optimization (SEO). The number of backlinks is one indication of the popularity or importance of that website or page (though other measures, such as page rank, are likely to be more important). Outside of SEO, the backlinks of a webpage may be of significant personal, business or semantic interest: they indicate who is paying attention to that page.

**Bing**

Bing (formerly Windows Live Search and MSN Search) is the current Web search engine (advertised as a "decision engine") from Microsoft. Bing was unveiled by Microsoft CEO Steve Ballmer on May 28, 2009 at the All Things Digital conference in San Diego.

# Glossary of Terms

**Blog or Blogsite**
A blog (a contraction of the term "weblog") is a type of website, usually maintained by an individual, with regular entries of commentary, descriptions of events, or other material such as graphics or video.

**Bounce**
The term "bounce" refers to the website visitor hitting the back button before navigating any additional internal pages. The goal is to have the lowest bounce rate possible by utilizing "sticky" content.

**CMA**
Competitive Marketing Analysis—also sometimes called a BPO—(Broker Price Opinion)

**Contact Management**
A Contact Management System (CMS) is an integrated office solution that allows organizations and individuals to record relationships and interactions with customers and suppliers. This information includes all e-mails, documents, jobs, faxes, calendar, and more. This type of solution is gaining more and more popularity as companies want to be able to control all information from a single, integrated application, rather than different proprietary applications, each with its own data collection system.

**Content Management**
A Content Management System (CMS) is a solution that integrates your content and content sources with your website, social networking, or e-mail. Ideally, a CMS is electronic and automated as found in the 1parkplace BOSS. The key is to streamline communication, marketing, and prospective activities.

**CRM**
Customer Relationship Management (CRM) is a widely-implemented strategy for managing and nurturing a company's interactions with customers, clients, and sales prospects. It involves using technology to organize, automate, and synchronize business processes, such as sales activities, marketing efforts, customer service, and technical support.

**CSV**
Stands for Comma Separated Values. The popular and widely accepted file format encodes primary contact information for storage in a computer file. Files encoded using the CSV format store tabular data separated by commas.

**CTA**
Stands for Call To Action. Using a proper call to action to highlight the most desired content is critical for Internet lead generation.

**Drip e-mail**
A set of e-mail campaign letters to be delivered to contacts with automated and scheduled delivery dates.

**E-mail Blasts**
A mass distribution of communication or marketing materials via e-mail.

**eMarketing**
eMarketing is the combination of e-mail, website, blog, and print advertising all co-ordinated together to effectively market one's business. Also known in 1parkplace vernacular as "Everything Marketing."

**Facebook**
Facebook is a popular social networking destination that could also be the basis for an eFarm. Invented by Harvard University student Mark Zuckerberg, Facebook was initially launched to Harvard students on February 4, 2004. The original objective was to connect students from university to university. As students graduated, the network exploded globally and virally, now boasting over 500 million members.

**Farm & eFarm**
A real estate Farm is the term used to distinguish a geographic marketing area in which an agent will concentrate his or her advertising and marketing efforts. The primary goal of farming is to secure listings within the targeted area. An eFarm is similar, however, the geographic boundaries are potentially eliminated and the marketing is conducted electronically via e-mail to a target group of prospects and past customers.

**FeedBurner**
FeedBurner is a Web feed manager that provides custom RSS feeds and management tools to bloggers, podcasters, and other Web-based content publishers.

**Flickr**
Flickr is an online community offering a variety of Web services, including image and video hosting. Its services are popularly used by bloggers seeking a host for content that they embed in their blogs and various social media outlets.

## Glossary of Terms

**Gist**
Gist helps build stronger relationships by connecting the e-mail inbox, social networks, and CRM systems to the Web to provide business-critical information about the people and companies that matter most. Gist provides an entirely new view on leads, contacts, and companies by intelligently prioritizing them, aggregating information about them, and auto-generating profiles (summarizing e-mails, links, attachments and related news) for those people and companies.

**Google**
The name of the company and search engine founded and developed by Larry Page and Sergei Brin. Due to its popularity and numerous products, it is listed as the most visited website on the Internet. The name Google came from the word googol, which is the numeral one followed by a hundred zeros in decimal representation.

**Hyperlocal**
Hyperlocal sites, also referred to as local-local or microsites, focus on a very narrow geographical area—a suburb, a small town or perhaps a rural county—that is not currently well-served by existing media outlets. Print publications, for example, publish separate "neighbor" editions for different areas and local television news stations occasionally broadcast "round-ups" of stories from surrounding suburbs. On the Web, these efforts can be expanded even further.

**IDX**
Stands for Internet Data Feed Exchange. This refers to the ability for an agent to display all MLS listings on his or her website for the purpose of lead capture and to ensure that they do not brand the listing agent. Generally requires permission from both the broker and the MLS. Sometimes a processing fee is required by the MLS.

**Indexed Page**
An indexed page is one that has been analyzed and filed into a database of a search engine. The page is then presented when a user searches for the content that was indexed.

**Inman (Inman News)**
Founded in 1996 by Bradley Inman, Inman News is an online source of independent real estate news.

**Landing Page**
A landing page (also known as a lead capture page) is the page that appears when a potential customer clicks on an advertisement or a search-engine result link. The page will usually display content that is a logical extension of the advertisement or link, and that is optimized to feature specific keywords or phrases for indexing by

search engines.

## Lead

A lead is classified as an online registrant or inbound phone caller who expresses interest in real estate property and who has not been sought after by the agent.

## Lead Capture

Capability to utilize a contact form to capture visitor information from your website.

## LinkedIn

Founded in 2002 by Reid Hoffman, LinkedIn is a business-oriented social networking site that is mainly used for professional networking.

## Listing Publisher

A solution that assists in the publishing of listings and other marketing content through advertising portals, such as craigslist and Backpage.

## Listing Syndication

Listing syndication is the process of distributing machine-formatted listings to website portals that offer real estate listings for sale. The purpose is to increase exposure to real estate listings via a multitude of websites across the world.

## Long-tailing

The marketing of websites on search engines that focuses on long-tail keywords that have less competition. Recent long-tail keyword research has found that long-tail searches often exhibit a higher conversion rate by up to 200 percent compared to short-tail (generic) keywords. This can be extremely profitable for search engine marketers in terms of a lower cost per action and higher return on investment (Wikipedia).

## Micro site

A micro site is a mini website that can either stand alone or integrate into a full website. It is specifically designed to feature a product or service with multiple pages of content and often a specific call to action for lead capture. Generally, a micro site will be accessible through either a direct domain or a link from another site.

## MLS

Multiple Listing Service is a suite of services that enables brokers to establish contractual offers of compensation (among brokers), facilitates cooperation with other broker participants, accumulates and disseminates information to enable appraisals, and is a facility for the orderly correlation and dissemination of listing information to better serve broker's clients, customers, and the public.

# Glossary of Terms

**MySpace**
MySpace is a social networking site launched in 2003. Its release was widely influenced by Friendster and was designed to mimic the more popular features of the social networking website.

**NAR**
The National Association of Realtors is North America's largest trade association. Founded on May 12, 1908, its objective was "to unite the real estate men of America for the purpose of effectively exerting a combined influence upon matters affecting real estate interests." A member of the NAR is called a Realtor.

**Off-page SEO**
Off-page SEO is comprised of search engine optimization techniques that are done off the pages of a website, such as linking and placing keywords within link anchor text. This maximizes a website's performance as its target keywords are scanned by search engines.

**On-page SEO**
On-page SEO is comprised of search engine optimization techniques that are done within the pages of a website. Examples of on-page factors are keyword frequency, meta tags, headings, links, and site structure.

**Organic Traffic**
Organic traffic is Web traffic that comes from unpaid listings in search engines or directories.

**Page Rank**
PageRank is commonly associated with how Google ranks the relevancy of a website in relation to specific keyword search requests; 10 is best and 0 is the lowest rank.

**Portals**
A real estate portal is a location that aggregates listing data and other industry information for the purpose of addressing a direct consumer interface. Portals typically earn their revenue through advertising and commonly, each listing is marketed directly to the listing agent. Examples include REALTOR.com, Zillow, and Trulia.

**PPC**
Pay-Per-Click is a form of advertising in which an ad buyer places an upfront commitment on the value of a paid link from a search engine or third party site. Every time their link is clicked from a site they are advertising on, money is deducted from the prepaid budget. Once the pre-paid budget has been exhausted, the link will lose

its presence on the site. There is no organic value of long-term site ranking with PPC. Google AdWords is a prime example of PPC.

## Prospect
A prospect is an entity of which bilateral communication has been established—for instance, a lead that has been contacted and conversation taken place, needs have been discussed, and perhaps pre-qualification has begun as well.

## Prospect Analytics
Technology that analyzes the value of a website prospect to determine their motivation and likeliness to conduct a transaction.

## Rainmaker
The person at the top of the team pyramid who is responsible for generating new leads for the rest of the team.

## Real Estate Broker
Generally meant to represent the owner of a real estate firm who has multiple real estate licensees operating as independent contractors.

## Real Estate Team
Consists of a lead agent within a brokerage firm who has associate agents working under a single MLS ID of the team lead. This group of real estate agents is the basis for the Rainmaker and Rainmaker concepts.

## REALTOR.com
REALTOR.com is the official website of the National Association of Realtors. The site enables all Realtors to effectively market their properties to millions of consumers who visit the site every month.

## RealTown
RealTown is an Internet portal that features everything about real estate. It is one of the oldest and most respected communities in the real estate industry.

## Retweet
Retweet, in the social networking and micro-blogging service Twitter, means to re-post something posted by another user. A retweet is usually preceded with "RT" and "@username" to give credit to the original poster.

# Glossary of Terms

**RISMedia**
RISMedia was founded in 1980 by CEO and Publisher John E. Featherston. It provides the industry with news, trends, and business development information through its publication *Real Estate* magazine, its website RISMedia.com, and its networking and educational events.

**RSS feed**
RSS stands for "really simple syndication" and it is used to publish frequently updated works in a standardized format. A website's feed or Web feed usually contains its most recently published works and is available for viewing without actually visiting the website itself.

**SEO**
Stands for Search Engine Optimization—the process of improving ranking in search engine results.

**SMART Tracker**
1parkplace website and blog analytics program for absolute website activity measurement. SMART Tracker can be installed on nearly every website and provides worldwide tracking activity.

**Social Media**
Social media refers to a group of Internet-based applications that build on the ideological and technological foundations of Web 2.0, and that allows the creation and exchange of user-generated content.

**Social Network**
A social network is a social structure made of individuals (or organizations) called "nodes," which are tied (connected) by one or more specific types of interdependency, such as friendship, kinship, financial exchange, dislike, sexual relationships, or relationships of beliefs, knowledge, or prestige.

**SOI/COI**
Stands for Sphere of Influence/Center of Influence.

**Sticky**
The term *sticky* pertains to the information on a website that keeps the visitors engaged. Historically, the stickier the content, the higher the lead conversion.

**Syndication**
Web syndication allows Web content from a website to be available to other sites or individual subscribers. Today, syndication is popular for marketing listings across the globe.

**Tagged**
A tag is a non-hierarchical keyword or term assigned to a piece of information, such as an Internet bookmark, digital image, or computer file. This kind of metadata helps describe an item and allows it to be found again by browsing or searching.

**Top 5 In Real Estate Network®**
The Top 5 in Real Estate Network® was developed by RISMedia, the leader in real estate information systems, and is comprised of leading real estate agents from throughout the United States and Canada. Members represent a variety of highly respected international, national, regional, and local real estate firms. Top 5 membership is based upon real estate professionals meeting a stringent series of requirements, including experience and results.

**Trulia**
Trulia is a real estate search engine and portal site that is designed to help customers find homes and provide real estate information at the local level to help buyers make better decisions in the process.

**Tweet**
A tweet is a text-based post of up to 140 characters on the social networking and micro-blogging site Twitter. The posts are displayed on the author's profile page and delivered to the author's subscribers who are known as followers.

**Twitter**
Twitter is a free social networking and micro-blogging service that enables its users to send and read messages known as tweets. Senders can restrict delivery to those in their circle of friends or, by default, allow open access. Users can send and receive tweets via the Twitter website, Short Message Service (SMS), or external applications. While the service costs nothing to use, accessing it through SMS may incur phone service provider fees.

**Viral Marketing**
Viral marketing is a form of marketing using pre-existing social networks to produce increases in brand awareness or product sales through self-replicating viral processes, analogous to the spread of pathological and computer viruses. It can be through word-of-mouth or enhanced by the network effects of the Internet. Viral

promotions may take the form of video clips, eBooks, brandable software, images, or even text messages. Often, your prospects and COI promote your message for you.

**VOW**
A Virtual Office Website (VOW) is a website that is used to conduct business activities. One example is a VOW used as a real estate property search site allowing the public to conduct searches of approved Multiple Listing Service properties in a given area under certain conditions. (Wikipedia)

**Web 1.0**
Web 1.0 is a retronym that refers to the state of the World Wide Web, and any website design style used before the advent of the Web 2.0 phenomenon. Web 1.0 began with the release of the WWW to the public in 1991, and is the general term that has been created to describe the Web before the "bursting of the dot-com bubble" in 2001, seen by many as a turning point for the Internet.

**Web 2.0**
Web 2.0 is characterized by any website, blog, or social media site that offers user-defined content and interaction, i.e., commenting, blogging, sharing, etc. Unlike Web 1.0 where the concentration was about branding and marketing, Web 2.0 allows individuals at-large to define and shape the content on a site based on topics generally defined by the site owner.

**Web 3.0**
Web 3.0 stands for the semantic Web as an evolving development of the World Wide Web in which the meaning (semantics) of information and services on the Web is defined, making it possible for the Web to "understand" and satisfy the requests of people and machines using the Web content. At its core, the semantic Web comprises a set of design principles, collaborative working groups, and a variety of enabling technologies. 1parkplace Nebula 3.0 is a Web 3.0 application.

**Web Analytics**
The statistical information gathered and analyzed based on website visitor behavior and length of time on a website. Google Analytics is one method of measuring visitor behavior, but 1parkplace has a superior product called the SMART Tracker, which can be added to any website regardless of host.

## Webify

Webify is often used to describe the porting or conversion of print or other pre-existing content to HTML (Hyper Text Markup Language) in order to present on the Web within websites, blog sites, mobile devices, or any other platform that accepts HTML as its native language. The act of webifying content is known as "Webification."

## Webinar

A seminar or training class that takes place over the Internet as opposed to a live physical venue.

## Website

A website is a collection of related webpages, images, videos, or other digital assets that are addressed relative to a common uniform resource locator (URL).

## XML

XML (Extensible Markup Language) is a set of rules for encoding documents electronically.

## Yahoo!

Yahoo! is an American public corporation, founded in 1994 by Jerry Yang and David Filo, that provides Internet services worldwide. It is best known for its Web portal, e-mail service, search engine, and other online services.

## YouTube

YouTube is a popular video-sharing website on which users can upload, share, and view videos.

## Zillow

Zillow is an online real estate database that was founded in 2005 by Rich Barton and Lloyd Frink. The website uses a proprietary algorithm called the "Zestimate" to appraise property values based on undisclosed factors.

For information on how RISMedia's Top 5 in Real Estate Network® can help with your social networking, social media content needs, and greater marketplace personal promotion, please visit www.top5inrealestate.com.

http://www.sellingcastlesinthesky.net/page/197509/About-Your-Consultant/AboutMe

For broker/owners interested in learning more about how RISMedia can provide relevant consumer content through RISMedia's Real Estate Information Network® (RREIN), kindly e-mail: rrein@rismedia.com.

For information on the most effective and "affordable" real estate coaching available to the industry:

# The RISMedia Coaching Institute

(which includes faculty from this book and many other leading industry coaches and practicioners)

please e-mail Paris Cheffer: paris@top5inrealestate.com.